Praise for Jean Tabaka's
Collaboration Explained

"*Collaboration Explained* is a deeply p̲̅ ̲̅ ̲̅ book that helps agile practitioners understand and manage complex organizational and team dynamics. As an agile coach, I've found the combination of straight-forward advice and colorful anecdotes to be invaluable in guiding and focusing interactions with my teams. Jean's wealth of experience is conveyed in a carefully struck balance of reference guides and prose, facilitating just-in-time learning in the agile spirit. All in all, a superb resource for building stronger teams that's fit for agile veterans and neophytes alike."

—Arlen Bankston, Lean Agile Practice Manager, CC Pace

"If Agile is the new 'what,' then surely Collaboration is the new 'how.' There are many things I really like about Jean's new book. Right at the top of the list is that I don't have to make lists of ideas for collaboration and facilitation anymore. Jean has it all. Not only does she have those great ideas for meetings, retrospectives, and team decision-making that I need to remember, but the startling new and thought-provoking ideas are there too. And the stories, the stories, the stories! The best way to transfer wisdom. Thanks, Jean!"

—Linda Rising, Independent Consultant

Collaboration
Explained

The Agile Software Development Series

Alistair Cockburn and Jim Highsmith, Series Editors

Agile software development centers on four values identified in the Agile Alliance's Manifesto:

- Individuals and interactions over processes and tools
- Working software over comprehensive documentation
- Customer collaboration over contract negotiation
- Responding to change over following a plan

The development of Agile software requires innovation and responsiveness, based on generating and sharing knowledge within a development team and with the customer. Agile software developers draw on the strengths of customers, users, and developers, finding just enough process to balance quality and agility.

The books in The Agile Software Development Series focus on sharing the experiences of such Agile developers. Individual books address individual techniques (such as Use Cases), group techniques (such as collaborative decision making), and proven solutions to different problems from a variety of organizational cultures. The result is a core of Agile best practices that will enrich your experience and improve your work.

Titles in the Series:

Steve Adolph, Paul Bramble, Alistair Cockburn, and Andy Pols; *Patterns for Effective Use Cases;* 0201721848

Alistair Cockburn; *Agile Software Development;* 0201699699

Alistair Cockburn; *Crystal Clear;* 0201699478

Alistair Cockburn; *Surviving Object-Oriented Projects;* 0201498340

Alistair Cockburn; *Writing Effective Use Cases;* 0201702258

Anne Mette Jonassen Hass; *Configuration Management Principles and Practice;* 0321117662

Jim Highsmith; *Agile Software Development Ecosystems;* 0201760436

Jim Highsmith; *Agile Project Management;* 0321219775

Craig Larman; *Agile and Iterative Development;* 0131111558

Lars Mathiassen, Jan Pries-Heje, and Ojelanki Ngwenyama; *Improving Software Organizations;* 0201758202

Mary Poppendieck and Tom Poppendieck; *Lean Software Development;* 0321150783

Jean Tabaka; *Collaboration Explained;* 0321268776

Kevin Tate; *Sustainable Software Development;* 0321286081

For more information visit www.awprofessional.com/series/agile

Collaboration Explained

Facilitation Skills for Software Project Leaders

Jean Tabaka

✦ Addison-Wesley

Upper Saddle River, NJ • Boston • Indianapolis
San Francisco • New York • Toronto
Montreal • London • Munich • Paris • Madrid
Capetown • Sydney • Tokyo • Singapore • Mexico City

The publisher offers discounts on this book when ordered in quantity for special sales. For more information, please contact:

 U.S. Corporate and Government Sales
 (800) 382-3419
 corpsales@pearsontechgroup.com

For sales outside of the United States, please contact:

 International Sales
 (317 581-3793)
 international@pearsontechgroup.com

Visit Addison-Wesley on the Web: www.awprofessional.com

Library of Congress Cataloging-in-Publication Data:

Tabaka, Jean
 Collaboration explained: facilitation skills for software project leaders
 /
Jean Tabaka
 p. cm.
ISBN 0-321-28677-6 (pbk. : alk. Paper) 1. Computer
software—Development—Management. I. Title.

QA76.76.D47T32 2006
005.3—dc22

     2005027650

This Book Is Safari Enabled

The Safari, Enabled icon on the cover of your favorite technology book means the book is available through Safari Bookshelf. When you buy this book, you get free access to the online edition for 45 days. Safari Bookshelf is an electronic reference library that lets you easily search thousands of technical books, find code samples, download chapters, and access technical information whenever and wherever you need it.

To gain 45-day Safari Enabled access to this book:

Go to http://www.awprofessional.com/safarienabled

Complete the brief registration form

Enter the coupon code A8DZ-HKYD-3B4F-QDEK-E68B

If you have difficulty registering on Safari Bookshelf or accessing the online edition, please e-mail customer-service@safaribooksonline.com.

ISBN 0-321-26877-6
Text printed in the United States on recycled paper R.R. Donnelley, Crawfordsville, IN.
Third Printing, May 2009

To Jim and Norma Tabaka,
my mentors in humor and love

Contents

Acknowledgments

"Who knows, today from yesterday may learn to count no thing too strange."

— Edwin Arlington Robinson

In moving from my yesterday, of no book, to the today of having this book, I realize that I harvested guidance from a number of people. With bottomless gratitude, I wish to acknowledge those who helped ferry me across that unknown land.

I couldn't have imagined how my life was about to change when I met Paul Petralia of Addison-Wesley at the Agile Development Conference in Salt Lake City, 2003. Relentless in his annoyance and support, Paul remained ever firm in his conviction that this was the right book, at the right time, and that I should be its author. I gratefully acknowledge his vision and fortitude. In addition, I am thankful to Michelle Housley, Chris Guzikowski, Jesssica D'Amico, Kristy Hart, and Rose Sweazy of Addison-Wesley for their patience and support in guiding me through the many editing cycles, schedule changes, and even the loss of a laptop. Your polish and aplomb continually guided me to safe harbors.

Paul was crafty enough to bring sure-footed sherpas to guide me on my authorship trek. I am so very grateful for the consistent, clear-voiced, and masterful guidance I received from my reviewers Mike Cohn, Alistair Cockburn, Linda Rising, Tom Poppendieck, Jim Highsmith, and Kent Beck. Each managed to nudge and poke me through some treacherous spots and potential pitfalls while making sure I lived to tell about it.

I am so honored to have been invited to contribute to Jim Highsmith and Alistair Cockburn in their Agile Software Development Series. Walking in the path of giants, I am grateful for their having cleared the way for me and for their conviction around this topic.

I am remarkably blessed to have met Janet Danforth, Lori Barnes, Bob Moir, Ellen Gottesdiener, and David Spann in my salad days as a novice facilitator. Each of them has provided a unique blend of experience and passion in this field that has served to inspire and motivate me to follow humbly in their footsteps. Similarly, I've been lucky enough to be a recipient of enthusiastic guidance from the wonderful participants in the

Retrospectives Gathering and Yahoo! group. In particular: Tim Bacon, Rachel Davies, Esther Derby, Diana Larsen, and Linda Rising. All of these people are the true guardians of collaboration through facilitation, and I am honored to be counted in their ranks.

For day-to-day, on the field of play support, I wish to express my thanks to the staff and patrons of Caffe Sole coffee shop in Boulder, Colorado. Just as the bench by the front window has a permanent indentation from my many early-morning and late-night visits there, so do each of you in me for being so genuinely interested in how the book was coming along. It's done!

Brilliant and supportive colleagues are never to be squandered, and so I gratefully acknowledge my wonderful colleagues at Rally Software Development. Tim Miller and Ryan Martens in quiet wisdom and with sincere support created a wide swath in which I was able to navigate my life as a consultant, mentor, trainer, and writer. They have opened amazing doors for me, and I am forever indebted to their great faith in my abilities. Michele Sliger gets the award as my most exuberant and vocal cheerleader. She would not let me stop writing! I am grateful for her persistence and cheer in moving me to complete these materials and to make the book something she truly sought to own. My deep and heartfelt gratitude goes to my colleague Hubert Smits. In addition to being an encouraging colleague, Hubert, through his detailed and insightful reviews and suggestions, managed to carefully provide that last push of support and energy my weary brain needed to finally see the book through. Finally, Jami Yannett, Brad Norris, Cindy Hagg, Richard Leavitt, and Dru Jacobs at Rally have all been selflessly supportive, especially when I was stressed and grumpy.

My deepest and most humble debt of gratitude goes to my friends who bore the brunt of my fears, fatigue, and frustration during the writing and rewriting of this book. Wayne and Laura Gifford, thanks for sitting me down in Kauai to breathe in ocean air and let inspiration flow. Sheldon Lutte, you so ardently believe in my abilities, I had to finish the book in order to not let you down. I hope you like it! Judith Oakland, I can't count the number of times we sat together talking through the blood, sweat, and tears that must accompany the creative process. I know that I couldn't have made it through without your love and guidance. To my secret fan club, Fuzuki, Boodle, Rocky, Über-Sponge, and You-Did, you will forever be in my heart. Each of you taught me new and deeper meanings of the word "friend" through your support during this challenging time. And finally, most importantly of all, I am "to infinity and beyond" indebted to my most excellent and most enduring friend, Alex Archaro. I know of no one else who could have so expertly applied such liberal doses of humor, annoyance, and love, all in the right proportions and at the right times in order to help me maintain my forward progress. Your steadfastness to me and my "book report" has made all the difference.

About the Author

Jean Tabaka is an Agile Coach with Rally Software Development, specializing in creating, coaching, and mentoring collaborative, agile software teams. Jean brings over 25 years of experience in software development to the agile plate in a variety of organizational contexts including internal IT departments, ISVs, government agencies, and consulting organizations. Having implemented both plan-driven and agile development approaches for Sybase, Siebel Systems, and Qwest, as well as a variety of smaller ventures, her work has spanned industries and continents. As an agile mentor, Jean coaches software teams through training and facilitation to adopt agile principles and practices using a hybrid of the leading agile methods. With a passion for collaboration practices through facilitation techniques, she guides organizations in creating high-performance teams. She is the co-author of *Physical Database Design for Sybase SQL Server* (Prentice Hall, 1995) and is a frequent lecturer and contributor on the topic of collaboration practices in agile teams. A Certified ScrumMaster, as well as Certified ScrumMaster Trainer, and Certified Professional Facilitator, she holds a Master of Arts from Michigan State University and a Master of Computer Science from Johns Hopkins University.

Foreword

The first value in the Agile Manifesto is "individuals and interaction," or collaboration. Yet there are precious few good resources on collaboration, how to set it up, how to manage, monitor, and improve it, and even more rarely, how to apply it to a software development environment.

Jean Tabaka, a trainer of professional facilitators, offers us a rare view into the workings of collaboration cultures, collaborative teams, self-organized teams, and collaborative leaders—what it means to be either of the first two and how to work with either of the latter. I am glad that someone as knowledgeable as Jean has had the energy and talent to capture how to build skills in these areas.

Jean shows the mechanics of running good meetings, ones that are welcomed and well-run rather than dreaded and dull, where the outcome is a net improvement rather than design-by-committee. She describes in easy-to-read prose how to set up the meeting room, identify and hold consensus, get the most out of small work groups, brainstorm and vote, and how to process the resulting information. She covers visioning, reflecting, retrospecting, managing, conflict, and extending collaboration to increasingly common but difficult situations such as distributed teams. My favorite chapter is Chapter 19, "Guerilla Collaboration": how to help nudge a group into profitable discussions when you are not the leader and the meeting's leader has wandered off the path.

Jean summarizes key collaboration sessions you are likely to encounter. She includes the common project meetings: project startup, status, action, and retrospective meetings. She also includes the special kinds of collaborative sessions found in several of the agile methodologies: blitz planning and reflection workshops for Crystal Clear, Sprint planning and daily standup for Scrum, planning and retrospectives for XP, and project chartering for Industrial XP. She presents each meeting's key questions and themes in a table you can use to prepare for the meeting. Even though I am supposed to know this material, I keep referring to these tables and to her descriptions of the elements to deepen my understanding and make sure I have not gotten off track myself.

These techniques are for every organization doing every kind of work. We are just lucky that Jean is bringing them to the agile development community to read first.

Alistair Cockburn

Preface

A Path of Learning

When I started my career in IT back in the 1970s, I began as an intern for a JCL helpdesk that supported a team of analysts who expected their programs to run smoothly (enough) in the massive farm of IBM 3270s built for that purpose. I never met the analysts I supported; I never really knew the business they were supporting. I just knew that a stream of data from one system through tape drives to another system had not completed correctly (ABEND!) and I needed to restart the job or redirect the stream from box to box as needed.

The only "collaboration" I experienced was in the form of directions from my supervisor when I didn't know how to solve the problem. There were no team meetings, no team decisions (except about the smoking policy that encouraged cigarettes but banned cigars), and no sense of team ownership of success. Each of the other members of the "team" had their separate set of analysts they supported, their own stacks of punch card carriers, and their personal, safeguarded mag tapes they used to manage their work.

In subsequent jobs, I moved into other 3GL environments, still working largely without access to a customer or other developers. With regard to the development teams, the work was divided up by our manager who made decisions about what we should be doing, how it should be done, and when it should be completed. Our team meetings were weekly bug report meetings where our manager would prioritize what needed to be done and its due date. We passed work from one job title to another (analyst, to designer, to developer, to tester), and teamwork for me was largely restricted to one-on-one debugging sessions with another developer. But a change was beginning to unfold about how software development projects, their teams, and their managers could work more effectively.

I first dipped into the notion of a learning-oriented approach to software development via *Wicked Problems, Righteous Solutions* by Peter DeGrace and Leslie Hulet-Stahl (Prentice Hall, 1998). The book became my bible about what was wrong with phase-driven, waterfall approaches and what might be right about a more empirically motivated approach. My next epiphany came in the late 1990s with a visit to the UK where I learned of a new methodology being adopted in Europe: the Dynamic Systems Development Method, or DSDM. What was startling for me about this methodology at the time was its emphasis on timeboxes versus scope for software delivery. It turned my notion of software development methodology on its ear. Moreover, as documentation was de-emphasized, rapid effective face-to-face communication was explicitly built into the approach through its facilitated workshops.

At this point, I made a conscious decision to steer my methodology focus toward facilitation practices that I could apply to software development teams. Because I had seen too many examples of how teams can crumble in bad meeting contexts and in bad control environments, I wanted to learn ways to make all the various team collaborations more reliable, more frequent, faster, and more productive. I took classes in facilitation, read books on facilitation, and attended facilitation conferences. I became a certified professional facilitator, and I began to teach facilitation as well as apply it.

And I learned a few things: facilitation has a place in how we create teams and coax collaborative work from and for them. Additionally, I learned that facilitation is not about control or manipulation. Rather, it is about applying tools, techniques, and processes in support of teams eager to engage in high performance. Good facilitators listen and echo in a way that helps a team hear itself and apply its best wisdom. Project managers and software team leads with facilitative skills become leaders who can listen and echo as they lead teams in vision and success.

Today, I find myself in teams that create a common goal, work to communicate frequently, and make decisions based on their collective wisdom. The agile methodologies we now consult (Scrum, Extreme Programming, Crystal Clear, Feature Driven Development, and Lean Software Development) emphasize project success through disciplines of engineering and communications that can effectively respond to change. In these contexts, I recognize the stabilizing force of collaboration and communication as fundamental practices in project success. Projects need teams; teams need communication. And while communication comes in a variety of forms from one-on-one to very large groups, at the team level of three or more people making decisions and acting on them, communication relies on collaboration.

This book brings together my specific lessons about the importance of applying collaboration in teams. Specifically, it catalogues the practices of facilitation I have learned to use in order to liberate teams into a variety of information gathering and decision modes that promote high performance. I have come to rely on facilitation not as a manipulation or control technique, but rather as a way to encourage participatory decision making among teams of experts. For me, facilitation, more than any other leadership or team practice, has proven to be my greatest gift to teams in creating a vision for them and encouraging their best teamwork.

A number of colleagues have warned me about negative experiences they've endured where a facilitator has used his role in a meeting to manipulate and control the team. That is not my intent here. I believe in leaders who engage facilitatively in service to the team, not in control of it. I believe in teams who recognize the wisdom of a powerful leader and how such a leader's move through various decision approaches strengthens them. A good leader absorbs a rich set of tools in creating success with and for their teams. In this guidebook, I offer one subset of those tools, the facilitation tools.

Overview

How Have We Arrived Where We Are Today?

Project Managers of software development projects have certainly always had some peripheral sense of the need to pay attention to how their teams collaborate, both within the team as well as across the wide spectrum of stakeholders interacting with the team. But the ever-growing urgency around innovation and speedy, reliable delivery of business value through software has caused even the most steadfast of document- and plan-driven Project Managers to seek a more invigorated emphasis on team collaborations. In fact a group of sage souls, the Agilists, confirmed a dramatic shift in software delivery approaches when they outlined the Agile Manifesto. Here, they explicitly thrust this sense of team and collaboration into the software project spotlight. Squinting into this brightly lit orb, Project Managers and their teams now scurry to answer the question: How can we actively and explicitly establish collaboration as a fundamental tenet of our project success?

What This Book Brings You

In this practical handbook, I offer leaders of collaborative teams (Project Managers, XP Coaches, ScrumMasters, agile Project Managers, traditional Project Managers, and team leads) a guide of step-by-step facilitation techniques for instilling collaboration in project teams. I review the fundamentals of collaboration in software development projects: what the various collaboration roles are, how leaders instill collaboration cultures in their teams, what the primary collaboration events are, and what the fundamental facilitation techniques are that you can apply in these collaboration events.

In short, this book harvests that intangible component of team power and wisdom known as collaboration by clarifying its fundamentals in guidance at the individual level, the team level, and the organization level. Applying these basics, you can safely steward project teams to new levels of collaboration and commitment, buoying your teams to consistently deliver business value through reliable and action-focused decision making.

Who Should Read This Guide?

Collaboration rests squarely on the shoulders of each member of a project team. However, we very often turn to the Project Manager to instill the practice of collaboration in the team. For that reason, Project Managers, ScrumMasters, XP Coaches, or other team leads may reap the most immediate benefit from the facilitation guidance provided here. Nonetheless, the book can serve as a useful reference for the full range of project team members. For the roles outlined here, consider reading this guide based on your participation in building collaborative teams:

Project Managers—Because you can have the most effective impact on grooming a team to behave collaboratively, Project Managers are invited to read this book. Without a strong sense of facilitating collaboration, a Project Manager may resort to management and decision styles that could inadvertently kill the team spirit and creativity. This can mean death to a technical team that needs to feel empowered to make decisions and take pride in carrying out those decisions.

Team Leads—Because you are very often tasked with owning all design and architecture decisions, collaboration can be a real challenge. Moving from a command-and-control stance to one of team collaboration in converging on key technical decisions may prove to be a powerful paradigm shift for technical leads.

Team Members—Because collaboration relies so deeply on your ability to be attentive to each other within the team, you need to adopt collaboration practices. You become fanners of the flame of team wisdom and "guerilla collaborators" (really!) who can guide leads and Project Managers about maintaining a collaborative culture.

Facilitators—Because to be truly effective, you must bring much needed neutrality to small and large teams alike, facilitation consultants are invited to read this book. You may review facilitation techniques suggested here that are directed at software teams wanting to move away from software by coercion to software by collaboration.

Managers—Because while you may think that you promote collaboration in your software teams and with your business representatives, you may need to rethink your premises and your policies moving forward. Managers have an opportunity for growth when they invite participatory decision making into their management style and then lead with the power of observation and expert input.

How to Use This Guide

You can use this book as a series of small guides on collaboration, depending on where your work currently steers you.

- **Section I, "Setting the Collaborative Context"**—If you're asking yourself, "Why collaboration, why now, and why should I care?" you'll want to read this preliminary section. Here, you'll lay the foundation upon which this current software development focus on collaboration has been built, particularly if you are starting to adopt agile software development practices. Namely:
  - **What is all this hoopla about collaboration?**—How does it relate to us in the software development realm as a fundamental project tool?
  - **What does it mean to have a collaboration culture?**—What is the difference between a collaboration-driven team versus a command-and-control team, and how does this impact our team culture and the way we make decisions?
  - **Who are the leaders that form and guide these cultures?**—Given that we choose to be collaborative, how do leaders of such teams (Project Manager, team lead, technical lead, or director) shift their thinking and hone their skills in order for us to succeed collaboratively while still maintaining a sense of leadership?
  - **And what do the teams look like that work effectively in these cultures?**—How do teams pay attention to their basic structure and behaviors in order to continually engender collaborative values and practices in their decision making?

  Building this collaboration context in effect bounds the realm within which the remainder of the book's work resides.

- **Section II, "Applying Collaboration"**—With what we have learned about collaborative culture, leaders, and teams, I define a set of fairly prescriptive tools and techniques for team collaboration. Specifically, I target the various team meetings (small, medium, and gargantuan) that can either amplify or squelch collaboration. These prescriptions include sufficient connective tissue around their components to build larger patterns for participatory decision making. Focused, highly participatory meetings lead to consistent and sustainable team collaboration, which ultimately builds high-performing teams. Therefore, in this section, I'll provide guidance on:
    - **Defining project collaboration events**—Where and when are we being called upon to engage collaboratively in our projects?
    - **Preparing for collaborative events**—What can each of us do when we are planning a project gathering to ensure that it is truly collaborative?
    - **Preparing participants for collaboration**—What needs to be done to tend to all participants when we have a major collaboration event in the offing?
    - **Setting the collaborative agenda**—Given that all these people are gathering, how can we plan to make the best use of their time in meeting a specific purpose or goal collaboratively?
    - **The organizing tools**—With a good plan, how can we ensure that we don't skid off track and that all participants have the ability to help the entire group stay on target and meet its objectives?
    - **Starting the meeting**—It's time to work, so how do we bring everyone together and help them to focus and to engage collaboratively? What steps can we use to gain focus on each new topic we explore?
    - **Gathering and processing the information**—Everyone has great ideas; decisions need to be made; how do we bring all the pertinent information together in a useful manner for tooling the team to make its best decisions? What can we bring together for estimating, dialogues, visioning, and retrospectives?
    - **Managing the participants**—Collaboration can be hijacked by intended or unintended dysfunctional behaviors; how do we anticipate these behaviors, address them, and keep teams fruitfully engaged without damage?
    - **Closing the event**—Given all the work that has been accomplished, how do we ensure that the collaborations continue once participants have left the gathering and are back at their desks?
- **Section III, "Extending Collaboration"**—If you understand all these collaboration practices with teams that are face-to-face, you may still want to extend your skills to shepherd collaboration into more challenging realms:

- **Collaboration for small teams**—How can we winnow down the large toolset of facilitation techniques to what is most useful for one-on-one or small team contexts?
- **Collaboration for distributed teams**—What can we do to promote collaboration with extended, distributed teams?
- **Collaboration growth in organizations**—How do we take these simple practices and encourage them outside of just one team or one group?
- **Section IV, "Collaborative Facilitation Guides"**—If you understand all these collaboration fundamentals and are ready to implement meeting agendas for specific agile software development approaches, turn to Section IV. This section provides a set of collaborative agenda formats to apply in generic meetings, Crystal Clear, Scrum, and XP. They serve as templates either to apply these specific methodologies or to build hybrid collaborative events of your own. Each template answers: "What is the purpose of this meeting, who are the meeting participants, what are the expected outputs of the meeting, what is the set of agenda items, and what are the processes that I can apply to help the participants meet the purpose collaboratively?"

How the Techniques Are Presented

Sections III and IV of this book provide the detailed facilitation techniques used to create and maintain collaboration. Each has a formula for delivering that information. For instance, Chapter 11, "Defining the Steps," defines four steps for helping teams focus and create information: Prepare, Prompt, Gather, and Process. These form the template for the guidance in that section. For example:

1. Prepare:
   - Label a flipchart clearly with the topic of the brainstorm ("User Interface Considerations," "What is Working Well," "Decision Strategies," "Name the Baby").
   - Explain that you are about to begin a brainstorming where each person will be writing their responses individually on Post-it Notes. (You may want to give some hint as to what the follow-on work will be with their responses, such as prioritizing, greater detail through small group discussion, grouping, or pros and cons to help them keep their responses short for the brainstorming.)

- Even if the exercise is conducted in small groups, there should be no discussion during the exercise; everyone is working as an individual.

2. Prompt with the brainstorm question.

3. Gather:
   - Hit the timer, say "Begin," and *say nothing else.*
   - End when time has run out.

The "Process" step is treated as a separate topic in Chapter 15, "Processing the Information," as in this example:

1. Process:
   - As items are posted, each participant is invited to start to group items as appropriate. Anyone can move any item to begin to form groups.
   - There are no predefined divisions; there are no predefined categories; there are no labels.
   - All participants are welcome to move posted responses around to form groups until the timebox is over.
   - Allow 20-40 minutes for this exercise, depending on the number of participants and the number of responses.
   - Once the timebox ends, or when there are no more changes in groupings, you can use the labeling approach described in the "Facilitator-Led Labeling" section of Chapter 15.

For the detailed agenda guides in Section IV, the guidance takes the form of a table, as in this example:

Agenda Item	
A. Opening	**Prompt Question:** n.a.
	Process: Meeting Startup
	Comments: Don't bother with personal objectives for such a short meeting. Just check in with everyone on the Purpose and remind them of the time limits.
	For teams that have been meeting daily, skip this formality entirely.

B. What is the status on the Action Items we gathered in the last status meeting?	**Prompt Question:** (No prompting question necessary)
	Process: Facilitator-led Review
	Comments: Use the Action list from the previous meeting as the prompt for reports. Keep reports short. Make sure they don't go into problem solving or detailed solution description; that should occur in a separate or follow-on meeting as appropriate.
C. What has been completed since the last status meeting?	**Prompt Question:** "Think back on the last status meeting we held on (date). We had a lot of work we accomplished since that time, as individuals and as a group. Now tell us, what has been completed since the last status meeting?"
	Process: Round Robin
	Comments: Use the timer. Capture any problem solving as discussions/meetings that need to occur after the status meeting. Also capture who should be involved in the follow-on discussions/meetings.
	For a Daily Standup, skip the Prompt question and go straight to the Round Robin. Encourage participants to address one another, not you.

This Is Only the Start

After you've worked through the sections of interest to you, there is still a lot of work ahead. Applying facilitative techniques for collaboration on your feet, day to day—that is where you'll really understand it, absorb it into your subconscious, and make it your own. As with any prescriptive set of tools and techniques, this book simply serves to encourage you to make those first steps down a new path. Choose facilitation tools and practices that look immediately applicable to you. Hone your craft around these practices. Apply them in small teams, small meetings, and then larger teams and larger meetings. Learn how to enjoy the benefits from these techniques even in one-on-one interactions.

Additionally, keep checking in with your leadership style and the practices that most comfortably complement that style. Build up your repertoire as your comfort level and your style permit. Although some of these practices may initially feel awkward or distracting, be patient with yourself and your teams. Over time, you'll feel teams trust more and more in the usefulness of your facilitative style as their leader. And through your guidance in collaboration, you and they can then reap the rewards that come with being highly participatory, highly focused, and hence highly performing.

Setting the Collaborative Context

Before digging into how to apply collaboration in software development projects, we need to set a useful context in which to bound the work. First, we have to agree on a good working definition of the term "collaboration" so that we can apply an appropriate focus to our project practices. Because our projects don't exist in a vacuum, we also have to look at what constitutes a general culture of collaboration and what makes it appealing to our way of working. Collaborative cultures rely on leaders who can understand the power of collaboration and nurture its growth in their teams. So, to complete the picture, we'll pull together a bit of guidance about the leaders who engender collaboration, and then take a look at some of the "DNA" that goes into promoting collaboration among team members.

Chapter 1

What Is Collaboration?

With the current interest in adaptive, more reliable software development practices, project teams and their managers are taking a renewed look at the many people aspects that either contribute to or detract from project success. We are re-reading Gerald Weinberg, Jim Coplein, Tom DeMarco, and Tim Lister, who have each been thought leaders around the roles that communication, negotiation, and collaboration play in software development.

Collaboration, the Definition

So now that we have progressed through the software ages and have this sense of collaboration beating a rhythm in our projects, what is a good working definition of collaboration?

> **Collaborate**—to work together especially in some literary, artistic, or scientific undertaking[1]; to work jointly with others or together especially in an intellectual endeavor.[2]

---

1. *Webster's New World Dictionary of the American Language* (Cleveland, OH: William Collins Publisher, 1979).

2. Merriam Webster Online Dictionary, www.merriamwebster.com.

These two general definitions help to set our focus on what is most useful about collaboration within the context of software development: how can we usefully share ideas, information, decisions, and solutions among the stakeholders and members of a project? And what is it about this joint work that creates benefits both for the collected individuals of the team as well as for the organizations or companies within which the team operates?

Through shared working, teams create a sense of community and identity for their projects. They are able to collectively converge on a purpose and a driving challenge for the project. In this way, collaboration becomes a practice that team members apply among the many tools and techniques that define their project.

When teams declare a collaborative imperative in their work, it is their pledge to employ consensus-based decision approaches through participatory decision-making. They apply high-bandwidth information gathering coupled with well-formed and well-articulated priorities. And, they are guided by a leader who fosters participation in defining the project work and who encourages open discussion around the project direction: its organization, its roles, and its deliverables.

How Collaboration Has Guided the Agile Movement

In February 2001, a group of software developers and managers formulated the Agile Manifesto as their expression of what they had come to truly value in terms of successfully delivering software. Their formulation was striking both in its simplicity as well as in the shift in priorities it proclaimed:

> Individuals and interactions over processes and tools
> Working software over comprehensive documentation
> Customer collaboration over contract negotiation
> Responding to change over following a plan

That is, while there is value on the items on the right, we value the items on the left more. Through this simple set of rules, the signers explicitly declared collaboration and communication as fundamental practices for successful software development, particularly the first and third declarations.

Individuals and Interactions over Processes and Tools

How do we buoy individuals in such a way that they can maintain their sense of self while still interacting effectively? Jorg Strübing reports that a very large part of a software developer's work is centered around "negotiation," hence the need for effective interaction skills:

- Respect the opinions of the other.
- Provide differing opinions in a non-attacking mode.
- Discourage command and control or bullying in interactions for the sake of moving forward (there are other ways to move forward!).
- Be able to reach consensus without any individual feeling that they had to compromise their true sense of what is right.

Customer Collaboration over Contract Negotiation

Define a relationship from the start that declares that the customer and the project team are full voting, working members in the success of the project. The team learns how to hear difficult information both from the customer as well as from the IT members without fear of recrimination. They create a safe harbor in which the team can negotiate, disagree, diverge, and then converge on a collaborative solution.

Collaboration, so powerful in its impact on team productivity, became an integral component of what would be considered a responsive, adaptive software development approach. As a result, the canonical works around agile software development each revere the credo "People over process" by devoting extensive insights into the need for collaboration in any of these pared-down processes: Scott Ambler's *Agile Modeling: Effective Practices for Extreme Programming and the Unified Process*, Stephen Palmer's and John Felsing's *A Practical Guide to Feature-Driven Development*, Alistair Cockburn's *Crystal Clear: A Human-Powered Methodology for Small Teams*, Jim Highsmith's *Adaptive Software Development: A Collaborative Approach to Managing Complex Systems*, Kent

Beck's and Martin Fowler's *Planning Extreme Programming*, and Craig Larman's *Agile & Iterative Development: A Manager's Guide*, to name a few. While each approach has its specifics about process and practices, they all echo a commitment to self-organizing, self-disciplined collaborative teams as a core principle to the successful implementation of those practices in process.

In this way, collaboration has been the daily glue that agile teams apply in order accomplish their joint undertakings.

Chapter 2

What Are Collaborative Cultures?

To better understand what collaboration looks like in our software development daily work, it's worth comparing a collaborative mode of working to other modes we might choose instead. If we think of these general organizational working modes as cultures, we can look at the descriptions and comparisons established by William Schneider in his book *The Reengineering Alternative: A Plan for Making Your Current Culture Work*. In this study, Schneider describes four fundamental cultures of working—that is, how teams make decisions and how their managers guide those decisions:

Command-and-Control—The leader is in charge and makes decisions for the team to ensure tight authority and responsibility.

Competence—The team or project relies on the expert capabilities of the few to bring about success for the whole.

Collaboration—Decisions are consensus-driven, and the team works in partnership toward success.

Cultivating—Establishing personal and professional improvement for each team member is paramount.

Each culture has a pattern of leadership that tends to drive how the groups organize, create teams, and complete their work. Each has its strengths and weaknesses. Understanding how a collaboration culture works compared to command-and-control, competence, or cultivating cultures ultimately answers the following questions:

- What can we hope for as the benefits of collaboration?
- What pitfalls should collaboration-driven cultures work to avoid?
- What kinds of leaders work best to promote collaboration cultures?
- How should teams expect to work in a collaboration culture?

The Non-Collaborative Cultures

To fully grasp the unique world of collaboration culture, we first take a look at the other three cultures to understand their characteristics and how they distinctly differ from the collaboration culture.

Command-and-Control

These cultures rely on the ability of the leader to take control, establish a firm grasp on the problem domain, derive a solution through her individual expertise and knowledge, and then direct the team in delivering that solution. Some project management styles rely heavily on this approach, especially in plan-driven software development work. The project manager (PM) defines the project plan, phases, tasks, and deliverables. This style leads to PM-driven decisions about schedule, roles, and responsibilities. The PM owns the project success and is the sole arbiter with the business sponsor of the project, being the interpreter of how user requests will impact the project activities, schedule, roles, and budget.

Project success therefore rests squarely on the shoulders of the manager and her ability to articulate, plan, motivate, organize, discipline, and execute. As Rob Austin and Lee Devin describe it in *Artful Making: What Managers Need to Know About How Artists Work*, this is a style that guides the work of "industrial making": highly plan-driven, highly repeatable, low-creativity production work. However, this command-and-control culture shreds morale and dilutes the motivation of gifted, creative team members.

Competence

Competence cultures thrive in a world that values the "best and brightest." Such corporations build their repute and bet their success on their ability to attract and retain those people considered to be the top in their field. As a result, they necessarily prize and reward individual contributions over team accomplishments.

Unfortunately, building an entire organization based on the competence of a few can be a risky proposition. Competent individuals move on, leaving their groups or companies with the dilemma of having to find equally qualified candidates to replace them. In addition, as problem domains and team sizes grow, these cultures have a hard time absorbing the increased demands of communication and coordination.

5% "producers" were let go every three months. There was negative incentive to work as a team. As a result, when my particular sub-group was called upon to produce a special consulting package for a new product line with another sub-group from a different business unit, not only the managers but also the employees had a very hard time letting go of "ownership" issues. We chose to stay secretive about our work and to cooperate as little as possible with the other group for fear that they would take credit for the entire project. When the final product was released, the results of the infighting and competition were glaring. The work looked disjointed, unorganized, and lacked a polished flow.

Cultivating

Cultivating cultures tend to create success by encouraging the growth of the employees. They target the health and welfare of each individual and create community by concentrating on personal well-being. By cultivating and motivating individual accomplishment and expression, they believe that the best work will emerge. Think about religious or academic cultures that promote experimentation, introspection, and personal interests as a means of defining the organization and what it accomplishes.

In software development, these tend to be highly research-oriented organizations where work is defined by the interest and motivations of the individuals. Deadlines or deliverables are not as prized as the information and learning that can emerge as a result of someone's passion about a particular topic or domain.

My Anecdote

My closest experience to a cultivating culture involved one of my early experiences as a programmer. I was assigned to a government organization whose express mission was to research new computer technologies. Each person in the group concentrated on a particular research project. For instance, one member was devoted to studying the emergence of the relational model for databases. Another person was evaluating the source code of the newly written Unix operating system—very provocative! In this environment, projects were defined not so much by purpose or by deliverable but rather by an individual with a specific research interest. Individuals were rewarded not for meeting deadlines but for bringing more and more new ideas into the organization from other disciplines. Teamwork was only happenstance because most of the researchers just wanted to work in their own specific domain.

The Collaboration Culture

In collaboration cultures, the success of the organization hinges on how teams formulate, organize, decide, and deliver. In such organizations, teamwork is prized, with an emphasis on how individuals share information, process it, and converge on the best thinking. Decisions are either team-driven or manager-driven with team consultation. In addition, consensus plays an important role in creating sustainable agreements about the solutions that emerge through the greater wisdom of the group.

Managers in such organizations believe in the explicit and tacit knowledge of the team as a fundamental tool for discovering the best solutions and creating the most innovative products.[1] They mine the team wisdom in order to take advantage of team members' backgrounds and experiences, and they foster an expert ability to communicate and coordinate. Rather than working to control their teams, these managers work to remove impediments and any external hindrances so that their teams can concentrate on the task at hand.

In software development, think about highly motivated teams of cross-functional individuals who, protected by their project manager, can converse openly about various possible solutions for a problem domain. They work to converge on a solution, decide how to complete the work, and then deliver it. There is a thriving sense of dedication based on the sense of community nurtured through open and frequent communication. Such teams turn out to be highly adaptive; they can absorb new information, brainstorm about it as a team, and create a solution.

My Anecdote

In the early 1990s, I was fortunate enough to work with two different groups that, for me, epitomized the collaboration culture. In one group, we were a team of quite diverse cultures and personalities from around North America and Europe. Very often, we had to produce work as a team with a variety of components, from software to library services, methodology materials, and training materials to support all the other components. Our manager was an open and encouraging leader who believed in the experts with whom he surrounded himself. So too, the group members had a way of valuing each other's area of expertise by inviting the recommendations of each on how to proceed and then move into action mode. With our manager in the lead and despite our geographic distances, we built a real sense of commitment to one another as a means to accomplish success. We explicitly sought synergy and worked to maintain it through our discourse and decision-making.

---

1. Nonaka and Takeuchi, *The Knowledge-Creating Company*, 59.

In the other group, a large software development team was on a very aggressive schedule to produce a radical overhaul of a system for a financial services group. Though the team didn't call it such at the time, the mode of working was clearly a collaboration culture; we worked in a very open workspace and engaged in very wide communication channels. The project manager, three team leads, and customer sat with the development team regularly in the open space, and so would collaborate with the group day-to-day with regard to how it should solve a particular problem or make a decision at a particularly crucial crossroad. Every team member was valued for their background and education, as diverse as they were, and each was encouraged to participate in the decision process as best helped the team.

Characteristics of the Collaboration Culture

In *Artful Making*, Rob Austin and Lee Devin describe two realms of work that differ dramatically from one another: one, the highly prescriptive, highly controlled work that they refer to as "industrial making"; the other, called "artful making" (as defined through their observations of theater groups), emphasizes teams and how they work. In artful making, success is a result of emergence over planning. Teams of experts continually revisit a problem to keep looking at it from different angles to learn more about it. They minimize the role of control and supervision in order to accomplish a goal. Instead, artful teams work collaboratively and move as a whole toward producing something.

In software development projects, when we create a sense of community (what Austin and Devin refer to as "ensemble") and collaboration, we get to harvest the richest talent of each of the "players" on the team. Just as theater groups capture their most creative knowledge about the play, so we instantiate our most creative knowledge in the form of the software products we deliver.

Collaboration cultures therefore exhibit these characteristics of release, ensemble, and play as they apply collaboration. They thirst for interaction and full-team participation to deliver results, maintain a sense of integrity, and absorb change. They value the power of such a culture and how collaboration can boost that power by helping teams move through conflict into productivity, through indecision to action, and through defensiveness into trust.

Chapter 3

Who Are Collaborative Leaders?

To promote a collaboration culture, we have to engage leaders who are ardent evangelists of this style of working. If you are already a firm believer in collaborative leadership in project management and in teamwork, you may want to reflect on the path that led you to this particular leadership style. What was it about your successful and non-successful previous projects that influenced your style? And, given what we now know about the strength of collaboration cultures, what leadership fundamentals did you apply toward collaboration that absorbed what you learned from the past?

Many of us transform into roles as leaders in software projects via our technical roots. We are schooled in and rewarded for our technical, not management, capabilities. Our research revolves around the ever-changing domain of technical solutions rather than leadership skills. So a path to leadership and particularly collaborative leadership may prove to be Promethean in size and attainability.

With any luck, however, our transformation never stops, neither in the technologies we master, nor in the professional and personal skills we pack into our workplace toolkits. So given our technical background coupled with an interest in acquiring a leadership style that promotes collaboration cultures, it's worth thinking about:

- How and why do non-software-oriented leaders promote collaboration?
- What do facilitators do that applies to collaboration?
- What can we in the software development domain learn about collaborative leadership styles that is applicable in our domain?

In defining how to engage as a collaborative leader in software development projects, we need only look around at the examples where such leadership styles have been used successfully in contexts that, traditionally, might not seem obvious candidates for collaborative cultures: sports, the military, and corporate America.

The Sacred Hoops of Collaborative Leadership

My first inspiration for the collaborative leader came during my five years living in Chicago in the mid-to-late '90s, working for a software consulting group. It was Phil Jackson, the coach of the then-mighty Chicago Bulls. I was so impressed with his ability to pull together diverse, highly volatile, highly skilled individuals and turn them into a team that could consistently outperform any of their NBA competitors. They were a juggernaut, and to my way of thinking, it was emphatically his ability to provide his players, Michael Jordan (a.k.a. "Michael"), Scottie Pippen, Dennis Rodman (a.k.a. "The Worm"), Tony Kukoc, and the others, with a sense of challenge and self-discipline that made it so.

What did Phil Jackson know about leadership that made him so consistently successful as a coach? I found the answer in a small book he wrote about his coaching style, entitled *Sacred Hoops: Spiritual Lessons of a Hardwood Warrior.*[1] Jackson tells how he relied on Buddhism, Lakota Sioux wisdom, and some good common hoop sense to create that sense of "team" that fueled the Chicago Bulls to their famous "3-peat" of three consecutive NBA titles. Simple lessons from an early coach, Red Holtzman of the New York Knicks, guided him:

> **Lesson one:** Don't let anger—or heavy objects thrown from overpasses—cloud the mind.
>
> **Lesson two:** Awareness is everything.
>
> **Lesson three:** The power of We is stronger than the power of Me.

These lessons formed the basis of what later drove Jackson to choose a facilitative, non-aggressive leadership style with the Bulls. He took it as his personal responsibility to build a highly integrated and self-organizing team that could define its own path to success.

---

1. Jackson, *Sacred Hoops.*

The same responsibility is in the hands of our software project managers, technical leads, and other team leads. Project success (and failure) may lie heavily on the shoulders of the project leader. But it is his ability as a leader to personally instill trust, vision, and challenge along with collaboration style that is the true measure of the project success.

Software teams, steered by collaborative coaches, leaders, and managers, learn to act in collaboration to produce the best results. They naturally engage in participatory decision-making, self-organization, and self-discipline as team norms.

The Collaborative Military Leader

If an NBA coach isn't a compelling model for collaborative leadership, consider the case of Captain D. Michael Abrashoff.

When colleague Mike Cohn learned of my interest in furthering the cause of collaborative leadership for software development teams, he directed me to Captain D. Michael Abrashoff's book, *It's Your Ship: Management Techniques from the Best Damn Ship in the Navy*. Imagine a U.S. Naval captain promoting the benefits of teams and collaboration. In his book, Abrashoff recounts his commission as captain of the USS Benfold, an aging supply ship that had struggled to reliably perform its mission for the US Navy; discharge and accident rates were high, morale and "re-ups" were low.

Abrashoff's solution to this plague was to turn to his crew for advice. He accumulated a log of their recommendations and then tracked the ones that proved beneficial. As servant to his command, Abrashoff was able to achieve the impossible, "turning the ship around" to one with the lowest accident rate in the naval fleet coupled with one of the highest "re-up" rates. How did he do it? He maintained his role as leader but turned to the crew for participatory decision-making. He sought their advice and became the instrument that tooled their success.

When I read his 11 lessons, I thought about how collaborative leaders in software development can similarly balance "command" with collaboration:[2]

1. Take command.
2. Lead by example.
3. Listen aggressively.
4. Communicate purpose and meaning.

---

2. Abrashoff, *It's Your Ship.*

5. Create a climate of trust.
6. Look for results, not salutes.
7. Take calculated risks.
8. Go beyond standard procedure.
9. Build up your people.
10. Generate unity.
11. Improve your people's quality of life.

Good to Great Corporate Leaders

Building the case for collaborative leaders, I decided to turn to another improbable source: corporate America. Surely, command-and-control managers are the backbone of truly great organizations. Or are they?

In his book *Good to Great: Why Some Companies Make the Leap…And Others Don't*, Jim Collins brings together research and resultant findings around the universal characteristics that distinguish companies able to bridge the gap from being just a good company to becoming a truly great company. Collins and his research team zeroed in on three fundamental practices of these successful companies: Disciplined People, Disciplined Thought, and Disciplined Action.

Despite the group's deliberate prejudice toward quantitative analysis (compensation, business strategies, financial ratios, and acquisitions), they discovered a startling golden thread: the key underlying characteristic of great companies was the person they came to refer to as the "Level 5 Leader." That is, as Collins describes it:

> …a paradoxical blend of personal humility and professional will. They are more like Lincoln and Socrates than Patton or Caesar.[3]

In other words, Humility + Will = Level 5 Leader = Great Companies.

When asked about how they were so successful in turning average businesses into wildly successful ones, each of the 11 CEOs interviewed was quick to deflect any credit or praise. As Collins points out:

---

3. Collins, *Good to Great*, 13.

The great irony is that the animus and personal ambition that often drive people to positions of power stands at odds with the humility required for Level 5 leadership.

Good teams, like good companies, rely on managers who can deliver humility and leadership to their teams. Neither command-and-control nor strong-handed personal ambition can create teams we can trust and upon whom we can rely. As the Swiss say about leaders and their styles: "The fish always starts stinking at the head." Indeed.

I am convinced that, like Phil Jackson, Michael Abrashoff, and Jim Collins's Level 5 leaders, we need good fish leading our software development projects in order for us to apply collaboration successfully and profitably.

Collaborative Leadership Through Facilitation Lessons

The collaborative leader instinctively moves to a management style that elevates the team wisdom through the use of a facilitative management approach.

As a profession, facilitators work as guardians for teams. They manage a collaborative process that guides decision-making, consensus building, and productive team outputs such as work processes, software, User Stories, design models, or team charters. A facilitator owns the process, not the decisions for which the process paves the way. A facilitator who moves out of managing process into owning decisions does so inappropriately and counter to the intent of the role. All decisions must be owned by the team.

Probably my favorite source of reference for collaboration and facilitation is Sam Kaner's canonical work, *Facilitator's Guide to Participatory Decision Making*. To quote Kaner:

> A facilitator's job is to support everyone to do their best thinking.[4]

And this is why facilitation skills play such an important role for project managers in agile software development.

A facilitator hones skills such as listening, paying attention, encouraging interaction, asking questions, and providing an environment in which trust and collaboration thrive.

---

4. Kaner, *Facilitator's Guide to Participatory Decision-Making*, 32.

This is how they promote the best thinking of the people around them. Project managers who apply facilitation techniques in their leadership styles promote the best thinking of their teams; they build a sense of ownership into the team. In return, they enjoy the benefit of getting the best decisions and work from the team as a result of being able to count on the best from each individual.

Collaborative Leadership in Service

Think about how agile approaches such as Scrum, XP, and Crystal guide us in how to be ScrumMasters, coaches, or project managers of our software development projects. There is a clear need for us to be more in a role of shepherd or guardian rather than commander or controller. Collaboration in agile software projects doesn't just occur within the team membership; it relies on appropriate nurturing from the leadership down and from within the team out to the customers. In this context, then, it is appropriate for software project managers to ponder the notion of leader as servant to the team: the servant leader.

Enter Robert K. Greenleaf, the grandfather of the business movement of organizational empowerment and author of *Servant Leadership: A Journey into the Legitimate Nature of Power & Greatness*.[5] Greenleaf accumulated his recommendations about servant leadership through his decades of service as an AT&T executive and as a noted lecturer, resulting in his founding of the Center for Applied Ethics. Thought leaders no less than Peter Senge and Steven Covey have turned to Greenleaf's writings for direction in defining growth-oriented and collaboration-driven cultures in modern business. We too can take advantage of Greenleaf's insight for how to build teams as powerful yet serving leaders.

Who Is the Servant Leader?

Simply stated, the servant leader as leader drives to serve the group first. Leadership evidences itself in servant leaders through their use of power; that is, in a position of strength, they determine that the greatest power they can wield is in service to their teams as leader. For technical leads, team leads, and project managers who have used power to control versus serve teams, this paradigm shift can seem antithetical to their role. Ultimately, however,

---

5. Greenleaf, *Servant Leadership*.

as evidenced in the agile software development context, a shift to this altered style of leadership reaps the greatest rewards.

How do project managers in agile software development projects exhibit their service to teams? Ken Schwaber in *Agile Project Management with Scrum* addresses this dilemma of a project manager schooled in formal project management. In Scrum, the collaborative leader (ScrumMaster) makes the shift from having authority to being a facilitator; he or she shifts from a mode of having authority to delegate instead to a role of being personally responsible.[6]

Similarly, in *Extreme Programming Explained: Embrace Change*, Kent Beck describes the role of the project manager in an XP project as someone who facilitates "communication within the team, increasing cohesiveness and confidence. The power gained from being an effective facilitator exceeds that of being a controller of even important information."[7]

Thus, there is a natural coupling between servant leadership and agile software development. Agile teams succeed when their leaders are attentive to incorporating service and facilitation into their leadership style, thus fostering collaborative, empowered teams.

Characteristics of the Collaborative Leader as Servant

So what are servant leader attributes that we can apply in our software development projects? Greenleaf highlights 10 main characteristics or strategies worth considering:

1. **Goal Setting**—Have a larger aim, a greater purpose, that guides you with equanimity in how you work with your project team. A broader goal steers collaboration when tactical situations threaten to undermine it.

2. **Principle of Systemic Neglect**—Attentive leaders have a knack for highly focused prioritization of what needs to be done. This feeds directly into the timeboxed, prioritized mode in which agile teams must work. When I work with agile software development teams, I lure them away from the many distractions that can derail them. With my belief in prioritization and my fervor for timeboxed activities, I subversively guide the team to apply their own useful systemic neglect.

3. **Listening**—Servant leaders hone their ability to use listening as a means to lead. They gather answers through the questions they offer the team and through the

---

6. Schwaber, *Agile Project Management with Scrum*, 30-31.

7. Beck, *Extreme Programming Explained*, 77.

expertise the team brings. XP Coaches and ScrumMasters walk around and listen to who is not communicating and then facilitate the useful and necessary communication, whether it is within the team or with outside contributors. They pay attention when a solution is recommended, and they guide their teams in evaluating recommendations with them.

4. **Language as a Leadership Strategy**—We must be articulate, if for no other reason than to grasp the goal of the group and to evangelize it early and often within the team and beyond. When we are walking around to make sure others are communicating, we apply our own effective, non-destructive language to help others communicate effectively.

5. **Values**—Collaborative leaders, like servant leaders, have the attribute of being responsible, in that they are responsible for building, not destroying. I bring my sense of values to the team each time I communicate with them. And my values include the conviction that the team creates its own sense of values.

6. **Personal Growth**—Servant leaders continually educate themselves, not only on their work, but also on paths of personal growth. More than any other software development approach, the agile methodologies each stress the need for values that include balance of life. Agile managers and coaches read from diverse disciplines to better equipment themselves in technical settings (such as Abrashoff, Jackson, and Kaner, for example) and bring their personal values into the teams as tools to support their teams.

7. **Withdrawal**—This leadership strategy ties in with our ability to apply systemic neglect: knowing when to let go, when to trust the instincts of the team. A leader withdraws to force the team to turn inward and seek its own strengths. Teams that stay too reliant on their manager may never learn the power of collaboration and the effectiveness of collective ownership. When leaders withdraw, they encourage teams to seek their own internal useful mentors and natural drivers.

8. **Tolerance of Imperfection**—Collaborative leaders learn to let go of their own sense of "perfection" or "right" and rely on the team's guidance for what is best. The team, not the leader, resolves what must be done and what the best solutions are. The leader uses power to guide through questioning and listening in order to help the team set the proper goal for accomplishment.

9. **Being Your Own Person**—This has been a great lesson in terms of moving from a strict plan-and-control view of project management into a more facilitative, collaborative approach. How I lead, how I implement these servant strategies has always come back to who I am and how my personality works with project teams. Each of

us takes in these collaboration strategies and defines how they can work most effectively for us and then apply the techniques accumulated from others that help us remain whole.

10. **Acceptance**—The final strategy of the collaborative leader as servant: acceptance. A servant leader in duty to the team and the team's goal learns to tolerate her own sense of imperfection and to offer this gift of acceptance to each team member. Because agile software development teams are so inter-reliant and cross-functional, this sense of acceptance must flow from the leadership down to each individual. Acceptance greases the skids of collaboration.

Pulling It All Together

As you consider your leadership role in collaborative software development projects, revisit these lessons from Phil Jackson to Robert Greenleaf. Additionally, these strategies need not apply just to the leader. Team members acting as servants to the team can support servant leadership in a guerilla fashion, in the guise of servants as followers. They groom their servant leaders, guiding them to embrace collaboration through their insistence and examples.

Returning to the topic of personal growth, here is one more source for guidance on basic practices of a collaborative leader. The Toltec wisdom as captured in Don Miguel Ruiz's book *The Four Agreements: A Practical Guide to Personal Freedom* reinforces at a very personal level what a servant each of us can be to ourselves and to team members with four simple guidelines:

1. Be impeccable with your word.
2. Don't take anything personally.
3. Don't make assumptions.
4. Always do your best.

How you absorb any of these four guidelines into your role as a leader depends on your particular leadership style. How will you promote collaboration in teams? How will you nurture the sense of trust necessary for collaboration to take place? What tools will you use? And how will you "be you" as you shift your management focus?

Decide which of these various leadership models (sports, military, corporation, service) you can absorb now into your own style. Revisit Robert Greenleaf's guidance from time to time and check in to your true sense of service to your team as their facilitative, collaborative leader. Maintain some Toltec life lessons as you make collaboration decisions moving forward. Above all, continue to check in with your teams to learn what they need from you in order to build and nurture their collaboration culture.

What Are Collaborative Teams?

Collaborative leaders who understand their responsibilities as collaboration guardians for their teams apply facilitative guidance about how to create, promote, and sustain broad participation and decision-making among team members. So, as leaders do this, what are they ultimately trying to engender?

In this chapter, I want to answer these questions: what defines a team, how can a disparate group of individuals become a high-performance collaborative team, how can we identify groups of individuals who can most readily create a collaborative and productive team culture, and finally, what does that collaborative team look like once all the other team glue has set?

What Defines a Team

In their book *The Wisdom of Teams: Creating a High-Performance Organization*, Jon Katzenbach and Douglas Smith provide a wonderful grasp of what teams are and why we should care. Through their research and years of experience, they uncovered some fundamentals about teams.

A team is more than just a working group. A team is

> …a small number of people with complementary skills who are committed to a common purpose, performance goals, and approach for which they hold themselves mutually accountable.[1]

---

1. Katzenbach and Smith, *The Wisdom of Teams,* 45.

Agile software development turns individuals into teams by promoting values such as those associated with Extreme Programming: communication, simplicity, feedback, courage, respect, and so on. These teams evolve through a strong sense of purpose, performance, and discipline; they tend to one another as individuals while demanding the best of one another. And as Scrum and Crystal Clear emphasize, teams engage through self-organization and through shared commitment to their common goal, respecting each other's past project experiences to create the successes of their current project. Teams create trust and eschew betrayals.

When teams are able to truly adopt the agile principles and values as guided by their collaborative leaders, we watch them move along what Katzenbach and Smith refer to as the "The Team Performance Curve" (see Figure 4.1). They move through their nascence as a potential team into a real team, ultimately emerging as a high-performing team.

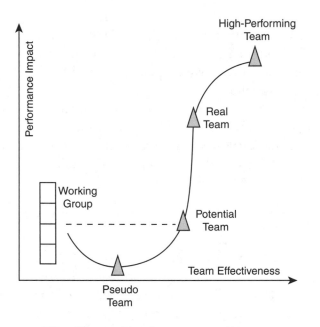

The Team Performance Curve

Figure 4.1 The Team Performance Curve (Reproduced by permission from Jon Katzenbach and Douglas Smith, *The Wisdom of Teams: Creating a High-Performance Organization* (New York, NY: HarperCollins, 1993), 45).[2]

---

2. Katzenbach and Smith, *The Wisdom of Teams,* 84.

How Teams Evolve to High-Performance

Trust, sharing, self-organization, and mutual accountability, all these things that define the high-performing team at the top of the Team Performance Curve, sprout and bloom as a result of what Bruce Tuckman has defined as the "Forming, Storming, Norming, Performing" model of team work, as depicted in Figure 4.2. In short, teams can only reach the Performing phase of working by first passing through the other three growth modes. A team must first Form and go through the characteristics of how such a team works, before it can progress to Storming, then Norming, and then finally to Performing.

Here are characteristics of each of these team maturity phases:

- **Forming**—Group members are learning how each of them works and are trying to figure out who will play what role in the team. Such teams need strong facilitative leadership and guidance to keep them on track.
- **Storming**—The jockeying for power and control begins, and team members express disagreement, distrust, and prejudice as they form alliances. Divergence is the primary characteristic of a Storming team, and so the group leader must be adept at conflict management in order to shepherd the team through this phase of discomfort.
- **Norming**—Team members now have a sense of consensus and the ability to make decisions. They trust one another about how to delegate work to sub-teams. The leader exerts less and less influence and acts mainly as a facilitator. Conflicts are resolved quickly and without distraction.
- **Performing**—The team now can focus its full attention on the performance challenge; team culture is healthy and self-managing. The team can self-navigate its work within a larger vision or strategy. All the characteristics of a Katzenbach-Smith high-performing team are in place: trust, sharing, mutual accountability, self-organization, and commitment.

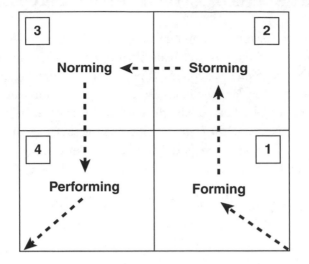

Forming Storming Norming Performing Model

Figure 4.2   The Forming, Storming, Norming, Performing Model.[3]

What Teams Do to Evolve

Given that teams must be able to pass through these stages in order to become mature enough to be high-performing, what actually moves the team along that path? In *Facilitator's Guide for Participatory Decision-Making*, Sam Kaner describes this growth in terms of how teams move from divergence to convergence. This model of divergence and convergence can serve as a simple map with regard to how you begin working with a new team, and how you create a safety net for the team to move across the tightrope from Forming to high performance.

During divergence, teams exhibit widely varying viewpoints and opinions; members may find themselves in direct conflict with one another. While a team is still Forming, this divergence is mild; it provides an opportunity for the leader and members to gather data on how they think and act as individuals. As the group work continues, the divergence actually expands. The team is now in Storming. This is where conflict is rife and can be destructive. The team enters what Kaner calls "The Groan Zone." It is hard for members

---

3. Alan Chapman, "Bruce Tuckman's 1965 Forming Storming Norming Performing team-development model," http://www.businessballs.com/tuckmanformingstormingnormingperforming.htm.

to imagine how they are ever going to work together! Strong facilitation and conflict resolution guidance are required to buffer the team through this tumult and discomfort.

Table 4.1, "Divergent Thinking versus Convergent Thinking," lists some ways to identify where your team may currently be working.[4]

Table 4.1   Divergent Thinking versus Convergent Thinking

Divergent Thinking	Convergent Thinking
Generating alternatives	Evaluating alternatives
Free-for-all discussion	Summarizing key points
Gathering diverse points of view	Sorting ideas into categories
Unpacking the logic of a problem	Arriving at a general conclusion

Notice that divergent thinking has many positive characteristics; we need to gather diverse points of view and unpack the logic of various problems and various solutions. What gets messy is when a team can't then move into the solution or convergent mode: taking the alternatives and turning them into a solution or conclusion. That is the essence of Storming, and that is where divergence that is not solution oriented no longer plays a valuable role.

So think about your software projects. Coming up with creative new solutions clearly requires that the team be able to converse fluently in divergence. But if team members turn alternatives into defensiveness or obstinacy about their particular technical solution, team creativity and productivity are ultimately squashed. (Later in Section III, "Extending Collaboration," I'll cover what to do when these dysfunctional behaviors threaten a team's ability to act convergently.)

What Kaner and other facilitators have learned in working with teams as they navigate their way through divergence into convergence is that this dynamic can neither be ignored nor forced. In his book *Adaptive Software Development: A Collaborative Approach to Managing Complex Systems*, Jim Highsmith emphasizes this need to foster divergence and convergence specifically in software development teams. Teams that come together to develop software are in reality complex adaptive systems and as such must learn to reside comfortably at "the edge of chaos." They are neither complacent and inert, nor chaotic

---

4. Kaner, *Facilitator's Guide to Participatory Decision-Making*, 6.

and accidental. Rather, they must reside actively and explicitly in just the right amount of anxiety to keep the team convergent yet challenged.[5]

My Anecdote

I am very often brought into organizations as an agent of change. I am asked to bring agile principles and practices to the organization, usually by providing training, then mentoring and consulting with one or more project teams at a time. Fairly consistently, these teams are highly divergent when I come into their group. They may have been convergent and able to work well together before my arrival. But because I represent a new way of doing things that may seem dangerous or at the very least uncomfortable for the team, my mere presence as the agent of change can throw the group into divergence. (Sometimes they quickly regain convergence by deciding to gang up on me to make the agile approach fail!)

In these early trainings and meetings with these new teams, I tend to encounter a bit of resistance, frustration, annoyance, doubt, defensiveness, and general malaise. All of these uncomfortable "feelings" can then evidence themselves in a variety of divergent behaviors. No one wants to agree on anything; everyone wants to question and contradict some aspect of any of the decisions moving forward. The tendency is for them to want to spiral away from the change and from my involvement.

What they don't know is that I recognize this "Groan Zone" and I know how to sit in it with them. I encourage their expression of what is troubling or painful. I listen to them and document their issues, risks, and concerns. And just by doing this (being with them, listening, documenting their voices), I watch for any signs that the opinions are getting destructive or damaging and pull them back by using my "Managing the Meeting Participants" techniques and "Managing Conflict" techniques. I help them begin to listen a bit more as we move on with one another into new ways of working as a team. I reinforce to them what is true about what they are saying and how their opinions are no less valid just because I believe that we can come to agreements about how to apply agile practices in their projects.

In small companies or large companies, in small teams or large teams, in single teams or multiple teams, I have been a witness to and partner in this process. I have watched teams work over and over again through this "goo" to a moment where they relax into their knowledge, power, and collaboration. They are able to express varieties of ideas without falling into accusation or confrontation and to stay convergent.

These are some of the lessons about teams and divergence that have helped me foster collaboration in newly forming teams:

---

5. Highsmith, *Adaptive Software Development*, 126.

- When beginning work with a group, don't trust someone else to tell you that a team is already working in a very convergent, collaborative mode; watch the team for any clues that an underlying current of distrust may still be flowing.
- Make sure you build time into your meetings for team members to openly diverge: evaluate the reference materials, examine your approach, check the preparations, and question the attendance.
- As a group sits in the discomfort that such discussions evoke, do not fall back on command-and-control as a means to move forward; trust in the wisdom of the team.
- Aggressively believe in the team's ability to find consensus by continually bringing their suggestions and solutions back to them and asking them to formulate a useful consensus.

Don't let anyone tell you otherwise.

How Teams Falter

So, what is happening when a team never makes it out of divergence? Or, what if they have moved through divergence into convergence (with healthy productive conflict), and then have reverted to the discord of divergence (with destructive, unproductive conflict)?

With a bit clearer sense of what teams are and what conditions nurture them into the high performance of true collaboration, think about how our software development organizations attempt to coax more productivity out of teams: team members may be matrixed (borrowed across multiple organizations), multiplexed (assigned to multiple projects at the same time), distributed (not co-located), or all three. As organizations create these shifting organisms of individuals, they cripple a team's ability to become high performing; teams tend to keep Storming in divergence. In agile software development terms, this means that teams cannot be consistently and reliably responsive to change.

As I have watched various IT organizations struggle with economy and scale, here is what I have noticed about the impact such policies have on team collaboration dynamics:

- **Remove a member**—When we remove even one member from a high-performing team, it impacts more than just the departing member; the entire team must stop to evaluate: how will that person's role be absorbed by the rest of the team, did the person leave under difficult circumstances, and does this mean a shift in power, influence, or control?

- **Add a member**—When a new person joins a high-performing team, similar questions arise: will the new member respect the existing working relationships, standards, and contracts within the team, what new standards will need to be put in place to accommodate the new person, and what power does this person assume as they join the team?
- **Change the team's goal/purpose**—A team that has made commitments to a particular performance challenge has formed its intra-team contracts and accountability based on that challenge. When this changes, questions emerge: What is the new compelling reason for the team to exist, what will be the useful roles to organize around in order to meet that challenge, and how can we best formulate our complementary skills around the new goal?

Any of these changes in team makeup can result in an unfortunate string of consequences for the team dynamic. They may move back to divergent behaviors and not come back out in a healthy manner. This means that they have regrettably abandoned their high-performing mode and have once again assumed a Forming mode. And finally, once back in Forming, this time they may not be able to successfully navigate their way through Storming all the way to Performing.

What We Can Do

Let's revisit matrixing, multiplexing, and distributing as organizational strategies and propose practices that can reduce the negative impacts such strategies can have on collaboration:

- Apply retrospectives and reflections to reestablish team norms. Agile methodologies rely on a heartbeat of retrospection on team practices in order to learn and adapt. When new members are matrixed into a team, or existing members are matrixed out of a team, hold a reflection or retrospective for all members to track a past, present, and future timeline of project milestones. The retrospective helps the entire team reflect on its practices: what has worked, what is worth altering, and what new practices could be adopted from the new member.
- Engage in a project chartering event that taps all members to declare how the group will work and what its standards of behavior, quality, status reporting, and problem solving will be. Pay particular attention to the demands that the matrixing, multiplexing, or distribution may impose.

- Be mindful of existing teams that had been self-organizing and mutually accountable but suffered as a result of reshuffling. Hold a new chartering event and reintroduce a more facilitative and engaged leadership style, one that can explicitly guide the team through the Forming and Storming that will need to take place in order to usefully absorb the team changes.
- Hold daily short status meetings to ensure that all resources meet with one another and share information about their current commitments at least once a day. Even 15 minutes can create enough of a rhythm of contact that members begin to build some sense of community and trust.
  (I will cover techniques for all of these collaboration practices in Section III and Section IV.)
- Strive to preserve the sanctity of the team from major deliverable to major deliverable. In Scrum, a 30-day Sprint to complete a set of potentially shippable functionality begins with a commitment by the development team, the Product Owner, the team coach (ScrumMaster), and all stakeholders that the team will not be altered during the 30 days.
- When a resource is a commonly shared resource (Technical Publications, Usability, Architecture), commit individuals to no more than three projects at a time. Ensure that they can commit to fixed durations of well-established teamwork, such as the 30-day Sprint defined in Scrum. Only change their work assignments as necessary and only on timebox boundaries.
- Engage a high degree of facilitation in the team meetings to help teams move through conflict into productive decision making. In distributed teams, self-organization is hard to achieve; trust tends to be equally elusive. Strong facilitation in local meetings as well as in video, web, or teleconferences can draw out the useful discussions and information sharing that improve trust and accountability, which then encourages useful self-organization.
- Plan regular meetings that bring all sub-groups of the team together to play out their diverse roles and opinions. Explicitly pay attention to conflict and encourage the constructive interchanges that help team members learn about one another and establish a sense of trust despite distances and infrequent contact.

Once these collaboration challenges are acknowledged, it is worth periodically revisiting strategies with regard to how they create or tear down the scaffolding that supports high-performing teams.

Personalities in High-Performance Teams

When some of the early adopters of agile software development were striving to explicitly draw out collaboration as a key element of the approach, they knew they had to pay attention to the individuals that make up the teams. How do different individuals' working styles clash or congeal as a team is forming? Their search led them to William Moulton Marston's DISC model of team roles in which four basic roles model the way individuals tend to participate in a team:

D—You can think of this person as primarily motivated by dominance and drive. They are always headed to a goal, like a horse to the stable.

I—This is the "influence" role of the team. They are pumped up around the "what ifs" of the project, all the possibilities no matter how wild or eccentric. They are optimistic and expressive about alternatives and new visions.

S—Teams need someone to act in a very reliable, very "steadfast" role. This person thrives on building relationships in the team, finding accord in what appears to be discord, contributing a very stable, sympathetic role to the team.

C—What would a software development team do without someone driven by detail and analysis? This "conscientious" role is checking out all the facts and figures for the team, keeping the team on the straight and narrow with regard to process, testing, and standards.

(You can learn more about DISC profiling at www.discprofile.com.)

My Anecdote

When I had first learned about the DISC model, I had a hard time believing that it could provide useful insight to how I worked in teams or how others worked with me. Here is how my thinking changed:

I evaluated which role I tended to play in a team. As a software developer, I was absolutely driven by a love of analysis and detail, and sticking with a task to do the very best job possible I could with it. That is what floated my boat! So, one thing for sure, I was not a driver, the **D** role. Even more revealing, I had to admit that being around **D** personalities really bothered me. I could see that I was a **C** with some **S** tendencies in that I worked to be supportive of other team members in order for us to be successful. To me, **D** personalities were pushy people who didn't really understand the value of my analysis and attention to detail and who preferred to just have visions and give orders. Not my style at all!

Then, I recalled which teams I'd worked in that were successful and collaborative. They turned out to be teams in which we were able to embrace all four roles and value each role's contributions. We tended to move constructively through divergence to convergence, supported one another during stressful times and through difficult decisions, and delivered software that we were proud of and that was valued by the customer. We even chose to stay together after the project was over in order to work together again.

Imbalanced DISC teams have a specific "smell" to them, based on the dominant personality role in the team. Unfortunately, these lopsided smelly teams are more common than not in that we tend to gravitate to like-minded and like-acting individuals as we formulate teams. We are driven by fear ("I don't want to have to deal with these other personality types; it's too uncomfortable.") and bad reasoning ("Dealing with these other personalities will simply ruin my work in the team."). And so we end up with teams primarily made up of drivers, or of influencers, or of sympathizers, or of calculators.

Here are some of the smells you may find familiar:

A Desperation of Drivers: These teams believe they have all the solutions and want to just get on with it, moving at lightning speed, wherever it may take them. They are desperate to just keep moving at any cost.

My Anecdote

I ran across such a team when working in methodology development for a software development consulting organization. (This particular organization had a tendency to hire D personalities, believing that only people with very high drive could work effectively in a consulting environment.)

While our group tended to be very results-oriented, we didn't tend to produce very high-quality work or very detail-oriented deliverables. Decisions were made based on speed and who had the strongest or most dominating personality in the group. Team meetings took on an incendiary feel with frequent power struggles, grandstanding, and little collaborative output. The team seemed to be constantly running as fast as it could, straight into brick walls and then on to the next great idea or initiative.

To me, the token C personality in the group, it felt as though we never completed anything to a useful level of detail. We were constantly starting new things, working intensely under tight deadlines to complete the work, and then declaring victory and moving on without finishing the work. In this environment, I was viewed as "slow, too detailed, too caught up in quality," or in other words, a classic C personality. I was soon "voted off the island" (moved to a different group) and was glad of it.

An Infestation of Influencers: This team is more prone to hypothesizing and cheer-leading than producing results. They become infected with ideas but can't move them into action.

My Anecdote

I came across this odd collection of folks in a development project I worked on years ago in a very large government organization. We couldn't keep focused and had no sense of drive to a goal, reward, or completion. As mathematicians, scientists, and researchers, we enjoyed any opportunity to debate and brainstorm. But, the lack of progressive results was maddening.

So, while we were eager to have everyone get along and to continually rework the problem statement in massive requirements documents, we had trouble really making any productive progress (a.k.a. working software). We had a hard time staying focused long enough to really grasp the details of the software in order to move forward with it and were instead mired in end-less conceptual design meetings.

Because I was just starting out in the software industry when I was associated with this team, I didn't realize how utterly immobilized we were; I couldn't yet gauge what productivity and accomplishment looked like. Later, when I moved to a private company in which we developed shrink-wrapped software under tight deadlines, I finally realized what had been so dysfunctional about the group.

A Swarm of Sympathizers: These teams suffer from an inability to make decisions, largely because no one is willing to take a stance for fear of the decision leaving someone out. They sit in a mode of constantly reworking their solution and talking through all the implications. Or, they simply have a hard time focusing on work. They concentrate more on how the team is doing, and how each individual is "feeling" in the team.

My Anecdote

As a facilitation consultant, I've been brought into such organizations in very well-established businesses as well as in state and federal government institutions. Groups sit in interminable meetings trying to get decisions from a group of users about strategies or requirements. Deci-sions come very slowly, only to be retracted and revisited the next time the group reconvened because someone's opinion hadn't been considered, or another person hadn't been consulted. We couldn't get the group to stick with a decision for fear of leaving someone out.

A Cacophony of Calculators: On the surface, this might be considered a developer's dream team: the highly competence- and engineering-driven team, awash in the analysis of detail and the grasp of every complexity of every solution. We like being left alone to poke around in a variety of solutions, making sure that we get everything "exactly right." The problem is, we may not be driving to a solution and may never truly take advantage of the power of the team's total knowledge.

My Anecdote

I have found myself in such a team on more than one occasion, one team in particular in support of electrical engineers engaged in chip design. We really had trouble sticking with a functional design decision because it never felt quite detailed enough. And when we did finally move into coding (back then we were heavily steeped in a strict waterfall process of detailed problem explication before moving to any solution development), we spent a great deal of time reworking our solutions in great detail before moving into the testing phase for fear of having produced anything that might not have grasped every possible complexity and nuance of the solution, whether specifically requested or not. Our delivery schedules were continually extended without the customer ever providing us any feedback.

Teams that can combine the best of each of these DISC characteristics and risk the discomfort of not being surrounded by "their own" turn out to have a unique gift of converging and collaborating to produce what is called "Best Thinking." The team is a complete organism with all its working parts in synch toward the same goal. When such a group has the guidance to move through divergence into convergence, they create the most powerful, the most high-performing of commitments.

My Anecdote

I had just joined a methodology team of seven people where I was the newest employee but had been asked to lead the team. As I began to work with various members of the group, I soon recognized that, while I had much more experience in agile software development, I had the least experience of anyone on the team with the particular industry we were supporting. I also began to learn that the team was in some peril: No one trusted anyone else in the team, and they devalued each other's work and perspectives; their individual working styles kept colliding. The collaborative nature of the group was actually fairly phony.

My first job as a facilitative leader was to wrest control of the decision-making away from the Drivers on the team and give it back to the entire group. I engaged in frequent information gathering and brainstorming exercises that encouraged equal voice to all members of the team, in particular the Influencers and Sympathizers who had been silenced by the Drivers. I engaged the participation of the Calculators to collect, maintain, and create large information radiators of group decisions, and I made sure that we tracked all contributions with equal vigor. In addition, I reached into my servant leadership handbook and applied "release" and "tolerance of imperfection" to let go of my own Calculator sense of what "acceptable" or "done" was.

Over time, what emerged was one of the most cohesive groups with which I have ever worked. By dropping our self-promoting, and instead encouraging the best thinking in each contributor, we began to really support one another and value these individual DISC differences. We learned to laugh a lot at our weaknesses instead of being defensive or attacking. And, we produced great work because we were able to pull from the best thinking of each team member.

The Collaborative Team—It All Comes Together

Now, with a good sense of what a team is, and who the individuals are that make up those teams, a collaborative team holds the following set of characteristics:

1. They are self-organizing versus role- or title-based in organization.
2. Teams are empowered to make decisions versus being dictated to by an outside authority.
3. Members truly believe that, as a team, they can solve any problem.
4. Members are committed to success as a team versus success at any cost.
5. Trust versus fear or anger motivates the team.
6. They aggressively engage in participatory decision making versus bending to authoritarian decision making or succumbing to bullying for decisions.
7. Decisions are consensus-driven versus leader-driven.
8. Teams maintain an environment of constructive disagreement versus falling into damaging conflict or no conflict at all.

1. Self-Organizing Teams

Collaborative teams are self-organizing versus role- or title-based in organization.

In my experience with agile software development teams, one observation I have made revolves around how such teams seem to be able to self-organize. Simply stated, these teams survey the skills of each member of the team and then allow the most useful team structures to evolve. As Pete McBreen states it:

> Hierarchical organizations do not work for software development. The command and control model of scientific management is outmoded for knowledge workers. It is not relevant when the employees—not the managers—provide the knowledge, skill, and ability to create software applications.[6]

In his book *Adaptive Software Development*, Jim Highsmith has helped us understand how complex adaptive systems by their very nature rely on the concept of emergence of roles and team in which

> ...project managers should become more focused on defining a mission and building relationships than on prescribing tasks.[7]

And, that:

> ...as the complexity increases in the environment in which a business or software development team operates, certain kinds of relationships produce better results.

A highly facilitative leader encourages this organizational discovery, letting the roles emerge as most beneficial for the team. Self-organizing and self-disciplining teams decide their own team norms and capture these in their project charter. Members are able to bring their past experiences into the group and make a team declaration about their methodology, their tools, their best practices, and framework. They decide how they will

---

6. McBreen, *Software Craftsmanship*, 70.

7. Highsmith, *Adaptive Software Development*, 121.

make decisions, how they will resolve conflict, how they will assign work, and how they will give and elicit feedback.

My Anecdote

In one XP team in which I worked, none of us were all that thrilled with providing the role of "tracker;" it was a dreaded yet necessary task for our distributed team. As a result, we took on a rotation approach in which each member was asked to complete two iterations of tracker duty per rotation. Ultimately, one team member in particular rose to the surface as the most comfortable with this job of collecting velocity information, updating it, and reporting the status to the team and to the outside stakeholders. This arose out of an ability to examine our skills and comforts and then make the best decision for the team.

---

2. Empowered Teams

Collaborative teams are empowered to make decisions versus being dictated to by an outside authority..

Collaborative teams operate through a sense of empowerment with regard to the decisions that they make and the paths they choose to success. These teams define success based on input from all team members. They build a sense of team through their commitment to one another as well as their sense of commitment to the team's challenge.

Because empowerment doesn't occur by accident, these teams rely on the project manager or coach to act as the facilitator and guardian of their power. Empowered teams can only discover their power under the careful guidance of a collaborative leader: The leader fully believes in the team's ability to do its work and believes that the team will make better decisions as a team than he alone could do.

3. Teams of Vision and Success

Members of a collaborative team truly believe that, as a team, they can solve any problem.

This is probably the greatest commitment a team must make in order to be a truly collaborative group; that is, each of the team members believes that ultimately the *team* can solve any problem. In fact, there must be a firm conviction that the team will always be better at

---

solving a problem than an individual alone. The team also grasps the usefulness of the individual experts in the group. Through its self-organization, the team recognizes when certain tasks should be performed by one individual, or when decisions should be delegated to specific individuals or sub-groups of the team.

4. Committed Teams

In a collaborative team, members are committed to success as a team versus success at any cost.

Collaborative teams build a sense of team through their commitment to one another as well as their sense of commitment to the team's challenge. This characteristic of a collaborative effort is vital in order for the team to reach its other resolve in item #3: that ultimately the team can solve any problem presented to it.

Team commitment can only occur when the manager practices release and allows the team to own its decisions. The collaborative leader fosters the team's commitment by letting go of the control and forcing the team to take control and responsibility. She facilitates commitment from the start by escorting the team through its Storming into the Norming that leads to Performing. A committed team is a Performing team. This is captured by Katzanbach and Smith, as follows:

> Within teams, there is nothing more important than each team member's commitment to a common purpose and set of related goals for which the group holds itself jointly accountable. Each member must believe the team's purpose is important to the success of the company.[8]

5. Teams of Trust

Trust versus fear or anger motivates the collaborative team.

Pete McBreen captures this in *Software Craftsmanship: The New Imperative* when he explains how software craftsmanship actually leads to collaborative development, which ultimately leads to the best solutions:

---

8. Katzenbach and Smith, *The Wisdom of Teams,* 44.

The key difference with software craftsmanship is that developers and users will understand one another better and can assist each other in making the necessary trade-offs. Sometimes hard choices need to be made, but these decisions are much easier when an underlying relationship of trust and respect exists.[9]

So, what are the characteristics of a trusting, highly functional team?

- Each member of the team contributes value to the decisions of the team.
- The team fully believes that the wisdom of the team as a whole is *always* greater than any one individual.
- Managing non-contributing members is as important as managing dominating members.
- Members firmly believe that all team members intend to act in good will.
- Members continually work to improve their ability to act without fear, anger, or bullying.

6. Participatory in Decision Making

Collaborative teams aggressively engage in participatory decision making versus bending to authoritarian decision making or succumbing to bullying for decisions.

Collaborative teams arm themselves with the powerful tools of information sharing, negotiation, and participation in order to make well-informed, team-driven decisions. Sociologist Jörg Strübing writes about the negotiation of decision-making in software projects in his paper "Designing the Working Process – What Programmers do beside [sic] Programming." He notes that this highly participatory negotiation for decision making is a fairly consuming part of a developer's total workload. Strübing characterizes this as:

> ...a process of constant assimilation of given constraints, requirements, restrictions, and opportunities. Thus, "doing" ("Tatigkeit") in this respect implicates acts of interpretation, redefinition and adaptive reconstruction of tasks.[10]

---

9. McBreen, *Software Craftsmanship*, 54.

10. Strübing, "Designing the Working Process," 3.

In other words, teams rely heavily on negotiation for their knowledge transfer and decision making throughout the whole programming process. Collaborative teams explicitly accept this attribute of their work and embrace it, whether in one-on-one communications or in group settings.

7. Consensus-Driven

In collaborative teams, decisions are consensus-driven versus leader-driven.

So what does it mean to be consensus driven? First, a simple definition of consensus: "I can live with that and support it." Consensus does not require that all team members must agree wildly on all topics. But, it does mean that no one has been compromised and no one disagrees vehemently with the recommendation.

Here are a few examples of statements I have heard people make with regard to a mistaken sense of consensus:

- "We have to run all our meetings with consensus, or else…" (This is threat, not consensus.)
- "You have to agree with us to move on." (This is compromise, not consensus.)
- "I insist on consensus in my teams." (This is command-and-control, not consensus.)
- "Since no one cares, I guess we have consensus to do option A." (This is non-participation, not consensus.)

Collaborative teams use consensus not as a weapon but as a tool that lends focus, clarity, and broad vision into decision making. Collaboration via consensus is the key to powerfully binding and enduring decisions.

To reach consensus, teams need to recognize their conflicts and work through them to evaluate their alternatives and converge on a solution. But just as each of us has our own working mode in collaboration (as in the DISC model), so we each have our own mode of managing conflict. And this variety of conflict resolution modes plays a pivotal part in how we act collaboratively.

The Thomas-Kilmann conflict mode instrument (TKI), shown in Figure 4.3, provides useful insight into these conflict resolution styles. We bring these conflict modes with us into our teams either through familial influences or through what seemed to have created success in previous professional environments.[11] Through the TKI, you can evaluate your level of cooperativeness in comparison to your level of assertiveness:

---

11. http://www.cpp.com/detail/detailitem.asp?ic=4813.

- Non-assertive, non-cooperative personalities work through conflict by *avoiding* it.
- Non-assertive but very cooperative personalities act in an *accommodating* mode to resolve conflict.
- The person who is uncooperative and very assertive resolves conflict by *competing* for their position.
- Individuals who have some ability to cooperate while remaining somewhat unassertive engage in a *compromising* conflict.
- The very assertive and very cooperative person uses the *collaborating* mode of conflict resolution.

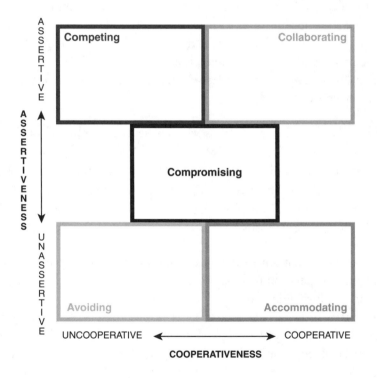

Figure 4.3   The Thomas-Kilmann conflict mode instrument (TKI), Reproduced with permission from Thomas and Kilmann, *Thomas-Kilmann Conflict Mode Instrument (TKI)*.

We benefit our teams most when we recognize our individual styles of conflict resolution and explicitly learn their positive and negative impact on our decision-making mode within our teams. A collaborative leader nurtures a collaborative team by watching these modes play out and by helping them mature into a cooperative and assertive team mode.

8. Relying on Constructive and Useful Disagreement

Collaborative teams maintain an environment of constructive disagreement versus falling into damaging conflict or no conflict at all.

When a team has truly moved to a collaborative conflict resolution style, it is able to then take full advantage of constructive and useful disagreement. The team is able to quickly negotiate through the variety of alternatives surrounding a decision, take the offerings, and craft one offering that takes the best pieces of each. Members agree that the resulting recommendation truly meets their needs in a useful way. And they are able to reap the rewards of their alternatives and recommendations without destructive conflict or worse, team dissolution.

So as a team moves through divergence and their natural tendencies toward avoidance, competition, compromise, or accommodation, its members are able to move into convergence that powerful collaborating mode of managing their conflicts with health and growth. They are able to pay attention to a variety of opinions, dig into the dirt and disagreement of their viewpoints, and emerge with the richest, best thinking of the team behind their decisions. In short, they are a truly collaborative team.

Applying Collaboration

The collaboration toolkit presented in this section provides a set of fundamental techniques and practices for building highly participatory team interactions in meetings of all sizes and shapes, with a variety of purposes and any number of outcomes. I have relied on these collaboration guidelines in my work as a project manager, as a consultant, and as a facilitator for all sizes of teams. In small team contexts, I learned that once I became adept at applying a strict set of rules around collaboration, I was able to relax the amount of planning and formality and rely instead on my instincts. I expect the same will be true for you.

As you read through the chapters in this section, you'll see a high order of discipline and rigor that may at first feel unnatural and a bit constraining. Most of these fairly formulaic guidelines are derived from experience in bringing together large project teams, up to 120 people for some large programs. In these contexts, I relied heavily on highly repeatable practices that could be customized for the particular occasion. Over time, I recognized that the discipline required to be facilitative in these larger team contexts made my small teamwork and my one-on-one work more collaborative, more focused, and more participatory.

So as you read, think about how you too will absorb the discipline, apply the guidelines, and then create a style that is truly your own.

My set of collaboration tools and techniques can be divided into the following categories of collaboration work:

- How to define collaboration events in a project
- How to prepare yourself for collaboration
- How to prepare participants to be as productive as possible
- How to plan a collaborative meeting agenda
- How to prepare the environment

- What techniques to use to gather and manage information from collaborative teams
- When and how to engage teams in conflict resolution
- How to help participants leave bad behaviors at the door
- How to help a team build a bridge from the meeting's decisions and outputs back to their desks

Chapter 5

Defining Project Collaboration Events

The true test of collaborative software teams lies in their ability to move through decisions, complete work, deliver software, all without causing undue damage to the fabric of the team. How teams move from decisions to action speaks volumes about all the other topics visited to this point: the facilitative, servant style of the leader; the collaborative, self-organizing nature of the team; and the inherent respect and trust built into both the team level communications and the one-on-one communications.

In 2002, Grady Booch surveyed developers worldwide about how they were engaged in their variety of project domains. In his survey, Grady discovered that developers tended to spend 10% of their day in "productive meetings" and an additional 7% of their day in "useless meetings."[1] A full 17% of a developer's day, then, is in these collaboration and decision-making opportunities for great success or dismal failure. Meetings are failures when participants leave the meeting feeling no productive results were achieved; or, that the results that were derived were accomplished without the full engagement of the partic ipants. In short, these useless meetings do not engage collaboration and participative decision making.

To talk about meetings as a means through which a team communicates in itself or with its stakeholders or external influencers, it is good to start with a basic sense of what these collaborative events are. You can think of meetings as falling into five basic categories:

1. The Status Meeting—"We need to find out what is going on."
2. The Planning Meeting—"We need to plan what we will do next."

---

1. Booch and Brown, *Collaborative Development Environments,* 7.

3. The Working Session—"We need to complete work."
4. The Retrospection Meeting—"We need to learn about how we did."
5. The Meeting That Shouldn't Have Happened—"We always meet at this time; that is the purpose of the meeting."

Status Meetings

If you think about the variety of status meetings you attend within the course of a project, you may have stumbled across one or two that you knew were just not working for you. Without putting a finger on it, you know that the meeting just wasn't serving a purpose for you. Here are some straightforward guidelines about how to recognize a bad status meeting, how to recognize a good one, and what to do to ensure that your future status meetings reside in the latter category, not the former.

Characteristics of a Bad Status Meeting

Project status meetings are often mistakenly run as catchall meetings. As such, they can quickly start to smell of a number of bad behaviors. Imagine being in the following status meeting:

- One or two people in the team start to delve into a detailed design problem about the production environment versus the development environment.
- The project manager begins to discuss budget issues with the client.
- The tester engages in a discussion with the deployment team about what will be automated versus manually tested.
- Three programmers pull out their laptops and begin to work on a bug from the previous day's work.
- Many side conversations ensue.
- As the project manager goes around asking each person their status, they respond "Nothing new."

What makes this a bad status meeting? In the case of the first four behaviors, the team has devolved into small problem-solving groups and stopped paying attention to the status nature of the meeting. They probably aren't hearing what others are trying to say about their current problems. Or, in the case of the last two items, team members have checked out of the meeting because they aren't really sharing information, or the meeting is taking too long, or they simply don't feel heard or understood and are left wondering "Does my status even matter to this project manager?"

The good news? The problem-solvers clearly know with whom they should be working through their problems; they've sought them out and are engaging in conversation. The bad news? They are doing it at the expense of the others in the meeting, taking up their time while they seek out detail on their problem domain and potential solution domain. Their eagerness as software professionals to solve problems has become a backbreaker for status meetings.

Characteristics of a Good Status Meeting

So, to hold a highly effective status meeting, a team takes on a very clear code of conduct:

1. *The purpose of the meeting is to share information, not to solve problems*—All participants engage in the information sharing. This means listening to others' information as well as sharing their own. If you don't need each other's status, then you either didn't need the meeting in the first place, or the team isn't acting in a mode that declares "The decisions of the team are always better than a decision by an individual."

2. *The meeting is leader-managed*—This is usually the project manager or coach, the person who is playing the role of the "process owner" as well as the role of "information owner" (not the decision owner). It is her job to call the meeting, ensure information is shared, and make sure that the meeting abides by an information-only mode. But don't confuse managed with owned; in a true status meeting, the team members own the meeting and are reporting to one another, not the manager.

3. *The meeting has only two outcomes*—Status meetings produce a status accounting, either informal or detailed, and optionally, an action plan. The information sharing in the meeting may stimulate the need for action after the meeting, such as follow-up sessions, requests for more information, or requests for added participants who can contribute needed project status.

Standup/Status/Daily Scrum Meeting

The standard agenda for a daily standup or status meeting consists of three questions answered by every participant:

1. What did I do yesterday?
2. What do I plan to do today?
3. What is getting in my way?

Think of these three questions as the daily read-out of the team members' commitment to one another: What did I commit to do for all of us yesterday, what am I going to commit for the team today, and what may be preventing me from meeting my commitment to the team? While these are the straightforward, *de rigueur* set of questions, you may want to add one or two others to specifically spur your team with respect to its useful, actionable status information. For instance, Craig Larman adds two additional questions into his meetings:

4. Have any additional tasks been identified for this Sprint/Iteration (in the Sprint Backlog)?
5. Have you learned or decided anything new of relevance to some of the team members?[2]

These three basic agenda items sit within a larger guiding context for a successful status meeting:

- Make sure the right people are attending ("Whose information do we need to move forward as a team?").
- Make sure they understand the purpose of the meeting ("We deliver information to the rest of the team; we don't solve problems in this meeting.").
- Make sure they understand the agreed-upon constraints set by the team ("We stand during our meeting." "We allow two minutes for each status report." "We charge a fine if you arrive late.").

---

2. Larman, *Agile and Iterative Development: A Manager's Guide,* 121.

Practical Guidance for Status Meetings

Teams very often need some guidance in discipline around letting go of problem solving in their status meetings. Table 5.1, "Techniques for Efficient Status Meetings," provides a few helpful hints that can bring a team to value the very efficient status meeting.

Table 5.1 Techniques for Efficient Status Meetings

Technique	Explanation
Start on time	People straggling into a status meeting five minutes after it has started is a killer, particularly when you consider that the goal is to keep the meeting concise and focused on information sharing. In one project, we instituted a 25-cent fine for anyone who showed up even 30 seconds after the start time. Most importantly, we did this very good-naturedly, letting the offender know how much we appreciated their contribution to the beer fund! Before long, offenders who knew they were going to be late would walk in the door tossing their quarter into the middle of the table ahead of them as a declaration of their "sincere" apology to the team!
Keep the meeting short	Our teams work on the 15-minute rule. Any status meeting over 15 minutes long is a status meeting "gone bad." To help maintain this meeting timebox, we began with a timer and *strictly* allowed only two minutes per attendee status. Period. We had two or three verbose contributors who, despite their initial grumpiness with the timer, learned to get to the meat of their status without the wandering fluff that used to creep into to their reports. Adopt a timer early on. Have it be the enforcer. No exceptions.
Have the meeting every day	This keeps the status meeting as short as possible. In one project in which I worked, as we approached a major deadline, we resolved to have three quick status meetings a day: 7:15 am, 11:00 am, and 4:00 pm. Why? Because the team felt it needed to find out the answers to our three status questions that often in order to make quick decisions about what to do for the impending deployment. Additionally, we had become adept enough in holding these quick check-ins that we didn't see them as a burden or waste of time. Rather, they were liberating in that, through a quick meeting with our sponsors and stakeholders, we could go back to our work and maintain a very clear focus on our tasks without a constant stream of interruptions or multiple, uncoordinated changes. *Continues*

Table 5.1 Techniques for Efficient Status Meetings (*Continued*)

Technique	Explanation
	While daily meetings are the recommendation, some teams resolve instead to meet only two or three times a week due to logistics, time zone conflicts, or very established work patterns. In these cases, ask the team what works best for the members.
Post the three questions	Yes, these are well-known and easy to understand. But any time a team makes a decision about how it will conduct itself in a meeting, post it on the wall, especially for this daily meeting that can so easily go off course. When you post the three questions, all members of the team can help keep the meeting stay on track by pointing to the questions.
Post any other agreed-upon procedures	This may include Start time/End time, fines for lateness, and any other protocols of the team ("We stand," "We sit on the floor," "We have three people who have to call in from another city," "Thursday is donut day," "You arrive late, you sing").
Collect action items	Besides sticking to the purpose of the status meeting by adhering to the three questions, the second greatest tool in managing a status meeting is to maintain an Action List. Post an Action List on a flipchart or whiteboard with three columns: • **What**—What action must be done • **Who**—Who needs to own this to ensure it gets done • **When**—By what date/time must it be done Here is where the team holds onto the various problem-solving discussions that otherwise could take over a status meeting. You can think of this list as a set of daily little User Stories: a placeholder for future discussions. Keep the actions very time relevant, something that can be completed before the next status meeting. One person owns every item/action/discussion, no matter how many people need to be involved. The Action List then becomes a good reminder for the team in the next day's status meeting: "We said we were going to do these things yesterday. Did we get them done? What is standing in our way?"

Technique	Explanation
Apply guerilla tactics	While a status meeting is led by the project manager or coach, the team as a whole should take ownership of the success of the status meeting. Without heavy-handedness, team members can keep each other to the purpose, the time limit, and the capture of action items. This works far better than the leader being forced to be the heavy hand. (You'll learn more about guerilla facilitation/collaboration in Chapter 19, "Guerilla Collaboration," along with the basic techniques for promoting collaborative decision making in teams.)

When your status meetings are running smoothly, and you feel that the team is gelling, don't be afraid to introduce some additional information sharing into the status. It's an everyday meeting and can get boring easily.

Status Meeting Flourishes

Here are some flourishes you can add to status meetings to spice them up once the team is established in the discipline and ready for some diversity:

- Every day, start the meeting with a song to see who can guess the artist/title. That person gets a free coffee/soda for the day, or the collected quarters for the week.
  - One project manager used Beatles tunes until he started running out!
- Each person takes turns bringing in a joke once a week.
  - On one project, our project manager was from North Dakota, so he decided to school us on Lena and Ole jokes about an old Norwegian couple in the upper Midwest. We couldn't handle more than one a week!
- Declare a team theme and create names for each other based on the team theme so that the status can start to reflect the team nicknames.
  - In one team, we used fish and developed an entire collection of fish names and fish culture references that then began to pepper our status information. We had Olle Musselskipper, Virgil Crabscubber, Molly Flukehausen, Penelope Fish-washer, and Noodles (yes, it is a fish culture reference!) give their status. When new members joined the team, we started using characters from "Finding Nemo" to augment the roster: Peach, Nemo, Marlin, Bubbles, Gil, and Dory.

- In the "What did I do yesterday?" report, encourage team members to point out someone in particular to thank them for something they had done the day before.
  - In our project, we referred to this as "Greats and Gifts." To compliment someone was to give them "a great." And to help them understand something that they could have done differently/better was to give them "a gift." Using this in our status meetings helped us to pay attention *daily* to how we were acting as a team.
- Take turns bringing in food, or once a month, turn the meeting into a breakfast.
  - Our favorite donut shop in Denver is "LaMar's Donuts," so once a month, the client sponsor would load up on "LaMar's" and orange juice to bring to our meetings. These meetings lasted longer than 15 minutes, but no one minded!

Planning Meetings

Planning meetings come in a variety of packages and can occur at any of the stages of a project's lifecycle. For instance, you can think of a project retrospective conducted at the end of a project as a planning meeting: It helps a team collaboratively accumulate knowledge about the inner workings of the project that is then used to plan how to shut down the project, how to engage project team members, and how to plan future projects. A planning meeting may take several days when strategizing for the start of a very large development effort to encompass multiple teams dispersed across multiple geographies delivering a wide number of functions. Or it may take 10 minutes, such as when planning the activities for the day of a four-person development team.

Planning meetings and working sessions have much in common in that the purpose of the meeting is to produce something: a work product, a plan, a strategy, a deliverable, a process, or something similar. Like the status meeting, the planning meeting has a very specific purpose and can appear a bit more restricting than the working session in that its intended outcome or product is strictly the plan. And like a status meeting, the planning meeting can so easily be taken off course, lose its purpose, not produce the much-needed work of the team, and frankly annoy the heck out of all attending.

This means that as the project team comes together for a planning meeting, you should help the members adhere to some simple cautions and guidelines (see Table 5.2).

Table 5.2 Planning Meeting Cautions and Guidelines

Planning Meeting Caution	Guideline
Avoid extended status sharing—This should have already been done prior to the meeting, in anticipation of it. Don't waste participants' time with status. Combining status sharing with a planning session can easily dishearten participants into believing that they aren't really there to get to the planning.	If you must share status, make it short and *specific to the purpose of the planning that is to take place in the meeting.*
Make sure information sharing is specific to the purpose of the planning—Don't use the meeting as an excuse to inundate the team with information that is not necessary in order for the planning to proceed.	Complete as much information sharing (architecture design, use cases, object class guidance, business model, etc.) as possible prior to the meeting. Additionally, make sure it is *specific to the purpose of the planning that is to take place in the meeting.*
Plan, don't build—Software teams seem to be naturally drawn away from planning scope or design or schedule and instead drawn into the detail of the solution domain. We are natural problem solvers and we love to get our hands around a solution! Unfortunately, this can derail a planning meeting. So while the team may have created some interesting other artifacts while moving off purpose, the plan itself will ultimately be hastily drawn (if at all) and potentially not represent the best thinking of the full team.	If the planning session needs to include some detailed diving into the solution (such as a quick spike), timebox it and make sure it is *specific to the purpose of the planning that is to take place in the meeting.*
Don't finish a plan without defining actions to support it—Creating a plan and not executing against it is the greatest killer of enthusiasm for any future planning meetings.	Build an action around the implementation of the plan where the actions have an owner and a date and are *specific to the purpose of the planning that is has taken place in the meeting.*

Clearly, the overarching guidance for a planning meeting is to make sure that all work, all discussions, all information sharing, and all follow-up actions are specific to the planning intended. Sticking to the purpose engenders collaboration in such a wonderfully subtle way. When you stick to the purpose of the planning meeting, or any meeting, you:

- Instill trust in the team that you are not hijacking the meeting for your own "agenda."
- Encourage the team to fiercely own the purpose and make sure that they help each other meet the purpose.
- Declare that you are not wasting the team's time by injecting other information or activities that don't shepherd them to their purpose.
- Provide them clear information that can help them decide whether their gathering would be better served by altering the purpose or by ending the meeting entirely.

As with status meetings, the team must police itself to stick to the purpose and to not allow the meeting to be derailed into solving end-product issues, business issues, resource issues, or any other issues deemed to reside outside of the domain of the planning.

Be aware! You are not alone. Planning meetings very often wrestle with how to set and maintain the boundaries of the planning: what issues reside within the problem domain and therefore must be addressed, what issues reside within the solution domain and therefore must be addressed, and what issues are moving us away from planning and into working in a way that distracts versus supports the planning? (Later, I'll cover some techniques for managing these risks about the issues before the team ever sets foot in the planning meeting. Using these collaboration techniques for boundary placement and conflict resolution will ultimately be some of your most powerful collaboration tools.)

Following are some of the planning meetings I see in very collaborative software development environments. While you may think of others more à propos of your particular work environment, these give you a taste of what I mean by planning. (Later in Section IV, "Collaborative Facilitation Guides," I'll delve into the very specific guidance that can bootstrap you toward conducting your own version of each of these planning meetings.)

Project Chartering Meeting

In *Agile Project Management: Creating Innovative Products*, Jim Highsmith describes a project planning meeting that kicks off the Envision phase of the project. Agile projects and non-agile projects alike have an opportunity to set the project in motion on a positive footing by using such a meeting as a planning device. In this meeting, team members and stakeholders come together to define a common vision for a project and the plan that can sustain the team in that vision.

Here are some elements of a collaborative project chartering meeting:

- Who are the members of the project team for this project?
- What is the product vision box these members can define for the associated product?
- What is the elevator test statement that can guide this product vision?
- What is the scope of this project within this product vision?
- What is the one-page project data sheet that describes this project?
- Who will be included in the project community?
- What are the community values that support this project?
- How will the team deliver the product in this project context?

Scrum Sprint Planning Meeting

The biggest planning event in the Scrum project is its Sprint Planning Meeting, where the project team convenes to establish the key characteristics of the Sprint to come. In the practical guide for this meeting located in Section IV, you'll see a detailed agenda can very clearly support this purpose.

Here is an example overview of what such an agenda would hold:

- Who is the product owner for this Sprint's Product Backlog?
- Who is in the project team for this Sprint?
- What other stakeholders maintain "skin in the game" of this Sprint?
- What is the full set of items in the Product Backlog to be considered for this Sprint?
- What is the length of this Sprint?
- What concerns does the team have about the Product Backlog and the length of the Sprint?
- Based on these concerns, what changes must be made to the Product Backlog?
- What is the final priority of the items in the Product Backlog?
- What priority items from the Product Backlog are being placed in the Sprint Backlog?
- Given the items placed in the Sprint Backlog, what are all the risks to be managed during the Sprint?

- How shall the project team report its progress and risk management during the Sprint to the Stakeholders?

While this agenda may at first blush appear massive or too defined, it actually can act as a powerful liberating tool for the Scrum team. It clearly leads the meeting participants through planning a completed, prioritized Sprint Backlog with project roles established, risks identified, and status reporting agreed upon. There is no doubt about the purpose of this meeting; anyone attending the meeting could immediately tell if the team is not meeting its purpose. And, through the use of techniques for collaboration to be detailed in the later chapters, each decision along the path to meeting the purpose of the group is reached via participation by the entire team and through consensus building.

This is a collaborative planning meeting.

The XP Release Planning and Iteration Planning Meetings

Extreme Programming uses its powerful Planning Game as a means to inject various stages of planning throughout a project's life. It prompts business decisions about dates, scope, and priorities and technical decisions about estimates. Teams engage initially in Release Planning about what Kent Beck and Martin Fowler refer to as one turn of the business crank.[3] The Release Plan then reveals a series of development cycles that support mid-course corrections along the path to the release. Each of these identified iterations then has its own planning meeting.

Release Planning Meeting

The purpose of the Release Planning meeting is to identify, estimate, and prioritize the user stories to be considered for the coming release, as well as to confirm project roles and a project charter for how the team will engage itself during the release.

---

3. Beck and Fowler, *Planning Extreme Programming,* 22.

An agenda that drives to that purpose would have some of the following elements:

- Who are all the members of the team to be engaged in this release?
- What are the roles of each of the members of the release team?
- What are all the User Stories to be considered by this team for this release?
- What are all the issues associated with the potential list of User Stories for this release?
- Given these issues, what are the estimates for the User Stories to be considered for this release?
- Given these estimates, what is the priority of the User Stories to be considered for this release?
- Given these estimates and priorities, what is the recommended length of the timebox for this release?
- Given these priorities and the release length, what are all the other considerations for selecting the final set of User Stories for this release?
- What is the final prioritized, estimated set of User Stories for this release?
- Given this set of User Stories and the length of the release, how many iterations will be in the release?
- How shall the project team members report progress on the release and its Iterations?

Here again, a very detailed agenda leaves no doubt to anyone attending:

- We are planning an XP release.
- These are the components of our plan.
- We know our purpose and so will also know if we waiver from it.

Later, when I touch on guerilla collaboration, you'll learn the incredible power that a detailed agenda lends to a project team in self-managing its way through a planning meeting, or any meeting. The team members, in their roles as "servant followers," keep each other on task and also keep the servant leader honest about the level of collaboration being sought when moving from agenda item to agenda item. Radiating this agenda information so clearly and openly becomes one of the most subtle yet powerful collaboration tools the planning meeting can have.

Iteration Planning Meeting

The purpose of the Iteration Planning meeting is to identify specific tasks and owners of the tasks for the subset of user stories to be completed in the iteration along with the initial user acceptance criteria. An Iteration Planning meeting agenda can take the following form:

- Who are all the members of the team to be engaged in this iteration?
- What are the roles of each of the members of the iteration team?
- What are all the User Stories to be considered by this team for this iteration?
- What are all the issues associated with the potential list of User Stories for this iteration?
- Given these issues, what are the detailed tasks to be associated with each of the User Stories in this iteration?
- Given these detailed tasks, what are the estimates for the User Stories to be considered for this iteration?
- What are the acceptance tests associated with each of these detailed, estimated User Stories?
- Given these stories, tasks, and tests, what are all the concerns about the length of this iteration?
- Who are the owners of each of the tasks and tests to be completed in this iteration?
- What is the final prioritized, estimated set of User Stories with their tasks, tests, and owners to be completed in this iteration?
- How shall the project team members report progress on the iteration?

Three other types of planning events can be used to drive the flow of a project from a high-level view to an iteration view:

- **Agile Practices Planning Meeting**—How will we apply agile approaches?
- **Business Scoping Meeting**—What is the business vision?
- **Timebox/Schedule Planning**—What will we complete in this timebox?

Agile Practices Planning Meeting

In an Agile Practices meeting, the entire team evaluates its approach toward using agile software development practices as a structure of its overall practices. The team's goal is to produce a report of its recommendations and to outline a plan for the development effort.

A simple approach to the planning that occurs in such a meeting includes the following items for consideration:

- What is the business scope for this project?
- What is a high-level view of the project team structure?
- What is a high-level view of the technical structure of the project?
- Given the scope and team make-up and technical structure of the project, what are all the possible agile practices that can be suitably applied to this project?
- What concerns are there about implementing these practices?
- What supporting practices can be applied to mitigate these concerns?
- Given these concerns and supporting practices, what is the final set of agile practices the team will apply for this project?

A retrospective meeting conducted about this topic helps the team to revisit its original recommendations and adapt them according to how they have worked or not worked to support the development effort.

Business Scoping Meeting

In this meeting, a team of business line representatives or product managers models the business processes to be automated (including functions, users, and information sources) and evaluates the associated risks and constraints in order to establish overall project priorities. The goal is to produce a project scope and vision that can guide subsequent planning meetings with the full development team. Notice that the meeting's goal, its last agenda item, is the full commitment of the business team to support the overall vision of the project.

To complete this work, you can think of a plan progressing as follows:

- What is the overall vision for this product/project?
- What are all the business functions to be supported in meeting this vision?
- Who are all the users that interface with these business functions?

- What are all the information sources associated with these business functions?
- Given these functions and interfaces, what are the major categories of functions to be scoped for this project?
- What is the priority of each of these major categories?
- Who will be the business representative for each of these major categories?
- What is the total commitment of the business to this scope and set of categories and representatives?

Project Working Sessions

Working meetings have an overall flow that revolves around bounding the work, managing the collection of data about the work, declaring useful groupings or prioritizations about the data for further consideration, declaring recommendations for the work, producing the work, and then determining actions related to delivering the work and reporting on it to appropriate parties.

Design meetings are a good example of this work meeting flow.

Design Meetings

Design meetings, like planning meetings, afford a team the opportunity to tap into the wealth of team resources in order to create a whole greater than the sum of its parts. In a complex design decision, no one person can represent the entire team's expertise with regard to technology, cost, time, risks, and so on. Similarly, the benefits a design may afford the team in reducing technical debt may not be clear to a tester, but the tester in turn may be able to provide test environment information that can help the team reach a more appropriate alternative.

- What is the scope of our design work?
- What are all the risks to consider in defining the design alternatives?
- What are all the technical benefits to consider in defining the design?
- What are all the budgetary considerations in defining the design?
- What are all the time constraints that may impact design decisions?
- Given this information, what are all the design alternatives within the prescribed scope?

- What are the benefits of each alternative?
- What are the concerns associated with each alternative?
- Given this information, what is the recommended design?

Requirements Modeling Sessions

Ellen Gottesdiener in *Requirements by Collaboration: Workshops for Defining Needs* provides a set of models (see Tables 5.3 and 5.4) that can be used for requirements gathering, based on the intended focus of the work as well as the intended view for a given team. With these models, Ellen creates collaborative agendas that guide teams through requirements working sessions. As they help the team focus on their purpose, the models gather and record the collective team wisdom. In essence, Ellen's models establish the working map of agenda items that will guide the team to meet its purpose:[4]

Table 5.3 Requirements Models by Focus

Focus	Requirements Model
Who	Actor map
	Actor table
	Prototype
	Stakeholder classes
	User interface navigation diagram
What	Context diagram
	Domain model
	Glossary
	Relationship map
When	Event table
	Statechart diagrams

Continues

---

4. Gottesdiener, *Requirements by Collaboration*, 30, 33.

Table 5.3 Requirements Models by Focus (*Continued*)

Focus	Requirements Model
Why	Business policies
	Business rules
	Decision table, decision tree
How	Process map
	Scenarios
	Use cases
	Use case map
	Use case packages

Table 5.4 Requirements Models by View

View	Requirements Model
Behavioral	Actor map
	Actor table
	Context diagram
	Process map
	Prototype
	Relationship map
	Stakeholder classes
	Use cases
	Use case map
	Use case package
	User interface navigation diagram
Structural	Domain model
	Glossary

View	Requirements Model
Dynamic	Event table
	Statechart diagrams
Control	Business policies
	Business rules
	Decision table, decision tree

So, one of these requirements workshops might have the following set of agenda items:

- What subset of the overall system scope are we defining?
- What are all the requirements within that functional scope?
- For each of these requirements, what are all the focal aspects of the requirement that need to be further defined?
- Given these focus guidelines, what is the recommended set of models to use in defining the requirements?
- For the defined subset of scope, what are all the useful views to define in laying out the system?
- Given these views, what are the recommended models to use in completing the requirements definition?
- What are our next steps in completing these models?

Agile Modeling Design Meeting

In his book, *Agile Modeling: Effective Practices for Extreme Programming and the Unified Process*, Scott Ambler does a nice job of helping both Agilists and non-Agilists alike learn how to engage in highly effectively modeling for both the planning of their projects as well as for their design. To think about what a planning session might look like in this context, a team can meet to collaboratively determine exactly how it will take advantage of modeling as a powerful means of articulating and gaining consensus in the variety of project domains.

- What is the scope of the functions to be delivered in this system?
- What are all the requirements within that functional scope?

- What categories do these requirements fall into within that scope (business, user, system, functional, non-functional, data, security, architecture, etc.)?
- What are all the possible models that might be useful for capturing each of these categories of requirements?
- For each of the identified categories, what is the best model to use in capturing requirements within that category?
- What are the highest-priority models needed within each of these categories?
- For each of the high-priority models in each category:
  - What is the primary focus of the model?
  - What is the context within which this model will sit?
  - What questions will the model solve?
  - Who needs to participate in defining this model in order to answer these questions?
  - What representation will we use for the model?
  - Given this representation, what new issues, risks, or questions have arisen as a result of building the model?

Self-Organized, One-on-One Meetings

One-on-one communications make up the yeoman's chunk of that work that Strübing refers to as the constant assimilation of given constraints, requirements, restrictions, and opportunities that goes on in development teams.

Agile projects in particular derive great strength from the continuous one-on-one collaborations that build the sufficient, continuous, and just-in-time detail of the project. Teams use one-on-one meetings to quickly engage in information exchange, so they need skills in how to accumulate information, evaluate the information, and make decisions with the data in a way that builds upon the convergence and trust of the overall team. In one-on-one meetings, such as pair programming, customer acceptance, or test definition, the participants must both be servant leader and servant follower; each must strive to ensure that decisions represent the best of their overall thinking.

In any of these one-on-one collaborations, you can check in with yourself and your colleague by asking:

- What is the purpose of our meeting?
- What different ideas or recommendations does each of us have about our purpose?
- What are the pros and cons of our recommendations?
- How shall we proceed with our work?
- What action items remain from our work?

While this may appear restrictive and formulaic, I have seen it work fairly effectively in helping pairs know when they are staying focused and knowing when they are not on track. In several companies in which I have either worked or consulted, it has become our team norm to sit down and have our first question always be: "What is the purpose of our meeting?" This works particularly effectively with managers who like knowing that the meeting has a specific focus, despite their unfortunate tendency to not stay focused!

Retrospection Meetings

Reflection workshops and retrospectives have been the unsung heroes of software development process improvement, team building, and collaboration-building events. Despite their unsung past, they now enjoy greater and greater importance in agile software development projects. These meetings are pivotal to how teams can continue to bond as a team, improve their skill set, adapt their project delivery approach, and continue on their path from divergence to convergence. Conducting such events collaboratively is key to their success and their positive impact on the team.

There is no finer expert in this work than Norm Kerth as articulated in his *Project Retrospectives: A Handbook for Team Reviews.* Norm's work leaves no doubt about the importance of collaboration in a retrospective from start to finish: how you plan the retrospective by surveying the sponsor as well as the attendees, how you prepare for the retrospective by inviting highly collaborative interaction and explicitly planning for it, and how you conduct the retrospective by constantly checking in with the group about what is working in the workshop and adapting the experience to ensure their trust and participation.

Iteration/Release Retrospective

Integrating learning into the project flow brings reflection directly into how the team works. Using some Jim Highsmith guidance, you can think about not just collecting the data, but also evaluating, as a team, how you would grade yourselves milestone-by-milestone using a Teams Self-Assessment Chart.[5]

- What were the major milestones of this release?
- What worked well in this release?
- What were some "Ah Ha!" moments in the release?
- What was frustrating for us in the release?
- What were our major distractions in the release?
- What do we still not understand?
- How well do we think we did?
- Based on these milestones, "Ah Ha" moments, and concerns and frustrations, what are our recommendations moving forward?

Sprint Demo and Review Meeting

- What commitments were made by the team for this Sprint?
- What functionality can be demonstrated from these commitments (stories)?
- What is the state of the remaining commitments (stories)?
- Based on what we have just seen, what have we learned about the project scope?
- Based on what we have just seen, what have we learned about the Product Backlog priorities?
- Based on what we have just seen, what have we learned about our estimates for the next Sprint?
- What practices in this Sprint helped the team?
- What got in the way of the team during this Sprint?
- Based on these observations, what are the team's recommendations for the next Sprint?

---

5. Highsmith, *Agile Project Management,* 221.

Reflection Workshop

Alistair Cockburn has instituted the idea of mid-course retrospection through the Reflection Workshop in the Crystal Clear methodology. This quick look back by the team helps it take a quick health check while staying focused on their priorities and goals:

- What practices would we want to keep or do again?
- What are our ongoing problems?
- What problems can we fix or escalate?
- What conventions or practices can we introduce now to address these problems?
- What three or four new things would we like to try?
- What is our action plan for instituting these recommendations?

Project Retrospective

Project retrospectives occur to help a team ponder its work and its style of working without having to report quantitative project results as is often connoted by the term "project review." As a result, Norm Kerth often refers to these project reflections as postparta, suggesting a sense of birthing something new into the world from the development project. Others refer to them as postmortem meetings, referring to the "after death/end" of the project view taken in the meeting. Each of these terms helps a team understand the intention: to pause, think about what has happened and how it has happened, and learn.

While Norm describes a number of powerful assumptions and supporting handouts that can guide a productive project retrospective, here is a basic flow of agenda items that takes advantage of that preliminary material and creates an overall reflection on the project:

- Who were all the project team members, stakeholders, and any other influencers or information resources?
- What is your definition of success for the project?
- What are all the significant artifacts you have collected from the project?
- What is the effort data associated with this project?
- What was the timeline for this project?

- What is all the information we can mine from the timeline?
- Based on our work, what are our appreciations for our colleagues on this project?
- What are our messages about the project?
- Based on our timeline, information, and messages, what are our recommendations from this project?

The Meeting That Shouldn't Have Happened

Unnecessary, unplanned, ill-run, unfocused, and non-action-driven meetings are potentially some of the most common and hence highly destructive of the meetings we encounter in software development projects. They are time consuming and disruptive. They distract and annoy team members and create distrust about meetings in general. You might think of them as "collaboration-killing wolves in sheep's clothing." They drain a team's energy and very often reinforce the team's sense that the project is not really a collaborative effort at all. They undermine any sense that the team is truly self-organizing and focused on action.

I have a colleague, Bob Moir, who argues that *every* meeting must "build a bridge" between the developer's desk and the meeting itself. That is, any team member attending that meeting must clearly see a benefit for being in the meeting versus remaining at her desk. Leaving the meeting, each participant must carry something back to her desk (an action, or a meeting output, or a shared piece of information, or a decision) that directly impacts her work. Without this clear "bridge," participants see no need to be in a meeting or to actively listen and participate.

If you can't build a bridge between a meeting and each attendee's desk, you may be creating the dreaded meeting that shouldn't have happened.

My Anecdote

In one company I visited providing some collaboration consulting, there was a sign above each meeting room door: "If you have not received a purpose and agenda for this meeting, please turn around and return to your desk." The company was determined to weed out the many meetings that shouldn't have happened.

Chapter 6

Preparing Yourself as the Process Owner

The work of collaboration in each of the defined collaboration events starts with a very facilitative and service-oriented guide, someone tooled and schooled to help a group of project members engage as a team. If you are assuming this role, you have a few simple tasks and practices to test and validate your responsibilities in this role. You may first want to refresh yourself in the "Servant Leader" information provided in Chapter 3, "Who Are Collaborative Leaders?," about the work of Robert Greenleaf. His characteristics of a servant leader form a solid context in which to prepare yourself to act as facilitator in your software project events.

Establishing Your Convictions About Collaboration

Before applying any of the practical tools related to collaboration events such as meetings or workshops, the collaborative leader establishes a very clear conviction about the use of participatory decision making in how the team proceeds. When you take on the role of collaborative servant leader, or if you are a team member guiding a leader by being a servant follower, your convictions about the reality of collaboration and its usage play a key part in any meeting's success.

Think about your role as follows:

You must firmly believe that the people gathered for this meeting are the right people.

You must believe that, as the right people, they can and will produce the desired outcomes that meet the purpose of the meeting. Without your firm conviction in this tenet of meeting planning, any stresses you encounter around the planning of the meeting or the flow of the meeting will result in bad decision making on your part.

Once you believe this, you'll discover a basic set of practices that can keep you honest in your work:

- Stay positive
- Foster self-organization
- Ask questions
- Encourage information sharing
- Drive to consensus
- Make everything else highly visible
- Take away the blame

In surveying each of these practices, you'll discover that language and attitude play a pivotal role. As you evaluate each of the practices, consider your own use of language in your leadership style. Is it calming, encouraging, rewarding, motivating, and positive? Or is it meant to agitate, confront, punish, or control? Paying attention to your facilitative tone plays a role in each of these practices.

Stay Positive

Facilitative leaders earn their team's trust through continual reinforcement that the team, not the leader, owns its decisions. When facilitating a collaboration of team members, your job is to remain, not just neutral, but positive about the team's ability to own its outcome. This means that you choose a role of process owner, not decision owner, in an encouraging and motivating mode. In all the preparation and planning, in all the actual work of the meeting, and in the follow-up from the meeting or workshop, your single responsibility is to ensure that the team has a neutral collaborative environment in which to produce their best work.

Owning the process, not the decisions, can be a challenge when, as the collaborative leader, you bring your own set of skills, knowledge, and prejudices to the table. You'll know that you have seriously moved to a truly collaborative style of decision making when:

- You value the opinions of the group more than your own.
- You provide process guidance through positive encouragement instead of controlling dictatorship.
- You provide your opinion only as an expert contributor and only with the permission of the group (more on this later).
- You don't use your opinion to sway the outcome of the meeting.
- You enlist others to dog your neutrality and ensure it is engaged throughout the meeting.

My Anecdote

Very often, when I am brought in as a consultant to help organizations transition to more agile approaches, one of the first roles I assume besides agile mentor is facilitator of their initial planning meetings, their daily standup meetings, and their first retrospective. When I originally began my work as a facilitator of large process meetings, I concentrated very hard on the neutrality aspect of my role in these meetings. Over time, and through the observations of others, I learned that, more than just neutrality, my role was to initiate and maintain a positive attitude about the group and its work within the process I was providing them.

This was no less true for one group I was facilitating through their first Iteration Planning meeting. The developers were getting very annoyed that they were being asked to think about their work as more than just one large code base. And the testers couldn't see why they should even participate in the meeting. As I worked to help the team look at their work in terms of a backlog, emotions were getting high about the frustrations and confusions and the inevitable disagreements. Time and again, the group challenged my conviction about the process, their knowledge, the work at hand, and the feasibility of really doing it all. I remained steadfastly positive about their ability to do the work and the efficacy of the approach. No matter how negative the comments were, I stuck with my positive viewpoint and tended to the process while guiding the participants through their decisions.

During a break, one of attendees came to me and said: "How can you remain so calm and positive in this meeting? Nothing seems to upset you! I could never do what you do!" I answered her as I answer anyone in these situations: "But *you* are the ones doing the hard work here! You are the ones who must make the hard decisions and then form an action plan around those decisions. I am just here to help you along that path. And I have every faith that you are the right people to do this."

Teams learn to let their distrust and cynicism melt away by having a facilitative leader maintain neutrality about their decisions while holding a positive conviction about their ability to make those decisions.

Through the early divergence and storming that teams must endure, they lose faith that they can constructively resolve their conflicts and create a sustainable pact. Remaining neutral in these storms provides comfort to a team that they really do own the future and that they really can solve problems without being herded into a decision. It is probably one of my greatest thrills as an agile mentor to steward teams as a neutral guide through these storms. When I am in a facilitative role, I am a servant to the team. I am very clear with myself that I stand my ground of neutrality through any storm.

Foster Self-Organization

Self-organization does not mean without flow, or form, or context. Nor does it mean leaderless. To foster self-organization means to:

- Encourage teams to figure out the best way to complete the defined work.
- Encourage decision making fit for the occasion.
- Remind teams to use their charter as their guide.

Teams that self-organize through the discomfort of Forming and Storming as guided by a true leader become the truly high-performing teams. As they Form and Storm, they create their own sense of team, a profile of fluid roles that works best for the team and its mission. Such teams work in that convergent mode of working that supports the useful critical decisions that must be made; they adopt collaborative agreements to craft and embrace more sustainable decisions. Each time you, as the collaborative leader, specifically step out of a decision and encourage the team to own it, you can more effectively step in when difficult decisions must be made.

When is the right time to start fostering self-organization? From the very inception of the team, you encourage team ownership of its roles and structure. How you manage yourself and your mode of leading the team continually drives this message home. So, while it is important to be a visible process owner as teams are Forming and Storming, you have ample opportunities within that context to move the team into self-organization. You step out of decisions to encourage self-organization. You step in when the divergence threatens to wound the team. You create a safe environment in which to poke and prod the team into formulating its identity, making them slightly uncomfortable but still maintaining a buffer of safety. Then you move back in to reflect their accomplishments as a team to them.

How do you urge teams into self-organization? Like little foxtrot steps, use early, quick wins to help the team build up some steam around their abilities as a group. In short, have them own a series of well-focused decisions from the start. This leads to ease of team well-being when later tackling the complex and potentially contentious issues they will likely encounter.

Here are a few steps to take along the self-organization path:

- From the start, confirm your role as process lead, not as team manager; this reminds them that they must take the lead on context and decisions.
- Use a stronger facilitative role at the beginning when the team still needs to learn about how they wish to self-organize; give them structured work to do and don't interfere with their way of doing the work and the conclusions they draw.
- Let the team take over more and more process responsibilities once they have successfully navigated through the potential destructive conflicts that can arise early on.
- Force team members to address one another in meetings by avoiding eye contact with the current speaker. When you turn away or toward other members of the team, you force the speaker (or speakers) to address the rest of the team, not you. (Colleague Mike Cohn talks about going so far as to pick up a magazine and read it during the daily stand-up meeting to force team members to address their status and issues to one another, not him!)
- Early on, lead the team in short brainstorming exercises that allow them to exhibit and confirm the breadth of their experience as well as flex a little mental muscle.
- Ask for recommendations early on about simple team protocols; this forces the team the turn to one another for decisions and recommendations.

My Anecdote

In one example of applying these techniques, I had been asked to help a cross-functional group of approximately 20 product owners and technical staff establish a set of high-level requirements for a new customer support website. The group had met several times and had not been able to produce any work. The meetings inevitably ended up in finger pointing and frustration. Additionally, I discovered that the meetings were being organized and run by one of the product owners who was very controlling and had a very specific end in mind for the meetings.

From the start, I asked the group for several recommendations about how to run the meeting: what will our ground rules be, when will we end the meeting, when should we have a break, and how long should the break be? When they were able to agree on these simple things, I could see that they liked owning their meeting and having the ability to make decisions as a group.

My next order of business was to have them sit in groups of three to brainstorm the purpose for the group. Again, they learned quickly that they had a lot in common, a number of overlapping interests and goals. The mood continued to lighten.

After several additional such exercises, I finally had them reach into the difficult work that they had not been able to wade through in the earlier meetings. Working in small groups, each with a specific aspect of the customer support equation to detail, they self-organized about how to complete their work: who had what expertise; what they should define; and how they should define it. At the end of the timebox for this small group work, they were then able to all come together and self-organize as a whole to produce the first cut at an end-to-end high-level view of the system. They were ecstatic that they had actually all agreed on something and that they had done the work themselves without coercion or railroading.

Ask Questions

Probably one of your most powerful tools in shepherding a team into self-organization and into high-performance is to use language as a tool. Positive feedback, reflective listening, and clear and precise language all are vital communications aids. Questions posed to the team capture the summation of these useful language techniques for communicating with the team. Questions confirm that the team, not you, owns its answers, its expertise, its destiny. This doesn't mean you never answer questions! Rather, you carefully gauge the usefulness of resolving an issue versus having the team resolve it for themselves. Your questions draw the team into owning its information and the decisions made with the information. And as you hone your skill as a questioner, you will discover that you rely less and less on your own problem-solving mode and more and more on your team.

Questions in general serve to:

- Get the team to move their thinking out of just one mindset (typically a destructive or negative one).
- Encourage the team to leave old thinking behind.
- Make a path toward new and different thinking.

You can also engage in questioning for more specific purposes such as when a team is just Forming and members are potentially still distrustful of one another. These questions come in a variety of forms and are used for a variety of purposes:

- Get them to tell each other information ("Can you tell us more about why that is true?" "How does that change your priority?").
- Find out something they don't know ("What new information do you have about this issue?").
- Have them think about an idea you may have as well ("Have you considered this option?"). Yes, this is sneaky, but sometimes you'll see a team is really missing something useful for their thinking. Asking a question allows them to decide whether your information is useful or not. If they reject the idea you present in your question, drop it.
- Bring others into the discussion ("Who else has some insights into that?").
- Keep a team on track with the decisions they are making ("Is this discussion necessary in order for us to make the decision we need to make?"). I had a colleague years ago who used to consistently rein in the rest of the team during discussions by asking "Is this discussion more interesting than it is useful?" We discovered that, when he was in the meeting, our discussions became much more usefully focused.
- Get to the underlying goo of a conflict (I have learned from a number of facilitator friends to use "The Five Whys" or a variant when helping teams see what is really moving an issue around in conflict. Ask "And why might that be true?" for each answer someone gives you until you have delved into five levels of "why" for the particular issue or viewpoint. The Five Whys help you and the team learn what is going on deep in an issue without jumping to emotion or conclusions.).

My Anecdote

I love being a team coach in new teams, particularly when they seem at cross purposes with one another. It gives me a chance to act stupid, and I do this so well! "The Five Whys" was particularly useful when I had a group of three testers trying to get the attention of the Product Owner and the developers about the impact of testing on the delivery of a certain set of identified functions. While the functions seemed easy enough to develop, it turned out that, in order to fully test each function, a number of complex environments had to be set up with different configurations of platforms, servers, and data. As the meeting facilitator, I just kept asking "And why is that?" of the testing team until we got to the level of detail and the root cause that helped everyone in the room understand what was making them frustrated and concerned.

In that epiphany, the Product Owner reevaluated her list of priorities by including the testing constraints and therefore the increased estimate of work this effort would take to be truly "done."

Encourage Information Sharing

When you pose questions to a team, you not only keep yourself out of the decision; you also encourage the team to own their data and their decisions by sharing more and more information with one another. You are out of the loop, so you are no longer the bottleneck to information sharing.

In agile software development methodologies, face-to-face communications are preferred over any other form of communication. These communications are meant to create a broad and ready access to the wealth of information that steadies and propels a team successfully to deliver systems and products. Team members become more effective in these face-to-face communications when they have been schooled by a leader who applies neutrality and questioning in order to share information. In addition, collaborative leaders school their team in how to quickly accumulate the data needed to make and reinforce decisions that move the team forward.

Team-wide, you can encourage information sharing through a number of facilitative practices:

- Use brainstorming to accumulate a great deal of creative and unstructured information before having the team come to a decision.
- For large amounts of data, keep the information as compact as possible; rely on quick prioritizing and categorizing of the information to manage it and to focus the team.
- Capture lists of information, such as a Product Backlog or prioritized list of requirements, by guiding teams in more structured information gathering that helps them hold onto information until it is needed.
- Use the variety of question types defined in the previous section, "Ask Questions," to draw out more and more information.
- Monitor the conflicts that shut down information sharing and instead guide team members to engage in convergent thinking as they accumulate data.

- Make all information and all subsequent decisions highly visible to all team members either through wall charts or highly accessible passive and active information portals.

In one-on-one interactions:

- Challenge team members to be sure to gather the useful facts with one another at the right level of detail before making a decision that impacts the entire team.
- Encourage members to use "The Five Whys" to establish a solid footing for further decisions.
- Guide members to post their information and decisions for the entire team to see.

My Anecdote

We have a technical publications person on one of our teams who is a persistent and pesky presence in all our planning meetings and debriefs. Because she is a fully engaged member of the team, we in essence pay her to keep us clear, careful, and attentive in how we share information. She has mastered the questioning art form and applies it liberally with the variety of team members involved in the project. During a particular Release Planning meeting for a major change in the product look-and-feel, her questions about workflow helped both the product owner and the development team see inconsistencies between the product functionality and the roles that were being defined in the newly defined security access rules.

Drive to Consensus

Because consensus plays such an important role in establishing the truly sustainable agreements that buoy a high-performing team, the collaborative leader must believe in it and drive to it. Using questions and encouraging information sharing, staying neutral, and reinforcing self-organization—all of these techniques set the stage for a team to believe in and apply consensus as their number-one means of reaching decisions.

As the collaborative leader, you have an important role in consensus by performing a check on the team's current position about an issue. Through a team consensus check, you:

- Find out where the group's passions are about a topic.
- Foster the information sharing that can clarify the issues about the topic.
- Determine the level of commitment the group is willing to offer to a recommended decision.
- Engage in conflict management when there is more than one recommended solution or when commitment is too low on the recommended decision.
- Help the team see how quickly they can make decisions and how these decisions don't have to leave anyone behind.

Consensus Check—The Fist of Five

The "Fist of Five," taught to me by my colleague Janet Danforth, has proven to be a quick and simple technique to help teams gauge their commitment to a decision. It is my favorite way to both help a team keep moving forward without leaving anyone behind, while also helping the team understand when it really shouldn't move forward without further discussion on a topic.

Here is how the Fist of Five works:

1. Tell the team that you would like to check on where they are with regard to the recommended solution/decision.
2. On the count of three, each participant holds up his or her hand in a vote as follows:
   - Five fingers means: I love this idea. I wish I had thought of it myself. It is the best we can possibly do.
   - Four fingers means: I am really happy with this and glad we came up with such a solution.
   - Three fingers means: I can live with and support this decision.
   - Two fingers means: I have reservations about this solution and would have trouble supporting it.
   - One finger (which is always the index finger!) means: I have grave misgivings about this course of action and can neither live with it nor support it. I do not think we should move forward.

3. When all members hold up their vote, look for any votes of two fingers or one finger.
4. If there are none, then the team is done. The decision is captured as such, and the team moves forward with its remaining work.
5. When members do oppose a decision enough to vote with one or two fingers, you'll need to engage in conflict resolution techniques to help the entire team evaluate recommendations and alternatives that can lead to a team-wide consensus of three fingers or higher. This guidance is covered in Chapter 18, "Managing Conflict."

Make Everything Else Highly Visible

Too many project managers and team leads believe that the success or failure of their teams relies on their strong presence, even when they truly believe in the power of a collaborative culture. There is a subtle art involved in making everything else visible about the project, not yourself. In order to encourage consensus in information sharing, you must preserve your neutrality and remove your ego from the team success, which in effect makes the process and decisions of the team highly visible instead of yourself.

To ensure that you reduce the power of your presence in a team, you can:

- Stand to the side, not in the front of the room, during meetings, particularly when a great deal of discussion is taking place.
- Sit down when someone else is providing information to the rest of the team; this reinforces that person's ownership of "the floor."
- Leave the room in order to force the team to address one another as they make their decisions.
- Post all decisions on the walls as they are made so that the team does not rely on you to maintain the decisions.
- When the team really understands the process of collaboration, have members take turns being the neutral leader of the team meetings for planning, demonstrating, brainstorming, and so on.

Think of all of this as a form of collective code ownership; it is essentially collective process ownership. No one person owns the process when each team member rotates through the role in a self-organizing team. And if you engage in pair leadership in order to mentor team members about the leadership role, you ensure that the team can always proceed without you. You build in your own obsolescence!

Take Away the Blame ("It's My Fault")

Your final job as a collaborative leader is to safeguard teams from a blaming mentality so that they can transform into an action mentality. To accomplish this, you should shepherd teams from a practice of discussing blame to a practice of discussing solutions. Early in the team life, you can engender a non-blaming mode by taking the blame yourself. (There is a quote in the Extreme Programming community "It's Chet's fault!" because of Chet Hendricks's stance on this issue in his early XP projects. Chet knew the power of taking away the blame.[1])

As the process owner and leader, taking away blame becomes easy. You can take blame for not having paid attention to the process, not having addressed an issue, not having removed an impediment, not having brought in the needed resources, or not having listened to the team when concerns were raised. You may also take blame for not having asked enough questions. You do all this by simply saying, "It's my fault." And when a problem seems to be fairly directly linked to one individual or group of individuals, the servant leader takes the blame, seeks solutions from the team members, and then addresses the responsible individuals in private as appropriate.

When you take away the blame in this way, you safeguard the team from self-destruction. You also confirm to them that they have the power to do amazing things. Taking away the blame is your testament to the team that you truly and wholly believe in their ability to do the work they have been gathered to do. If something goes wrong, it is not their fault; they are doing the very best that they can under the circumstances. You dissolve the fault and liberate the team from worrying any further about the blame. (This is so effective that I've discovered that in grabbing the blame first, there usually isn't enough left to go around for anyone else!)

So, when something goes wrong, and you take blame, you confirm that you and the collaborative process are always at the service of the team. And a wonderful thing happens. As you admit that you may have been at fault, others feel more and more open to accept their own responsibility for issues or problems that may arise. The team learns that taking ownership is possible without suffering the destruction of blame. Rather than drive

---

1. Jeffries, Anderson, and Hendrickson, *Extreme Programming Installed,* 194.

alternate behaviors through guilt, the group encourages constructive behaviors through encouragement. Your ability to act out of humility and servitude to the team invites others to do the same. Blame is no longer an arrow in the team's quiver of tools; they must instead turn to information gathering, respect, and problem solving to succeed.

Take away the blame, and you will discover that any number of team issues dissolve:

- Destructive conflict decreases
- Dysfunctional behaviors lessen
- Distractions disappear

A leader who removes blame while fostering self-organization and teaching consensus steers a team into the high-performance that necessarily brings success for all the team members.

Chapter 7

Preparing Participants for Collaboration

In my work with large project teams or with product teams composed of multiple project teams, I have learned the importance of paying attention to the participants long before they walk in the door for a meeting. This chapter provides a set of guidelines and formulas to think about when preparing such teams for the large meetings that move their work forward. As you read this guidance, think about how you can take the formality here and massage it, relax it, in order to apply it to small team contexts. Pay attention to the intent of the practices as you then move to alter them for your specific team contexts.

What It Means

Getting a team off on the right collaborative foot for an event or meeting requires some preparation work on your part prior to the meeting. To help team members understand the collaborative intent of the work and to encourage their enthusiastic participation, you'll want to find out a few useful things about each person's involvement. Additionally, you'll want to arm each participant with any information that can usefully prepare them to actively participate. Finally, you'll want to address the logistics necessary to smoothly pave the way for the actual event. When you prepare team members in this fashion, you help them believe that they own the meeting before they ever arrive in the room.

You prepare participants for collaboration by:

- Interviewing the sponsor
- Determining the participants
- Surveying the participants
- Setting the list of attendees
- Setting the expectations

Interviewing the Sponsor

In workshops, design meetings, retrospectives, or planning meetings, you may be the project manager who is calling the meeting with a specific end in mind (for example, "We need a design decision," "We need commitment from the executive leadership," or "We have to declare a go/no go on deployment of the latest build."). In another scenario, as project manager, you may have been asked by the customer or stakeholders to hold a planning meeting to kick off the project. Or, because the project manager has subject matter expertise that requires her to actively participate in the meeting, you may have been asked to help the team by facilitating the meeting.

In any of these scenarios, your first order of business is to clearly identify, "Who is the sponsor of this meeting, and how can I ensure that this person gets what they need from this meeting?" The sponsor is the person (or the group of people) who has the most to gain or lose as a result of the meeting's outcomes. In a sense, they are the party that needs the collaboration to take place and to succeed: They need some piece of information, or a strategy, or a decision, or a commitment from the participants.

For preliminary planning meetings, such as a Release Planning meeting, this is an executive or senior person representing the client group in the development project. They have secured the funding and the commitment from the business to proceed with the development effort. In addition, they've made predictions, assurances, or promises about the value the project can deliver. For the Release Planning meeting in an Extreme Programming project, the sponsor might be the customer who needs to learn how the team can define a high-level view of the next product release. In a retrospective, it might be the project manager who wants to learn more from the team about how to proceed with best practices in the future.

In collaborative, high-performing teams, the "sponsor" is very often the entire team; they have a specific need to have you very objectively manage the meeting agenda for them to ensure that they stay on track for their purpose. You merely own the process that gets them to their purpose through the means (agenda and practices) that can ensure their success.

To hold a successful collaboration, ask yourself or the sponsor:

> ## What is the purpose of this meeting?

You can also reflect on these supporting questions to provide further insight into the meeting's goals:

- What do you want to accomplish through this meeting?
- What problems do you intend to address in this meeting?
- What benefits do you hope to reap?
- What organizational issues do you wish to address?
- What is the current situation of the group?
- What is the future state desired?

What Is the Purpose of This Meeting?

Of all the questions you might ask about a meeting, the most important is "What is the purpose of this meeting?"

Even for your own meetings (you are calling a planning meeting with your team, or you want to hold a project retrospective, or you need to hold a refactoring meeting), this big yet simple question prompts you to clearly define for yourself the sole and singular purpose of the meeting. It keeps you focused and honest.

To figure out the purpose of the meeting, pose the following scenario and question to the sponsor (or yourself):

> "Imagine that the meeting has just ended."
>
> "You are walking out the door of the meeting, and you turn to your colleague and say, 'I am so happy with what the group has accomplished in this meeting!'"
>
> "What was it that the group accomplished that made you so happy?"

When you are able to answer this question, then and only then do you have the true purpose of your meeting. But beware! You may discover even at this point that your meeting is in peril of failure. Here are a few indicators that your meeting's purpose may still be a bit too fuzzy to warrant gathering your team:

- You can't articulate the purpose in a single statement (yes, it is a design meeting, but you haven't yet formulated with the team how the design should be captured, what the scope of the design is to be, or what agreements are expected to emerge as a result of the design discussion).
- You have too many things you want to accomplish in one meeting and they don't really relate to one another.
- You don't know the purpose because the real reason you are having the meeting is because your director told you to have it.
- You hadn't really planned on an outcome; you just wanted to get together to talk with your team.
- You always have the meeting because it is your weekly meeting; that is its purpose.

So, how will you know when you are on the right track for defining your meeting? You'll know you have a clearly stated purpose when:

- It can be stated in the following way: "The purpose of the meeting is to ...." where you can fill in an *action* ("create," "define," "select," "produce") followed by an *outcome* ("process definition," "iteration scope," "Product Backlog," "set of use cases," "conceptual object model").
- It represents the outcome that would convince you (or whoever is the meeting's sponsor) that the meeting has been a success.

Determining the Participants

Once you have a clearly articulated purpose, you can now determine who the intended participants are. To guide a team in working collaboratively, help them value their time by being clear about a purpose and how each participant can contribute to that purpose. Begin by determining:

- **Who plans to attend**—Usually there is an initial set of attendees you or your sponsor has in mind.
- **Who needs to attend**—These lists don't necessarily coincide! You may learn that some named attendees have no clear reason for attending, while some key roles may be missing representation.
- **Why they are attending**—Just as you focus a meeting on a clear purpose, focus the list of attendees on why each is attending and how he or she is contributing.

In short, a successful collaborative team has all the right people in the room in order to make a sustainable, actionable set of decisions.

My Anecdote

I was involved in the planning of a very large Release Planning meeting and began by interviewing the executive sponsor about her purpose and objectives. So far, so good. I then started asking about the attendee list, explaining that I needed to be able to interview attendees about their needs with regard to the meeting. In talking with the executive sponsor, I started to learn that the attendee list was massive! Attendees seemed to fall into one of three categories: those people who had subject matter expertise and could drive decisions, those people whose managers had demanded that they be allowed to attend, and those people whom the executive sponsor felt she had to invite for fear of offending another group.

In these latter two groups, I could see that no one was empowered to make decisions; people were required to attend, and yet their attendance didn't ensure that they could make decisions. To get the sponsor's attention about this problem, I tried to delve into what each of their roles would be in the planning. This was unclear. I kept returning to the stated purpose of the meeting and its intended benefits. In this context, I urged her to reevaluate the role of each participant.

I worked with the meeting sponsor for a week to help her edit the list and make the purpose of attending the meeting very clear and very directed. Ultimately, we managed to reduce the attendee list by almost 50%.

Surveying Participants

With the purpose of the meeting defined, and a list of attendees outlined, you can now survey participants to prepare them for the collaboration. Without this step in your preparation, you run the risk of having unpleasant surprises in your meeting. Perhaps someone who has been invited does not want to attend because of a personal issue with the sponsor. Another person thought the meeting was for a completely different purpose. Yet another person believes that the purpose is completely wrong and needs to be altered. You survey participants to remove these surprises and meeting challenges before they happen.

To help participants learn about the meeting and their participation:

- **Gather their personal objectives**—When interviewing participants, state the purpose of the meeting and then ask the participant a question similar to the one you asked when articulating the purpose with the sponsor. This will help you learn what each participant's real reason for attending might be and how it aligns with or contradicts the stated purpose:

> "Imagine that the meeting has just ended."
>
> "You are walking out the door of the meeting, and you turn to your colleague and say, 'I am so happy I attended this meeting! I got exactly what I wanted out of it!'"
>
> "What was it that the meeting accomplished that made you so happy?"

- **Find out hidden agendas**—Look at the personal objectives and ask the participant further questions:
  - What do you believe your role to be in the meeting?
  - What do you think might get in the way of accomplishing the meeting purpose?
- **Learn what the ongoing battles are**—This is what my friend Janet Danforth calls "getting the canary to sing." As Janet talks about it, there is always some dirt lurking somewhere in a group that is setting out to go through some major collaborative event such as a strategy meeting or kickoff meeting. Someone will eventually "spill the beans" and let you in on what hasn't been working in the group. This is valuable information in your planning!

When you find out these potential disconnects prior to a meeting, you can plan the problems away in how you set up the agenda, seat the participants, and plan activities. Don't skip this step! Very quickly, you will learn:

- How much Forming still needs to occur in the group
- What sort of Storming is already going on
- What damage has been sustained as the group has been dealing with its divergence
- What activities may help the group move from just Norming into Performing
- How much to let go of very defined activities if the group is already Performing

Setting the List of Attendees—Participants and Observers

Having surveyed the full cadre of potential participants, you can now winnow or expand the list as appropriate for the meeting purpose.

Your interviews may have revealed one or more people who don't have a clearly defined role in the meeting. They may not even know why they have been asked to attend. Participants who attend a meeting but do not have a clear *raison d'être* in the meeting are distracting. As partially engaged attendees, they have the power to deplete your and the team's energy. They may have a hard time determining their useful role during the group's Forming stage. And as a group moves into its Storming phase, figuring out how to work together, these attendees without clear focus can create confusing and potentially destructive dynamics for others. In their meeting "identity crisis," they get uselessly caught up in the conflicts that can arise and may even create conflicts in order to have a role in the meeting, albeit a dysfunctional one.

These are the people you need to help understand that their contributions are best applied elsewhere.

Your interviews may have also revealed that some of the attendees plan to just "observe." A seasoned facilitator will tell you that there is no such thing as someone who just observes a meeting. Inevitably, the observer has an observation to share. If someone claims that they are just an observer in your meeting, provide them with this helpful set of guidelines:

- You may not speak to participants during the meeting.
- You may not speak to other observers during the meeting.

- You may not enter and exit the meeting at will.
- You may not work on your own work during the meeting; this includes your laptop, your iPaq, your PDA, your Blackberry, your daytimer, or your cellphone.

If you still have observers undaunted by these guidelines, check in a bit further with their intentions with the meeting:

- **Find out why they think they need to observe**—This may take asking, "The Five Whys," but do it. Their answer can give you information about the politics or the power of the group.
- **Find out if their presence can be detrimental to the team's collaboration**—Observers often tend to be from management or stakeholder roles. If they are not directly providing expertise and are not directly taking responsibility in the meeting, their presence may only serve to squash the trust of the team about their work.

In most of these cases, you should be able to ascertain the true role of the attendee. Invite them to attend in a participatory fashion or, with approval from the team, welcome them as an observer and remind them of the ground rules that will guide their "good observer citizen" behavior.

Setting the Expectations

You've set the purpose, interviewed the participants, and finalized the list of attendees. You now have one more crucial task in preparing participants for the meeting. You need to help them understand what will be expected of them and what can they expect in terms of their ownership of the meeting decisions and actions.

Their Preparation for the Meeting

A meeting may not be able to meet its purpose without the participants having completed some homework prior to the start of the meeting. You can learn about exactly what that pre-work should be based on your interviews with the sponsor and the various participants. As you survey these people about their roles and personal objectives, pay attention to assumptions they may have about what has taken place prior to the meeting. Learn what the participants are expected to know. This may lead to homework concerning:

- **Reading to do**—Shorten your meetings and keep them focused by having attendees complete any lengthy reading prior to the meeting. Don't allow meetings to be used for reading and reviewing detailed documents; extensive reading kills focus and momentum. Require reading *a priori* and use the meeting for making participatory decisions about the material.
- **Materials to bring**—If the group is expected to make strategic decisions about the upcoming release of a product, be sure that someone has data about what has been defined so far, what has been completed to date, what the effort was concerning that work, and what the known risks and issues are related to the work ahead.
- **Questionnaires to complete**—Some meetings need feedback from the participants even before they arrive at the meeting; make sure participants know this, complete it, and provide it.
- **Presentation materials to prepare**—For individual contributors, such as subject matter experts, who need to present group-wide, high-level material, encourage the use of brief, focused presentations. Support the presentation with materials (handouts, wall charts, posted files) that can be used for reference guidance in subsequent decision processes. If the material is not expected to be used as a guide later in the meeting, question its applicability to the purpose of the meeting.

Their Role in the Meeting

The meeting purpose isn't the only thing that shapes an attendee's participation. Prior to the meeting, help participants learn the work of their meeting role by addressing:

- **The subject matter expertise**—Each participant should be very clear about the expertise he brings to a meeting. This means arriving equipped with information in his area of expertise that can guide the team as it converges on team decisions.
- **The time commitment**—A well-run, highly collaborative meeting relies on full participation by all attendees. Make sure all participants understand the time commitment they face, especially for very large strategy meetings, Release Planning

meetings, or retrospectives. Discourage "in/out" behavior. When attendees are coming in and out of a meeting, this does more than just distract the other participants; it makes a statement that the transient participants find the meeting less important than other work they are doing. (For participants who have to time slice their involvement, bring the question to the other meeting participants about the impact on the meeting's purpose. Team members should then decide how the meeting should proceed.)

- **The "machinery" of a collaborative meeting**—When teams rely on collaboration for decision making, they are expected to engage fully in all information gathering, processing, and consensus checks. This requires participants to stay focused throughout the meeting and to believe in the power of the team to make the best decisions. And this requires that you ensure that they are well schooled in tools and processes for consensus building and consensus checking.

- **The scope of their authority**—In some collaborative meetings, teams may be making the final set of decisions that drive the next actions in a project. However, some meetings are meant to have a team create a recommendation to another individual or another team. In these situations, you should help set expectations prior to the meeting about the team's scope of authority. Will the team own the decision? Are they just being consultative? Will they be asked to facilitate others in making the decision?

The Potential Consequences

When looking at a meeting purpose and the roles of the attendees, find out whether the meeting may bring up potentially negative consequences to someone in the meeting. Knowing this information in advance can help you manage the discomfort or dysfunctions that may arise due to difficult revelations or decisions that come to light:

- Is the team in a go/no go for the next phase of the project?
- Are resources being reallocated due to missed deadlines?
- Is there discord among the business owners that could cancel the project?
- Are there concerns about the role of the architect?
- Has the QA team been targeted for outsourcing?

When you discover these consequences, determine how they may come out in the meeting and who specifically may be impacted. Develop an agenda that clearly manages the flow of information toward these decisions. Apply a more engaged facilitative role, as in a Forming mode. Ensure that the right attendees are engaged in the meeting to deal with the decisions and the actions that these decisions bring about.

Chapter 8

Setting the Collaborative Agenda

You are now about to enter into the rocky terrain of conducting a highly collaborative meeting: planning the meeting agenda. The goal of this chapter is to provide you with a grounded set of essentials that will guarantee you productive, collaborative meetings at the outset. So, while the planning, analysis, and juggling detailed here may seem arduously lengthy, pulling this mode of thinking into your sense of your meetings will be well worth the effort.

Read these guidelines in terms of the larger project meetings you must lead. Then make adjustments for how to use the guidance in smaller teams. Understanding the work necessary to build a large, focused agenda has helped me be more cognizant of the value of focus and order in small team meetings.

How Much Planning Is Enough?

Here is a good rule of thumb: You'll need to apply two days of planning for every day of a highly effective meeting. That means that to plan a highly collaborative two-hour meeting, you should set aside four hours of planning time.

My Anecdote

The first time I shared this brute force calculation with a classroom of XP developers and coaches, I expected immediate bristling at the idea of so much planning time just to have a collaborative meeting. On the contrary! One attendee lit up at the idea. In short, his view was, if someone expected him to devote a full day of his time in a Release Planning meeting, he'd want to know that someone had spent a good amount of time making sure that he wouldn't be wasting his time.

Once we go through the set of essentials you need to address in planning a very collaborative meeting agenda and all its sub-parts, you'll understand why a 2:1 ratio of planning-to-execution is advised. This may look like a lot of BDUF (big design up front) that could be perceived as overkill. But, the goal of such planning is to ensure that when your team enters the room for that meeting, they have the best opportunity to make the most effective, most sustaining agreements as a team.

Therefore, when we ask teams to engage in meetings, we show our respect for their time by being fully prepared, ready to feed tools of focus and collaboration into their decisions. The highly productive interactions we set in motion through this 2:1 ratio of planning versus meeting time help teams move into that self-organization mode of operating that creates high-performance. Such positive team-oriented results then encourage more and more collaboration and greater high-performance in what a friend calls a "virtuous circle."

As a facilitative, collaborative meeting leader, setting a good agenda is just plain hard work. Insufficient or near-sighted planning can lead to meetings with poor agendas, such as the following:

- An agenda that doesn't drive to a clear purpose
- An agenda with no clear desired outcome
- An overcrowded agenda
- An agenda that does not allow for open discussion and disagreement
- No agenda at all

Any of these can easily undermine all your other work in nurturing a collaborative team. For this reason, you'll discover that the yeoman's portion of your meeting planning will revolve around creating a useful, actionable agenda.

Consider the service you provide a team in creating a focused view of their role in a meeting. Your planning for their success is evidence of your servant leadership in action. Coupled with that plan, your ability to then hear the team when the plan needs alteration may be your strongest tool in gaining trust from the team. And when a team gains trust concerning this interplay of plans, feedback, and change, it naturally moves through Storming behaviors into the power to consistently create strong, sustainable, participatory agreements.

Thus, rather than being manipulative or a creativity killer, an effective, informed, well-planned agenda creates the nutrient-rich environment in which these agreements can emerge.

Steps for Planning the Agenda

Setting an effective, highly collaborative agenda requires a good bit of planning and listening well in advance of the meeting. You'll have to resolve:

- What is the purpose of your meeting?
- What deliverables/outcomes will support your purpose?
- What are the questions that lead to those outcomes?
- What is the natural order in which these outcomes should be accomplished in order to meet the purpose?
- What process approach should you use for accomplishing each outcome?
- How much time should be allocated for each outcome's process?
- Given the time allotted, can these outcomes be produced to meet the purpose?

What Is the Purpose of Your Meeting?

A meeting's purpose drives its entire agenda; that is, if the agenda doesn't drive to the defined purpose, you have the wrong agenda. Recall that the meeting purpose comes from questioning the meeting's sponsor (whether it is you or someone else) about the outcome of the meeting and that it conforms to the following criteria:

- It can be stated as: "The purpose of the meeting is to ...." where you are able to fill in an *action* ("create," "define," "select," "produce") followed by an *outcome* ("process definition," "iteration scope," "Product Backlog," "set of use cases," "conceptual object model").

- It represents the outcome that would convince you (or whoever is the meeting's sponsor or set of sponsors) that the meeting has been a success.

As an example, you may find that your team needs to figure out a way to capture the GUI design. Several possible sets of artifacts could be used to do this; team members in prior projects have used lots of approaches. And while you could just pick a set and make the decision, you are bringing the team together to decide. Leaving the meeting with a clearly defined, agreed-upon set of design artifacts would really float your boat! Your meeting purpose then is:

To select the artifacts the team will use to capture the GUI design

Hold onto this statement. It is the litmus test you will apply frequently while planning your agenda that ensures you haven't gone off track.

What Deliverables/Outcomes Will Support Your Purpose?

You can think of the next step in agenda building as analogous to some of the engineering practices brought into XP teams:

- **Test-driven development**—Knowing what the ultimate outcome needs to be for your agenda (the purpose), you work backward from that purpose in order to derive an agenda. As you build the agenda, you keep checking it against the test: "Does this agenda sufficiently drive to my meeting purpose?"
  Never build an agenda without a committed, clearly stated purpose against which to test its validity.
- **YAGNI**—As you build your agenda items, keep checking in through the simple test: "Is this agenda item necessary for my meeting to drive to its purpose?" If you can't answer in the affirmative, then the agenda item may fall into the crippling YAGNI category: *You Aren't Going to Need It.* Overpacking an agenda, incorporating too many items that have nothing to do with one another, forcing in items to satisfy political situations: These are all death to a workshop where true teamwork has to be accomplished. Stick with a YAGNI, low-fat approach to designing your agenda.
- **Pair programming**—Build an agenda with the help of another set of eyes. We took on this practice in one company where we were aggressively trying to reduce the time and resources dedicated to large planning meetings. None of us finalize a

Release Planning meeting agenda without at least two other colleagues looking at it to validate the approach. We learned so much from one another in this way.

- **Frequent refactoring**—Your agenda will have to take shape through iterative scrutiny. Even though the purpose or final expected output may not have changed, your work will lead you to continually reinvestigate what must be produced in order to meet the outcome, in what order the items should be produced, and how you expect to help the team produce them. Additionally, once you are in your meeting, you'll discover that refactoring will continue as you and your team learn what will be most effective for participatory decision making about the meeting purpose.

As a reminder, pay attention to your intention when determining the meeting's outputs and deliverables. Your goal is to determine the set of agenda items that can help you facilitate your team in achieving these goals. Remember, you aren't deciding what the content of the outcomes should be, or what the decisions will be. Rather, you are clearing a path that can guide your team to create the desired content or to make the useful decisions. If your planning starts to define the deliverables as well as the specific content, you've taken a wrong turn and need to revisit your role as servant leader.

For the example purpose:

To select the artifacts the team will use to capture the GUI design

consider that the team must have a list of artifacts from which to choose the final set of artifacts. To get that list, you might want to find out all the possible artifacts for design that team members have used in the past. Then find out from the team what artifacts they felt had worked well versus what artifacts hadn't worked well. You may also want to ask them what other considerations or risks might help the team select its set of artifacts (for instance, they may tell you that time or skill sets or the distribution of the team should impact the final decision; let them tell you).

What Are the Questions That Lead to Those Outcomes?

In the example provided, you've identified four potential intermediate steps to help the team come to its final decision on the set of artifacts used to capture the design. When you have done this, simply state each step as a question. For example:

"What are all the possible design artifacts we could use?"

Stating the agenda items as questions that the team will answer reinforces your role as a servant to the team: You ask questions in order to provoke their thoughts, information, and decisions rather than stating what you want. An agenda item stated as a question makes it clear to everyone reading the agenda that "At this point in the agenda, we are going to produce whatever is necessary in order to answer this question." There can be no doubt about what the team has been drawn together to do.

Applying this question approach, you would end up with an agenda that looks like the following:

Agenda Item	
A.	Opening
B.	What are all the possible design artifacts we could use for the GUI design?
C.	Based on past experience, what are the benefits of these design artifacts?
D.	What are the downsides to these design artifacts?
E.	What other considerations should be used in selecting the set of design artifacts for this project?
F.	What is the set of design artifacts we will use for this project?
G.	Close

(I'll talk about the *Opening* and the *Close* agenda items in a lot more detail later. For now, use them as placeholders in defining your overall agenda.)

In this agenda, we know exactly what is going on each step of the way. When you begin to build agendas with your own questions, follow this rule about the detail:

Use more words, not less.

Because words are the hooks participants use to keep them engaged in the meeting or bring them back into the meeting, make them rich and clear.

In contrast to the previous agenda, consider an agenda formulated as follows:

A. Introduction
B. Discussion on Artifacts
C. Close

Simply stating *Discussion on Artifacts* as an agenda item gives no guidance to the team regarding what they will be doing with the artifacts discussion (defining them, producing them, selecting them, grading them, archiving them), why they are dealing with artifacts in any way that will benefit them, or how they'll know when they've adequately addressed artifacts. It offers no guidance concerning "How will we know when we are done?" or "Have we been successful in our meeting?"

Returning to the seven-step agenda example, think about your reaction to it. If you are used to the latter example of only three, short agenda items, the seven-step agenda can look controlling, nit-picking, and overly detailed. But as you get into the flow of what defines a good agenda, and how a good agenda buoys you and your team through a meeting, you will discover that the detail becomes a strong ally to all of you. At any given moment in the meeting, the agenda is very clear about what is happening in the meeting and what is going to happen in the meeting.

So, a collaborative leader builds these clear, detailed, word-rich steps into an agenda in order to do the following:

- Validate and reinforce the purpose of the meeting
- Help the team see how they are going to accumulate all the information to make their decisions
- Guide the team in self-governing how it stays focused in the meeting
- Assure the team that they create the decisions through their work in the meeting
- Maintain a position as a servant to the team by presenting questions for their consideration (later, we'll investigate how you can also contribute to the team as a subject matter expert while still allowing them to own the final content and decisions of the meeting)
- Help the team determine when and how the agenda should be altered

My Anecdote

I have learned to be very clear about the specific steps it takes to fulfill a meeting purpose, so my agendas do take on a look of detail and many words. And indeed, I have received some really negative reactions from people not used to this detail.

I was once setting up the agenda for a Release Planning meeting for a client, and a colleague of mine, not used to this very directed and word-rich style of agenda building, looked at my agenda and declared that he would never attend such a meeting. His impression was that it just looked too controlled, too manipulating, and too boring. But I had seen how he ran meetings and knew that he tended to not stick to the meeting purpose. Moreover, at any given point in his meetings, one never knew if the meeting was on target for attaining the purpose of the meeting.

In contrast, I had run lots of Release Planning meetings in the past, and I had seen what the very detailed agenda hanging on the wall was able to do. As would happen at times in such meetings, if someone was called away from the meeting, he could come back and ask any participant, "Where are we now in the meeting?" Anyone could point to the agenda on the wall with all its guidance and would quickly catch the newly returned colleague up on exactly what the group was doing.

In another group, I had been asked to help the group define a high-level product strategy (vision). Early in the course of the meeting, the group determined that while the agenda was indeed leading to the purpose, they hadn't prepared adequately prior to the meeting in order to move into any useful, collaborative decisions about the plan. We stopped the meeting, gathered around the agenda, zeroed in on the trouble spot, and reworked the questions and their order, building a set of new detailed word-rich agenda items that would guide them in doing the work they hadn't yet done. The remaining questions from the original agenda were then preserved for the meeting we planned to have the following week; we already knew exactly what we would be doing and how we would do it.

Without the original detailed agenda as a guide, the group would have not been able to so quickly rebuild a useful roadmap to a purpose they felt they could achieve in the time allocated. When we left the meeting, the team's sponsor told me it was one of the most productive meetings she had ever seen the group hold.

What Is the Natural Order in Which These Outcomes Should Be Accomplished in Order to Meet the Purpose?

A good agenda sets a focused, uncluttered path to a meeting's purpose. It is the map that guides steps through a natural progression of *Discovery* to *Exploration* to *Decision*.

Selecting the proper order of agenda items helps you discover if your agenda is redundant, contradictory, or assumptive in setting the intermediate items for achieving the purpose. For instance, do you need to define the training environment in order to define GUI design artifacts? Does debating the pros and cons of the company's standardized architecture contribute to the team's decision on GUI design artifacts? Investigating how to maximize the use of the company standard models or discussing their pros and cons might be more appropriate.

In applying the *Discovery* ➜ *Exploration* ➜ *Decision* roadmap to the example meeting purpose, you can see how the items came to be ordered as they were. First, the agenda leads the team through their current experience and what they know (*Discovery*). Then the team investigates what might be useful versus what might not be useful, as well as any other considerations that could impact their sense of the value of a particular artifact or set of artifacts (*Exploration*). Finally, the last agenda item represents *the* question that must be answered in order to meet the purpose of the meeting (*Decision*).

With an established order of agenda items, you now have to determine what approach you will use in each of the agenda items in order to ensure that it directs the team through a collaborative completion of the item. Each phase of the agenda roadmap has process approaches geared toward accomplishing that work, as listed in Table 8.1, "Agenda Types and Their Process Approaches."

Table 8.1 Agenda Roadmap Phases and Their Process Approaches

Agenda Roadmap Phase	Process Approach
Discovery	Brainstorming, Listing, Categorizing, Surveying, Researching
Exploration	Pros and Cons, Listing, Prioritizing, Small Group Discussion, Debate, Visioning, Questions and Answers
Decision	Round Robin, Prioritizing, Multi-voting, Recommendations, and Alternatives

(I'll go into more detail on each of these approaches in Chapters 12 through 16. For now, understand that you'll want to select a technique for each agenda item from your toolkit of collaborative techniques in order to complete the work.)

Returning to the example agenda, you may think about setting up the accompanying processes as follows:

Agenda Item	Process
A. Opening	Walk the Walls, Introductions
B. What are all the possible design artifacts we could use for the GUI design?	Brainstorming

Continues

Agenda Item	Process
C. Based on past experience, what are the benefits of these design artifacts?	Listing, Pros
D. What are the downsides to these design artifacts?	Listing, Cons
E. What other considerations should be used in selecting the set of design artifacts for this project?	Small Group Discussion
F. What is the set of design artifacts we will use for this project?	Multi-voting
G. Close	Re-cap

How Much Time Should Be Allocated for Each Outcome's Process?

Pulling together each agenda item and the process to be used for accomplishing it, you now need to apply a first best guess at the time needed for each process you intend to implement. Going back to the example of the design artifacts meeting, here are the agenda items, their processes, and possible timings for each:

Agenda Item	Process	Time Allotted
A. Opening	Walk the Walls, Introductions	10 minutes
B. What are all the possible design artifacts we could use for the GUI design?	Brainstorming	20 minutes
C. Based on past experience, what are the benefits of these design artifacts?	Listing, Pros	15 minutes
D. What are the downsides to these design artifacts?	Listing, Cons	15 minutes
E. What other considerations should be used in selecting the set of design artifacts for this project?	Small Group Discussion	20 minutes

Agenda Item	Process	Time Allotted
F. What is the set of design artifacts we will use for this project?	Multi-voting	20 minutes
G. Close	Re-cap	10 minutes

This design artifacts meeting example now represents a 90-minute meeting at its optimum (i.e., no process overflows its allotted timebox).

Given the Time Allotted, Can These Outcomes Be Produced to Meet the Meeting Purpose?

The truth about highly participatory meetings is that collaboration and group-wide information sharing by their nature beg for cushions and buffers around the participation. And that means time. You've invited information flow. Your team needs time to take in all the useful information from one another in order to equip them to make the best decisions for the entire team and for the project. Additionally, you are helping the team Form, Storm, Norm, and Perform. Finally, when starting out in planning meeting agendas, we have no data ("yesterday's weather") to help us gauge how well we estimate timings. Think of these process estimates as you would velocity estimates in Extreme Programming: Your planning and estimates improve as you and the team learn how you work together and how you tend to arrive at decisions.

Therefore, when defining the meeting time, apply the following axiom:

Process Timing Axiom #1: Timings are a guide only; assume they will change.

Building in some cushion around your timebox estimates is particularly important as a team is still acting divergently (Forming and Storming). Once the team moves to a convergent mode of operation, your timeboxes will be more stable and require less buffering.

To build in slack for the sample agenda, you should allow two hours for the meeting. Had you planned on that much time? Are the participants prepared to devote this much time to the meeting and to be 100% participatory for that time? Do the outside stakeholders and sponsors understand the importance of allotting this much time to the meeting?

This is often a hard lesson when building very participatory approaches for decision making. Failing to allot enough time for the meeting can cause the following unintended consequences or "D"-structions:

- **Distrust**—The team will feel railroaded into making a decision and end up distrusting that they truly own it.
- **Detachment**—If the team really didn't own the decision in the first place, they may build a sense of apathy about any future meetings and just mentally detach from the whole process.
- **Divergence**—A convergent, performing team can easily move back into a divergent, storming team if they cannot work through conflict in a safe environment. Lack of time to work through conflict makes your meeting environment unsafe.

Managing the Work of Meetings—Keeping an Agenda Backlog

The Scrum methodology advises the maintenance of a Product Backlog that teams consult from Sprint to Sprint. You can use this approach to maintain an "Agenda Backlog" over the course of a project as a team moves from meeting to meeting. When teams run out of time in working toward a meeting purpose, they may chose to revise the agenda, restate the purpose, and then move on. Something must be done with the leftover agenda topics. Maintaining an Agenda Backlog provides the resilience to change agendas without abandoning useful work. The backlog documents the intent of the team to return to its unfinished business.

My Anecdote

A group of us in one company had a standard meeting every two weeks to come together for an hour and discuss what we were doing with our projects in terms of applying agile principles and practices. The idea was to share ideas, come up with recommendations, and then determine any useful follow-up actions. We quickly discovered that we had a growing list of items we could address in our gatherings, though we had to stay timeboxed in how long our meetings could last. We began an Agenda Backlog that we maintained from meeting to meeting that helped us manage what we wanted to discuss, what our priorities were, and what should be covered in the next meeting (i.e., our highest-priority items from the backlog).

In Chapter 9, I'll cover the use of an Action Plan as an organizing tool that can help you manage work that should follow a meeting. Updating the Agenda Backlog can be one such action item.

The Organizing Tools

The Underlying Communication

In real estate, as they say, it's all about "Location, location, location." In collaboration, we might borrow this mantra to say instead that it's all about "Communication, communication, communication." With this in mind, communication for any workshop or collaborative meeting relies heavily on what I refer to as the *organizing tools* you apply to ensure effective communication. Although teams can benefit from any number of information radiators or billboards during a meeting, the organizing tools discussed here are a specific class of information device for managing the meeting.

Organizing tools form a life raft of underlying communication for collaborative meetings, a framework around which the remaining trappings of the meeting are hung. They radiate basic meeting information to sustain and guide the team and the leader when they might otherwise either veer off track or begin to sink into non-effective, non-collaborative modes of work. As such, they need to be useful, informative, legible, directive, and easily visible anywhere in the meeting venue and at any time during the meeting. For instance, maintaining the agenda or a "Parking Lot" on one person's laptop will not do. Even if the laptop image is projected on a large screen, it very often projects only one screen at any point in the meeting, thus hiding other organizing tools that need to be continually available for reference.

As I describe a basic set of organizing tools, you'll see how the clarity, usefulness, and directiveness of your tools will guide your preparation and use of them. If your organizing tools provide fuzzy or vague information that is either non-directive (it is too general or too complicated), unclear (it is hard to read), or non-useful (it may be interesting but not useful to your meeting's purpose), you risk sinking your team's collaboration ship before it is out of dry dock.

This chapter takes a close look at organizing tools in terms of how to capture and exhibit them and what constitutes a good basic set of tools. The specific tools covered here are:

- Meeting Purpose
- Agenda
- Ground Rules
- Parking Lot
- Action Plan
- Decisions Board
- Communication Plan
- Consensus
- Other Tools

General Guidance About Organizing Tools

Before exploring the various organizing tools individually, there is some basic guidance that applies to all of the tools. Think about these guidelines as you then proceed to learn about the specifics of each tool.

Choosing the Medium

Clarity of your organizing information relies not only on the words through which you choose to convey your information, but also through the medium you choose to make the information available. Select your media based on how to best make these organizational reminders available anywhere and anytime in the meeting setting.

Here are a few standard vehicles for delivering the meeting organizational information to the team:

- **Flipcharts**—These large sheets of paper provide persistent, highly visible access to the organizational backbone of your meeting as you display them around your meeting area. Using a separate sheet of paper for each organizing tool helps that particular communication stand out and makes it modular so that it can be moved, updated, or removed independently of any other materials.

The Post-it style flipchart, with self-adhesive at the top, makes the paper easy to hang and move around as needed. If you do need to use tape for non-sticky flipchart paper, use artist's tape, a white tape slightly thicker than masking tape; it sticks more reliably and is more easily removed from walls. Flipcharts roll up nicely for transporting back to where you complete the "as spoken" documentation of the meeting.

- **Flipchart PLUS**—Can be posted and read anywhere; maximizes use of wall space.
- **Flipchart MINUS**—Still needs to be transcribed; requires sticky notes or tape for posting information on it.

- **Sticky Wall**—A large sheet of parachute fabric sprayed with an adhesive specifically designed for this purpose. Sticky walls create a bright focal point upon which to display any information such as the organizing tools. Information can be posted on the wall using regular 8×11 paper, or index cards, or even large flipchart sheets. No tape or additional adhesives are needed for posting new information; a major benefit, though you still have to tape up the fabric itself.

  Mixing up the colors of paper on the sticky wall can help define what information is being displayed (green paper for "Ground Rules," orange paper for "Action Items," beige paper for "Parking Lot," etc.).

  - **Sticky Wall PLUS**—Holds any style of paper; easy to pack and carry.
  - **Sticky Wall MINUS**—Requires upkeep, limits use of wall space, and may require use of more than one in order to maintain all the meeting postings.

- **Butcher Paper**—Available in art shops, these rolls of white paper on a wall form a large canvas upon which to write or post information. The paper, measuring four feet wide, can be cut to any length, and so it could hold all the basic meeting infor mation on one sheet, dividing up items by drawing a border around each section. Butcher paper is ideal for creating large reference radiators that need to present great detail to a large group while also creating a sense of a continuum of information (such as an existing timeline, map, or series of models).

  - **Butcher Paper PLUS**—Displays large spreads of data; can hold lots of detail; takes maximum advantage of wall space.
  - **Butcher Paper MINUS**—Hard to hang and transport; sticky notes fall off easily.

- **WhiteBoards**—These are ubiquitous in IT settings and are a natural information radiator to use in collaborative meetings. You can quickly capture the organizational information you need and change it as the team alters its reference needs throughout the meeting (add a ground rule, remove a ground rule, add an item to the Parking Lot, etc.). Whiteboards work well for ad-hoc, small meetings with low formality and quick turn-around.

- **WhiteBoard PLUS**—Easy to use; saves paper; supports dynamic input.
- **WhiteBoard MINUS**—Usually not large enough to post all organizing tools; can't be moved around the room for better viewing; information may still need to be transcribed.

- **Electronic Whiteboards**—One giant step above regular whiteboards, you can use these whiteboards both to make information highly visible to the team during the meeting and then easily and readily available to the team after the meeting. Because of their ability to capture dynamic information for later documentation, electronic whiteboards are probably best saved for gathering data during the meeting versus displaying the fairly static organizing information.
  - **Electronic Whiteboard PLUS**—Dynamic updating supported; easy transformation to softcopy.
  - **Electronic Whiteboard MINUS**—Expensive and usually not large enough to post all organizing tools.

- **Projections**—A laptop projection onto a large wall or screen allows even very highly detailed information to be displayed in meetings. PC projections serve the organizational backbone best when they bring complex, detailed reference data (such as previously captured use cases, design models, existing functionality, demos) into the meeting for easy access by all.
  - **Projection PLUS**—Very large format can be useful for providing information to a large meeting; creates focus around the item being projected; supports dynamic updating.
  - **Projection MINUS**—Limited ability to post more than one reference item at a time.

Fit to Print

The basis for determining the set of organizing tools you'll use in your meetings relies on your answer to the following question:

> "What references do my team and I need readily available to us in order to collaborate effectively in achieving our meeting purpose?"

In other words:

- How can we stay on track?
- How can we stay focused?
- How can we remain productive while inviting divergence?
- How can we avoid damage?
- How can we strive toward consensus in making our decisions?
- How can we carry our collaboration back from this meeting to our work?

The suite of defined tools listed at the beginning of the chapter forms a good starting point upon which you can build and elaborate as you and your teams learn what works best for your meetings.

Here are a few guidelines with regard to what you use and how you use it:

1. **Information must be clearly legible from any part of the meeting venue**—Use bold, dark colors on light backgrounds to create the organizing tools. Practice writing legibly and large; this is an acquired skill, and it is worth having in your hip pocket.

   My Pet Peeve: conducting a meeting with many flipcharts for organizing tools or information gathering, but with markers that are too light and with handwriting that is too small and very sloppy. This is not information sharing; this is information taunting.

2. **Information must be available from the beginning of the workshop to the end of the workshop**—This is information persistence and one reason that laptop projections will not do as the supporting medium for the organizing tools that help to drive a meeting. Have all tools ready and displayed in the meeting *before* participants arrive. Keep them displayed until after the meeting is over.

3. **Refer to the organizing tools throughout the meeting**—These are your life raft and the team's life raft. Everyone needs to be able to gaze at or ponder the information they hold as the meeting progresses so that should the meeting need clarity, resuscitation, or re-direction, immediate aid is available. With the aid of the organizing tools, your team and you can quickly declare:

   "This is what we have been doing. This is what we need to be doing. This is how we can get there."

This guidance also refers to any work accumulated by the team during the course of the meeting. Keep all charts on the walls and visible for the duration of the meeting. Don't cover charts up with other charts. In addition, do not just flip charts on the flipchart stand once you have addressed them; pull off a chart when it is done and hang it visibly for future reference. Always hang all information.

Driving the Message Home

Organizing tools create an environment of comfort for your team. They create a bounty of information and reference that each member can apply as needed throughout the meeting. Helping team members learn the value of these devices starts with you and how you present the materials to the team. You gain the team's trust and interest in the organizing tools by using your voice and body language as a focus for them:

- At the start of any meeting, go through the tools one by one, explaining how you will be using each during the meeting.
- As you refer to each tool at the beginning of the meeting, touch it while you are talking about it. This simple technique has such power in creating a connection between the tool and the members through you. When you physically associate yourself with each tool, you are telling the team that you trust the value of the tool and that you are asking them to trust in the tool as well.
- For any tool with multiple items (such as the Agenda or Ground Rules), go through each item one-by-one, reading it completely word-for-word, touching it as you read. Again, this physical and vocal messaging creates focus for the team around how you are using the tool.
- When you have explained the purpose of the tool and how you expect to use it in the meeting, always ask permission to use the tool. This solidifies the sense of trust you create with your voice and body language in presenting the tool.
- If there are any objections, find out what is driving the objections or concerns. Give the group guidance about why you are using the tool to help them with their meeting, then ask the group for guidance on how to respond to the concern. If their concerns persist, ask them for their trust and promise that you will check in with them at some specific point in the meeting about how the tools are working for them.
- Each time you need to rely on a specific tool during the meeting to help the team refocus or reengage, you should again move physically to the tool and touch it. Here, you are helping the team trust that you are not abusing your privilege as their servant leader and that the tools are their power in the meeting.

Meeting Purpose

Chapter 8, "Setting the Collaborative Agenda," covered how to set the meeting purpose in order to establish the meeting agenda and hence all the collaboration processes for conducting the meeting. Because of its fundamental importance to the meeting (it is the sole reason for having the meeting), it is the first organizing tool to post for the participants. When you have the purpose clearly visible in your room throughout the meeting, you are establishing with every participant:

- Why the meeting has been convened
- Why they have given up time back at their desks to participate in the meeting
- Why their participation is vital
- What should be the driving force behind every discussion and decision in the meeting
- How to tell if the meeting is off track

In these ways, it is potentially the most powerful weapon any meeting leader can give a team to manage itself in the meeting.

Meeting Purpose to Start and Guide the Meeting

When conducting a meeting, either with your own team, or as an outside facilitator for another team, always insist that the "Meeting Purpose" is hanging very legibly and clearly in the meeting room prior to the start of the meeting. At the very start of the meeting during the "Introduction" or "Welcome" part of the agenda, use your physical presence with the "Purpose" to set the meeting in motion. Follow the general guidance about how to then present it to the team.

When you are guiding a team in working collaboratively, one of the hardest tasks placed upon your shoulders is to help them determine if and when they are in danger of going off track or "down a rat or rabbit hole." Collaboration is brought to its knees when individuals lose sight of their goal and have to step back from decision making into debate about what they really want to be doing. Some discussions, while being interesting and stimulating, may just not be useful. A clearly stated purpose delineates the interesting from the useful in a far more direct way than any other device. At any point in the meeting, anyone can refer to the purpose as their guide for, "Are we still on track? Is this discussion more interesting than it is useful?"

My Anecdote

In my days as a spelunker, we very often had to be careful about "going down a rat hole" on our caving trips. On any given expedition, we would have a destination in mind (a particular room or chamber of the cave). But because we tended to not have detailed maps of how to proceed within a given cave, the group would very often find various nooks and crannies, also known as "rat holes," to explore along the way. Rat holes could swallow someone up so that they were lost, couldn't be seen, or, worst of all, couldn't be heard. Or, too many people going down too many rat holes could take the expedition off course either by heading in a different direction or by proceeding too slowly to our destination.

Therefore, we made a pact going into any cave that any "diversion" from our end goal in the cave required at least two people to agree to it. Additionally, someone else had to know where the pair was going in case they weren't heard from after a given length of time. This prevented severe "rat-hole-itis": too many detours in the trip or too much risk or danger for the crew.

In Release Planning meetings with new teams, I talk about the "Meeting Purpose" as my "anti-rat-hole" device. I invite the entire team to be the additional eyes needed before proceeding with any topic that may be a rat hole for the purpose. The group must make an explicit decision to "go down a rat hole" and also decide how long to explore the rat hole before coming back up for air.

(By the way, rat holes in caving are named rat holes for a reason. A rat may be at the other end of the tunnel, as I learned one time when leading an exploration in a narrow channel. Think about that when your meetings start down a rat hole!)

Given the power of the "Meeting Purpose," keep checking in with it throughout the meeting to help the team stay focused. You can use questions about the Purpose in the following ways (while touching the posted Purpose) to check in on the current trajectory of the meeting:

- "Is the current discussion helping us achieve this Purpose?"
- "Does the current conflict need to be resolved in order for us to meet this Purpose?"
- "Is a consensus-driven decision necessary on this topic in order for us to meet this Purpose?"
- "Are we still on track to meet our Purpose?"

Posting the "Meeting Purpose" throughout the meeting also helps the team explicitly rather than accidentally change why they gathered. Again, think about the rat hole. If you suspect that the team is moving from the originally intended purpose to a new, perhaps more useful purpose, go to the posted Purpose, place your hand on it, and ask:

- "Has the Purpose of our meeting shifted in a useful enough way to explicitly change the purpose of our meeting?"
- "Can anyone help me redefine the Purpose based on the discussions that the team is now in?"
- "Should we revise the Purpose based on the current topics, or should we put the current topics in the Parking Lot and resume our work toward this posted Purpose?"

Never assume that only you know whether the Purpose is correct. Never assume that you can change the Purpose for the team. Never assume that you can force the team to stick to the posted Purpose. Always guide the team to make an explicit team decision about their purpose for the meeting, and use the posted "Meeting Purpose" as your organizing tool around this discussion.

Agenda

In preparation for a collaborative meeting, you've established the purpose, and you have outlined an agenda in your facilitation guide. Therefore, your next life-saving organizing tool is a posted Agenda. With the posted Purpose, it creates a consistent, focused guide for the team about the map of activities that can lead them to meet the Purpose. The posted Agenda establishes that there is a clear path to the Purpose, and that you are acting as the team's servant to guide them along that path. While it may not necessarily be the only path possible, through the pre-meeting interviews, you have helped the team accept it as a "good enough" path that can guide the team to their collective goal.

Always post the Agenda for clarity about your roadmap. Always believe that you have done your homework about its usefulness in bringing the team to its Purpose for meeting. Always help the team use the Agenda to their greatest advantage.

No Agenda Is Infallible

Part of being the process owner is knowing when the Agenda no longer serves the team. Displaying the Agenda invites scrutiny of it and change in it in order to better serve the team in meeting its purpose. When you clearly advertise your roadmap, you invite the team to help you stay on the path and to recognize when a change or detour is warranted; that is, the team helps you continuously evaluate the value of the planned Agenda.

You can test the fallibility of your agenda by asking:

- Is it not driving to the purpose?
- Are the wrong participants in the room for reaching the purpose with the posted Agenda?
- Has the team's work revealed a flaw in the Agenda that will not drive to the Purpose?
- Has the team's work revealed a flaw in the Purpose that warrants a change in the Agenda?

A posted Agenda invites observation around these questions. When those observations incite dissension, the posted Agenda is just doing its job: It is helping the team communicate about how they explicitly believe they need to work together to meet their Purpose.

My Anecdote

I had been working with a group of representatives from a variety of business organizations who were interested in establishing some common practices about how to define high-level programs that would ultimately secure funds for XP projects. The group wanted to learn from one another what work would be necessary and adequate for their various business types to be able to set the XP projects in motion in as agile a manner as possible. Working extensively with the executive appointed as the main contact for the team, I had crafted an agenda that could lead them through some brainstorming about their current practices and some consideration of their concerns, obstacles, and constraints. It would then lead them to defining a process, its deliverables, the roles involved, and a few other data points they had wanted to collect.

When we came to the meeting, I had posted the Purpose and the Agenda on the meeting room walls, and I gained consensus that these were our goal and path for the meeting. But when we started into the brainstorming, it became apparent that a large assumption about the definition of a "program" proved not to be widely accepted. The meeting was in danger of collapsing under the frustration and annoyance of an inappropriate assumption. (This was a common occurrence in the group's past and the reason that I had been invited in to help plan and facilitate the meeting.) In this case, however, we had a well-defined Purpose posted, and we had an Agenda that we could evaluate step-by-step. With these organizing tools, we were able to make a declaration as a team about what items in the Agenda were still useful to complete, and what would be the new Purpose of the meeting. The team agreed that, in the time allotted, they felt that the new Purpose was well worth pursuing and that the altered Agenda would get them there.

At that point, I then proceeded as their servant to guide them through the newly defined agenda. The meeting ended on a high note with great enthusiasm about the work that the team was able to accomplish. For the first time in their months of meeting, they were eager to reconvene to pick up their work and march to the next deliverable in the vision.

A few "lessons learned": Never assume the Agenda is 100% correct. (In *Project Retrospectives,* Norm Kerth provides strong advice about when and why we invoke this agenda resiliency.) Never change the posted Agenda without the explicit approval from the team in its items and wording. Always challenge the team about their ability to meet the posted Agenda. Always challenge the team about eagerness to change the agenda. And, always post any changes.

To maintain a balance of resiliency and order, rely on all of your organizing tools and your observations. Teams just learning to engage collaboratively in meetings may be too quick to abandon an agenda. (This seems to be a tendency of technical teams unused to relying on an agenda as a means to complete work.) They may still be in divergence mode and unable to see any path to success, much less the path as defined in the posted Agenda. They may also be distrustful of your intention to act as their servant and may want to test your intentions for them.

Don't let these divergent teams abandon their Purpose or their Agenda without clear and valid reasons. It is your job as their servant to help them investigate their concerns and then make appropriate participative decisions. You'll probably want to guide them in an explicit exercise to brainstorm about what doesn't work about the agenda so that they can be explicit about their concerns and air them openly. Be sure this exercise is timeboxed; have the team tell you how much time they'd like to consider the problems before a decision is called for.

Posting the Agenda—What Does It Look Like?

What constitutes a good Agenda posting?

- Post the Agenda directly with the Purpose.
- Post every item in the Agenda *word for word.* (Remember that every item in the Agenda other than "A. Open" and "X. Close" is stated as a question that leads to some specific output.)
- Post the Agenda items but do not post timings (e.g., 30 minutes for item B. and 45 minutes for item C.). Your initial estimates on timings need to have some ebb and flow to them throughout the course of the meeting.
- Also, though you have a plan for how you are going to guide the team to answer each agenda item question, do not post the process you will use to help the team answer that question. The process that you intend to use for each item may be too verbose or too distracting and may change on the fly as your meeting progresses.

Keep your Agenda posting straightforward and to the point, but be sure to maintain very clear language about exactly what is to occur with each agenda item. Here is an example:

AGENDA

A. Opening

B. What are all the possible design artifacts we could use for this project?

C. Based on past experience, what are the benefits of these design artifacts?

D. What are the downsides to these design artifacts?

E. What other considerations should be used in selecting the set of design artifacts for this project?

F. What is the final set of design artifacts we will use for this project?

G. Close

Ground Rules

This organizing tool, along with the Parking Lot, may be the most misunderstood and abused of all the tools designed to provide collaboration guidance to a team. My facilitation guru Janet Danforth has been my savior about my own Ground Rules abuse and has set me on the straight-and-narrow path of how to use this organizing tool in service to the team. Without this fundamental shift in perception about Ground Rules, teams will resent them, abandon them, and lose any sense of their usefulness for collaborative work.

Ground Rules should be the team's declaration of its self-governance. They are not a disciplinary weapon of the meeting leader to quell dissent or control the group. They are the boundaries a team believes can help it stay focused on their goal. They belong to the team. If this discomforts you, then you have been abusing your power as a meeting leader. There is a better way.

When used correctly, Ground Rules help a team answer the following question:

"How will we help ourselves meet our goals without destruction, either in conflict or distraction?"

You Don't Own the Ground Rules

When you post the Ground Rules, review them one by one and then ask the team whether they reflect their own set of guidelines for how to keep themselves on target. In this way, you reinforce that you are neither the owner of the meeting nor of the Ground Rules nor how participants conduct themselves. They are the owners. They set the Ground Rules. They agree on them. They enforce them. They merely ask you to help them use the rules effectively.

To help a team think about and quickly decide on Ground Rules, you can "pre-populate" this organizing tool with items or rules that you have seen teams use effectively in the past. For instance:

- Respect the speaker
- One conversation at a time
- Cell phones on stun
- Start and end on time

Explain the pre-populated items *only* as suggestions that have worked successfully in the past. For instance, we continually note that meetings that allow cell phones to ring end up being very distracted meetings. Similarly, having participants leave a meeting to go to other meetings and then return can make consensus building very difficult. These distractions and ever-shifting waves of participation block a team from swimming through the Forming and Storming waters into the open expanses of Norming and Performing.

So, although you can't require a team to use certain Ground Rules, you can be their guide about very strong boundaries to set that can help them be a high-performance team.

What Constitutes a Good Ground Rule?

A good Ground Rule is anything that the team feels will help them stay on track, reduce distractions, maintain respect, and work collaboratively to meet the purpose of the meeting. Do we need to limit parallel conversations? Do we need to have people "park their titles at the door"? Have we learned that only Round Robin responses work for us in our teleconferences?

One caveat: Very often the loudest detractors to the use of Ground Rules are the people who have the greatest interest in keeping the meeting on their own personal agenda, in their control. They tend to be the people who dominate meetings and so have been very happy without the use of Ground Rules. They don't want Ground Rules because they don't need them. They are fully participatory already, or at least happy with their level of participation.

My Anecdote

I was leading a Release Planning meeting for a multimillion dollar project in which the lead architect refused to follow the Ground Rules on laptop use (limit it to supporting the meeting) and active participation (stay actively engaged; you are here because we need you). He spent a good deal of the meeting either out in the hall talking with other people, or in the meeting reading email on his laptop.

As the facilitator of the meeting and guardian of the process, I chose not to single him out, but rather I reminded the entire team of their commitment to the Ground Rules for self-governance. Still, he continued to ignore the group, and no one dared challenge his behavior. During a break, I spoke with the Director from the customer organization, the business partner who was sponsoring the product release. I expressed my concerns about the architect's impact on the meeting with his disruptive, unengaged behaviors and asked for feedback on what he would like done. Specifically, I wanted to know if the Ground Rule was not useful and should be deleted. He agreed that the architect's behaviors were unacceptable and demeaning to the rest of the team and that the Ground Rule should be enforced.

We approached the architect privately during the break and explained the situation to him, offering him a choice to engage in the meeting or leave. He chose to stay. When the break was over, the Sponsor asked the team again to turn to their Ground Rules and to be active participants in the meeting and the use of the Ground Rules. From that point on, the team agreed to self-govern and to not let others abuse their rules.

Referring to Ground Rules via questions is your way of helping the team revisit how they said they wanted to conduct their meeting. Remember: You are not a Sergeant-at-Arms. You are not an enforcer. You are a servant to the team, and as such you are sometimes their "Guide from the Side" who steps aside and makes observations for the team to ponder, such as:

- "These are the Ground Rules you agreed to at the beginning of the meeting. I'm concerned that these are not helping the team toward its Purpose. Should we review the Ground Rules for their usefulness?"
- "I'd like to check in with you about how we are progressing on meeting our goal. Are there any additional Ground Rules that could help you meet the Purpose more effectively?"

- "We seem to be ignoring this particular Ground Rule, and I am fearful of the damage it may be causing to participation. Could you tell me what might be useful for proceeding?"

Meeting Norms Versus Ground Rules

You can also use "Norms" as a guide for helping team members manage their own meetings. These are agreements that the team sets up in advance of a meeting knowing something of their team dynamics and how they work best with one another. Norms tend to look a bit wordier than Ground Rules but can be used in the same way in a meeting. You can help a team derive these norms prior to the meeting by using an informal survey. Or they may be statements captured in the Project Charter about team behaviors. In either case, find out if the team has norms and if so post them in the meeting. In Ingrid Bens's *Facilitating with Ease!,* you can find some good starting points for helping teams define their norms, such as:[1]

- Everyone's opinions count.
- All team discussions will remain confidential.
- We will respect differences.
- We will be supportive rather than judgmental.
- We will stay focused on our goals and avoid getting sidetracked.

Diana Larsen, a phenomenal agile facilitator, has a wonderful set of norms that she brings into her meetings with new teams to help them evaluate their behaviors. She calls it her "Focus On/ Don't Focus On"[2] norms:

Focus On	Don't Focus On
Inquiry	Advocacy
Discussion	Debate
Convergence	Argument
Understanding	Defending

1. Bens, *Facilitating with Ease!*, 55.
2. Retrospective Gathering, Phoenix, AZ, February 2005.

Parking Lot

The meeting Parking Lot helps you and the team track important items that may not be:

- Useful to discuss at this time in the agenda.
- Useful for the purpose of the meeting; we're not yet sure.
- At all useful for the purpose, but we don't want to lose track of them.

Or, we may want to track items that may be causing conflict that is holding the team back and that may need to be visited later in the meeting or after the meeting.

Although all of these situations warrant attention from you as the facilitative leader of the meeting, there is important guidance for what that attention looks like:

Parking Lot Axiom #1: Never put a topic in the Parking Lot without asking the permission of the team.

Simply stated, the team owns the Parking Lot, not you. Meeting leaders sometimes have an unfortunate belief that to "lead" a meeting, they also have to perfect the role of "Parking Lot Attendant": They decide what enters the lot and when. Additionally, they police when and how something exits the lot. For this reason, Parking Lot Axiom #1 has a critical corollary: "Never take anything out of the Parking Lot without getting the approval of the team."

A truly facilitative leader maintains a far more service-oriented view of their role *vis-à-vis* the Parking Lot, more like a valet.

"I'll help you park your vehicle, only if you want to park here. And I'll make sure your car is safe while it is in my lot. Finally, I'll retrieve it for you when you are ready to exit the lot; you just let me know. In exiting the lot, I'll make sure your vehicle is delivered where you want it. I will never abandon your vehicle in the lot."

Sometimes a team member, in an effort to help "manage" a meeting, may decide to start putting other people's topics in the Parking Lot. Their zeal to help turns into control of others' intentions. Therefore, there is a second corollary to our axiom: "Never let anyone else decide on his own to move something to the Parking Lot." No one team member owns the Parking Lot, not the technical lead, the customer, the development manager, or the developer. The team owns the Parking Lot and therefore determines what goes in and what comes out.

Here are some ways that you can help the team decide whether a topic should be placed into the Parking Lot:

- "I hear a lot of discussion moving to this particular topic, and I am concerned about its relevance to our current agenda item. Can someone help me understand if we should continue? Or is there a recommendation to place the item in the Parking Lot?"
- "Alan has requested that we table this discussion and move on. Do I have your permission to place the item in the Parking Lot?"
- "I hear the concern you are raising, but I am afraid that it may not be something we can address right now. Can I put it in the Parking Lot if I promise you that we will get back to it before the end of the meeting?"

My Anecdote

As part of my work to attain certification as a professional facilitator, I was invited to participate in a day-long event with other facilitators seeking certification. Each of us was given a topic for a meeting that we were to facilitate, and several assessors (along with the other invitees of the certification) were the meeting's participants. In each of our meetings, one or more of the assessors would try out different issues/problems on you to see how you would respond as the meeting facilitator. Would you notice that someone was sleeping? Would you be able to manage someone who was very negative? Would you be able to use effective information gathering techniques?

In almost every one of the assessments, they watched how the facilitator used or abused the Parking Lot (if the facilitator had even hung one for the meeting). During that day, I watched one unfortunate man who was facilitating his meeting really struggle. Whenever anyone asked a question that he felt didn't pertain to the meeting topic, he announced that it was going into the Parking Lot.

During the meeting I was facilitating that day, one of the assessors decided to dominate the meeting with her specific concern (childcare issues) that wasn't on the meeting agenda (church capitalization budget). I kept trying to reel her in, but she was darn good at this stuff! Finally, I asked her for permission to put her concern in the Parking Lot, and I promised her that I would get back to the topic before we closed the meeting. She agreed.

After the meeting, when I went through the one-on-one interview with my assessors about how I had led the meeting, they told me that what had really convinced them that I "got it" was that I had asked permission to place the item in the Parking Lot and had promised that I would return to it before the end of the meeting. Whew!

Because the team owns the Parking Lot, they decide not only what goes into the lot but also how to "clear the Lot": when something can be removed from the lot and what its fate is as a result. That means that clearing the Parking Lot must be accomplished prior to the meeting close.

Parking Lot Axiom #2: *Never* leave an item in the Parking Lot past the close of the meeting; no meeting can end if any items remain in its Parking Lot.

Without the team's input, you can't appropriately reflect their collaborative intentions for the items that they placed there. You guide the team in clearing the Parking Lot as part of the Closing agenda item. Therefore, during the Closing, you will specifically review every item remaining in the Parking Lot in order to resolve one of three fates for the item:

a. **The item must be addressed now**—The team reviews the item and determines that, without addressing the item, the purpose of the meeting cannot be met. The team decides on a timebox for dealing with the item and then proceeds immediately into addressing it.

b. **The item needs to be addressed but not right now**—The team determines that, while the item clearly has relevance to the team, it doesn't need to be addressed in order for the meeting to attain its purpose. This item goes to the Action Plan.

c. **The item no longer needs to be addressed**—Either the team feels that the item has already been adequately addressed somewhere in the course of the meeting, or the item has now been made irrelevant. This item is removed.

(With regard to the actual mechanics of clearing the Parking Lot, refer to Chapter 20, "Closing the Collaborative Meeting.")

Decisions Board

Sometimes in a meeting, the team has had a breakthrough in an area not specific to the purpose of the meeting. They've had an issue that has been haunting them or plaguing them in their background processing, and now they have arrived at a decision. Or, some fundamental statement has been made with regard to the meeting Purpose that can help steer the team through the remainder of the meeting. The Decisions Board organizing tool hosts these decisions and broadcasts them so that the team does not fall into a pattern of continually revisiting decisions that have already been made. It reduces the team's collective mental noise by being the placeholder of their already accomplished work.

While a Decisions Board doesn't provoke as much emotion as the Ground Rules or Parking Lot, it holds no less important a place in the full deck of collaboration cards. When you are facilitating a team, your job is to reduce distraction, increase focus, and welcome continued collaboration toward the posted Purpose. The Decisions Board not only minimizes distractions; it also promotes a sense of accomplishment for the team by posting their successes for them. Decisions can be hard to come by! Don't let them slip through the team's fingers unnoticed, undocumented, or uncelebrated!

Sometimes, however, a decision may need to be revisited. When it is posted as a reference in the Decisions Board, you invite the team to readily be able to test their assumptions as appropriate.

- "The current discussion sounds as though you are moving away from the decision we captured earlier here in the Decisions Board. Do we need to revisit this decision now in order to meet the Purpose of the meeting?"
- "I've just heard a new decision taken on this topic. We have a decision here in the Decisions Board. Do we want to change the originally documented decision, or would you rather keep your decisions?"

These questions guide a team to remind themselves of where they have been and where they are headed. Without a Decisions Board and you working in service with the Board, the team runs the risk of inadvertently losing decisions, revisiting them, altering them, and then rediscussing them, all in the same meeting. Worse, this decision may not even be useful to the purpose of the meeting. Maintain a Decisions Board to help the team explicitly make choices about their decision.

Action Plan

The Action Plan builds a bridge between the meeting and each participant's desk. Through the Action Plan, a team determines what they need to do after the meeting in order to reap the benefits of the hard work accomplished in the meeting. Actions give the team's decisions both validation and persistence.

A few rules guide the use of an Action Plan in a meeting:

- Every item in the list should be stated as an action ("Complete the use cases," "Publish the acceptance test cases," "Alert the media").
- Every item must have an owner ("Complete the use cases—Linda," "Publish the acceptance test cases—Michele," "Alert the media—Brian").
- The owner *must* be present and must personally volunteer to take the action; no absentee assignments or forced assignments are allowed.
- If an action has no clear owner, it must be dealt with either as:
  1. A new action regarding alerting the possible owner of the action ("Contact Linda about completing the use cases—Erika," "Work with Michele to complete the acceptance test cases—Jill").
  2. An action that can no longer be tracked from the meeting—An action without an owner is *not* an action. This action can be documented in the notes as a Decision "No one took the action to complete the use cases because there was not adequate representation of someone who could volunteer." Or, it is dropped.
- Every item must have a due date, agreed upon by the owner of the item ("Complete the use cases"—Linda by Tuesday the 13th).

So, the actions in an Action Plan might look like the following:

Action Plan

What	Who	When
Complete the use cases	Linda	Tuesday
Document the acceptance test cases	Michele	Thursday
Alert the media	Brian	COB Today

(I'll cover more about how to actually put items in the Action Plan, how to populate them with their owner and due date, and how to ensure that someone owns the Action Plan when I cover the "Closing" of the meeting in Chapter 20.)

Meeting participants carry around a hefty amount of cynicism with regard to the usefulness of the many meetings to which they are invited or required to attend. That cynicism is often fueled by the lack of follow-up from the meeting. Sloppy follow-up includes *not* providing all the meeting outputs to the participants. Therefore, every meeting's

Action Plan I lead has at least one item on it, with my name or an alternate representative as the owner, and a definite date when it is due:

"Complete the documentation of the meeting"

The item should have a due date no later than three working days from the date of the meeting, though you should find out from the team when it would be most beneficial to them.

A clear commitment to timely delivery of all the meeting documentation by you the facilitator of the meeting sends a few powerful messages to the participants:

- "I value the work you have done here, and I want you to value it as well."
- "I believe you have use for this material in acting successfully as a team."
- "I believe it is my job, as your servant, to be timely in providing these materials to you."

Communication Plan

This is the second organizing tool, along with the Action Plan, that supports the bridge between the meeting and each participant's desk. The Communication Plan guides a team in acting upon the following question:

"Who needs to know what about the work we have done here today and in what form?"

In other words, the team is explicitly determining as a group *what* should be conveyed (for instance, all of the meeting notes, the action items alone, the decisions only) and *how* they should be conveyed (email, blog, wiki entry, news article, flipchart in break room) and for *which audiences* (VP of Finance, customer rep, entire team, staff rep in Bangalore).

In truly agile team environments, team members engage in as much face-to-face communication as possible. That means that they are participatory in each meeting as appropriate with the intent that little or no communications or decisions need to be formalized post-meeting. In these environments, the Communication Plan may be more about conversations that need to take place, or information radiators that need to be updated. You and your team can decide how useful it is to document such informal, low-ceremony communications. You can also decide whether such communications can be tracked more easily as simple actions in the Action Plan.

So, the entries in a Communication Plan might look like the following entries in five columns:

Communication Plan

What	Audience	Vehicle	Who	When
Meeting notes	Attendees, Stakeholders	XLS spreadsheet on team website	Anne	Tuesday
News article	IT Dot Net developers	IT Dot Net newsletter	Paul	Thursday
Updated estimates	Sprint team	Breakroom chart	Mike	COB Today

The rules of engagement concerning a Communication Plan follow suit with those of the Action Plan:

- No item can be placed in the list except by the team.
- Every item must have an owner.
- The owner *must* be present and personally volunteer to take the action; no absentee assignments or forced assignments are allowed.
- The owner of the item should consult with the team about the proper vehicle for the communication but is the ultimate person responsible for supporting the vehicle.
- Every item must have a due date, agreed upon by the owner of the item.

Consensus—I Can Live with That and Support It

A collaborative meeting strives toward highly participatory decision making. But what constitutes agreement about decisions? And how much agreement must a team have to move forward comfortably with other work? Consensus-driven decisions form the most sustainable agreements a team can use to create action. Therefore, a collaborative meeting includes a posted definition of consensus as one of its organizing tools.

I use a definition that removes the binary or black-and-white connotations from the notion of agreement and instead reinforces the notion of agreement without compromise and without violent dissention. Simply stated, consensus means:

"I can live with that and support it."

This helps participants understand that collaboration can be achieved in a team without everyone being wildly enthusiastic about the choice. The choice reflects a shared understanding by the team. The choice is good enough to live with and support. The choice is adequate to help us move forward. The choice has enough of a team sense that no one feels completely left out of it.

Consensus Is Neither Compromise Nor Coercion

Confusing consensus with compromise may be the great "wives' tale" that undermines the collaborative nature of meetings. The Thomas-Kilmann conflict mode instrument described in Chapter 4, "What are Collaborative Teams?," provides clear differentiation between the compromising individual and the collaborative individual. This is useful when considering a definition of consensus for an organizing tool:

- Individuals who have some ability to cooperate while remaining somewhat unassertive engage in a *compromising* conflict mode.
- The very assertive and very cooperative person uses the *collaborating* mode of conflict resolution.

True consensus, therefore, relies on a collaborative mode of reaching decisions versus a compromising mode.

(Later, in Chapter 17, "Managing the Meeting Participants," we'll revisit consensus with regard to how teams can move from disagreement to consensus through effective conflict management.)

Teams that agree to work in a consensus-driven mode make a few implicit statements to one another as they begin a meeting:

- "We believe that any decision made by the team is better than a decision made by an individual"—This does *not* mean that the team cannot have experts that give very strong recommendations to the team about how to proceed. Experts often provide the necessary rocket fuel to help teams move forward and maintain focus on the larger collaborative issues. This is especially true in our technical environments in which we have to rely on specialists in a variety of domains in order to converge on our complex "righteous solutions" for our "wicked problems." Experts ensure that the team has accessed its greatest wisdom in order to build the best overall solution.
- "We understand that gaining consensus can take more time"—In the section entitled "How Do I React to Conflict" in Chapter 17, I'll uncover the delicate yet very specific steps a facilitative meeting leader uses to guide conflict toward consensus. Because of the work and commitment it takes to gain consensus in a highly charged issue, a team has to understand at the start what is required of them. They may choose to reserve consensus for critical, high-risk decisions only.
- "We may not seek consensus for all decisions"—Some conflicts are not so important as to warrant the time to resolve it to a consensus level of agreement. Therefore, once meeting participants truly understand the meaning of consensus, they can then more knowledgeably choose when to use less time-consuming forms of decision making.

Trina Hoefling (author of *Working Virtually*), a facilitator who specializes in conflict resolution, leads teams through a decision process at the very start of any meeting to help them decide explicitly about their consensus organizing tool:

"When will we use consensus to resolve conflict? When consensus is not warranted, what other decision-making process will we use?"

By making these clarifications at the very start of the meeting and posting them, Trina helps the team move along at a pace that works for them with regard to consensus building. In sum, teams decide which decisions are important enough that they should only be resolved in consensus, and which decisions can be taken through a less enduring approach.

Teams who believe in consensus and use it appropriately are teams that are able to work more and more collaboratively.

Other Organizing Tools

The previous sections provided you with the bare essentials for bringing your meeting preparation and organization into the meeting room: Purpose, Agenda, Ground Rules, Parking Lot, and so on. But you'll soon discover that particularly for very large technical meetings, having a few other organizational ducks in a row will go a long way toward keeping a meeting and its participants productive, focused, and galloping toward a successful finish. In this way, organizing tools expand to include any materials that help a team self-govern and self-manage as they produce the meeting outputs.

Here are a few examples of useful organizing tools I've used in the past that have provided highly visible meeting information to participants.

- **Expert materials**   When a particular plan or set of designs is to be used frequently during a meeting, you should consider adding it to your stable of organizing tools as a large wall chart. Large plotted CAM/CAD drawings of system process, architecture, or user assumptions go a long way in reinforcing clarity of discussion in a meeting. I use these early and often when a large format printer is available to produce such charts.
- **Previous meeting decisions**—This tool can be a lifesaver for keeping the current discussion on track by not revisiting decisions unless an explicit choice is made to do so based on the posted decisions.
- **Timelines**—When a team has produced a timeline for a release, or set of releases, or set of dependencies around milestones, consider capturing this as a chart that can be made available in subsequent meetings. A very visible display of the agreed-upon timelines invites acknowledgment of previous assumptions as well as clarification and amendment when the assumptions shift.
- **Attendees**—Large meetings may make it hard to keep track of who all the participants are over several days. Besides providing name tents and name tags, consider hanging a chart of attendees by name and role or business representation. This has been particularly valuable for groups where technical leads from a variety of organizations are coming together and they want to be able to talk one-on-one during

breaks or lunch. The chart helps them learn who is present and in what capacity they serve.

- **Lunch instructions**—If you know the lunch schedule and accommodations (is it "buy your own," provided but outside the building, in the room next door, at a certain time, of a certain cuisine?), post this information so that you are not the sole gate to the detail. It saves you time and others frustration about a minor (but often grave!) detail.

- **Security guidelines**—Some companies have specific security issues from building to building, or from group to group. Posting this information in the room makes everyone aware of the constraints within which they should comport themselves without embarrassment.

- **Breakout room lists**—For very large meetings where different design teams need to work in small groups, I post a large chart of all the rooms available. For instance, at the beginning of the design work, explain that teams should self-organize about what topics need work and who should be involved. Suggest that teams reserve a breakout room for a given time slot and post it on the chart. Participants then resolve for themselves which group to participate in; locate the topic, room, and time slot in the posted chart; and then self-manage their participation. This self-organization chart also works well when large numbers of organizations come together with uneven representation of the technical staff or of the end-users. The posted breakout room list helps groups locate the subject expert they need for any particular decision about their work.

- **Message board**—Again, for very large meetings that overflow into many breakouts or small group discussions, provide a message board with Post-it notes and a pen on a string, taped to the wall. Anyone can leave a message for anyone else, regardless of whether they know their cell phone number (and if there is a ground rule that cell phones are turned off, it may be hard to reach anyone without this tool). This message board is also useful for finding an expert, even if you don't know the name of the expert. For instance, perhaps a team needs to talk with someone with a .Net background, or from a specific company, or a specific user group. The message board can serve as a broadcast for whoever is available to help; it invites self-management about such ad-hoc meetings or conversations.

- **"You Liked What?!"**—It is always worth encouraging people to tell you what is working well about the meeting (particularly meetings that extend over several days) while the meeting is still in progress. So while you may have a specific debrief at the end of a meeting where you ask for this feedback, consider also using this posted organizing tool to encourage postings during the meeting. I've posted this board on a number of occasions with large groups. It has proven to be fun and to provide some highly valuable in-flight feedback.

- **"What's Yer Gripe?"**—Sometimes people may not be getting what they want out of a very large meeting. If they are of the more reticent ilk, a "What's Yer Gripe?" board posted in an easily accessible location helps them just vent or expressly request something without having to draw specific attention to their discomfort.

Chapter 10

Starting the Collaborative Meeting

A few meeting preparations go a long way. So, once you have dealt with the participants, the sponsor, and the organizing tools, prepare for your collaboration event by bringing the meeting venue together and starting your meeting.

Setting Up the Room

I've discovered that the layout and feel of a room can, from the very start, have a big impact on how your team members perceive the meeting you are about to start. When people walk in the door, they gain some sense of how they want to participate in the meeting. So for instance, I've noticed that if there are lots of rows of tables, as in a classroom-style setting, technical people tend to sit half way back and beyond. Or, there may be people so certain they do not want to participate in a meeting, they choose a chair that had been shoved in the corner to make more room.

Any of these gestures tell you that participants expect the worst from the meeting. They are used to not owning a meeting because command-and-control has been the norm for decision making. Or meetings are typically so out of control that no decisions are ever made; so the meetings are non-productive drudgery. Sitting outside of the group creates a detachment from all the expected dissatisfaction.

Here are some guidelines about seating arrangements that invite collaboration:

- **U-shaped**—Use this for small to medium groups. The U-shape keeps participants in eye contact with one another and reinforces their ownership of the meeting; rows of tables do not. A U-shape allows you to enter the center of the space when you need to create focus on a process item, and then to clearly step outside and away from the space when you want to ensure that the group is taking over a decision. A U-shaped setting also lends itself to some simple approaches for managing dysfunctional behaviors, discussed in Chapter 18, "Managing Conflict."
- **One large grouping of rectangular tables with people on all four sides**—Use this seating when it is not possible to reconfigure the room into a U-shape and the size of the group is still small.
- **Multiple round tables**—This works well for very large groups where work will be subdivided into smaller groups. With ten or fewer people at a table, people who tend to be reticent still have a setting in which they can speak up without having to address the entire crowd. Additionally, it still allows you access to each table and each group.

There are some other seating techniques you should consider. When you plan on having observers, make sure that the seating you have for them is behind the main seating of participants. In Scrum meetings I have led, the teams love having the observers (often referred to in Scrum as the "Chickens") sit separate from and behind the actual working team. It is a very physical reminder of their non-speaking status in the meeting.

When you know that you are going to have a number of breakout activities, either have tables available in different corners of the room, or make sure breakout rooms are available in the near vicinity of the main meeting room. Make sure the seating in those rooms is equally conducive to groupwide participation.

In addition to the setup of the seating for a room, pay attention to the wall space you will have available. For large Release Planning meetings and retrospectives, you may want to build a release or project timeline using a series of flipcharts or a length of butcher paper. That means you need a wall that is long and wide enough to collect the many items that populate such a chart. Even without using a timeline, evaluate the wall space in terms of how you will keep all your organizing tools and accumulated information radiators visible throughout the course of the meeting. You may need to resort to using windows or hanging some very large items in hallways.

Setting Up Supplies

Collaborative meetings stay focused through the use of a variety of tools as underpinnings of the information gathering. Maintain focus and participation by making sure you have stocked:

- **Lots of flipcharts**—This includes a flipchart with flipchart easel for each sub-group.
- **Lots of pens**—Keep a carton of ballpoint pens available for participants.
- **Lots of markers**—Flipchart markers and dry erase markers make for large highly legible items to move around on wall charts or on tables for planning strategies, Sprints, or iterations.
- **Lots of index cards**—For capturing stories to be planned in Sprints, releases, or iterations.
- **Lots of Post-it notes**—Can also be used for capturing stories, but also hold Parking Lot items, decisions, risks, personal objectives, and any other brainstorming or listing data that needs to be accumulated and then grouped or prioritized.
- **Lots of tape (artist's white tape or blue decorator's tape; these don't mar walls)**— To hang any information that is useful for the team to access during the meeting: organizing tools, timelines, instructions, maps, etc.

"Do Food"

In their book *Fearless Change*, Linda Rising and Mary Lynn Manns talk about a pattern they call "Do Food" as a means to support teams in making change. Collaborative meetings thrive on food and beverage support. Here are a few "lessons learned" about food when working with technical teams:

- **Make sure that coffee, tea, and water are always available, not just during breaks**—In particular, make sure team members have access to lots of bottled water; water seems to keep people alert in meetings without the jitters that caffeine can bring. Fruit juice is also a good energizer. If possible, keep all of these items in the back of the room where anyone can access them at any time without disrupting conversation or work.

- **Provide low-sugar snacks**—Sugar can cause some adverse reactions in some people's blood sugar and can contribute to making people anxious in a meeting; offer some sugar-free substitutes in with the candies if you are going to make candy available. As an alternative, our teams are tending to offer more fruit than candies during our meetings.
- **Go light on carbohydrates**—These make people drowsy. If you don't intend to have team members up and moving during the course of the meeting, avoid high-carbohydrate snacks. If pizza is the snack of choice, make sure they are not sitting for long periods of time after eating. As a change of pace, I have moved to cheese, cracker, and fruit trays. This keeps the sugar and the carbohydrates at lower levels than candy and potato chips.
- **Use low-noise packaging**—At Chicago Symphony Orchestra concerts, audience members have access to large bins of free cough drops in the lobbies. The symphony has been clever enough to use only lozenges wrapped in wax paper instead of cellophane. I try to do the same when picking snacks for access at the table during meetings. Small, low-noise items work best.
- **Manage dietary restrictions**—Pay attention to dietary restrictions of team members and provide a choice of snacks for all palates.
- **Stock any team favorites**—In one team I worked in, our favorite food was Peanut M&Ms, so no meeting took off without these, even though they violated the sugar rule. In another team, it was sugar-free red licorice (definitely low on the noise scale!). Declaring a team favorite and replenishing its stock often has been a great way to build collaboration in team meetings.

Food provides not just comfort and sustenance; it can also help reduce distractions. The food on the table keeps the people in the chairs.

My Anecdote

As an agile coach, I like to ensure that food is available for any new teams just slogging their way through a new, agile way of developing software. The first meetings can have some discomfort, and food helps alleviate the pain. I was headed to a new client in San Francisco when I decided to buy some See's Lollipops at the airport on my way into town. They are larger than normal children's lollipops, and the flavors are more about chocolate and latte than about sugary fruit. When I started working with the group on their Release Planning, I brought out the See's, not knowing if a group of developers, testers, and their customer would like something as non-cool as lollipops for food. As it turned out, they loved them. The lollipops weren't an immediate rush of sugar; they were different flavors than normal pops, and they took a long time to finish. At one point, I looked around the room, and everyone had a lollipop either in their hand or in their mouth as they walked around in serious contemplation, planning the stories for the iterations.

As a result of that first meeting's "Do Food," I am not allowed back into their offices unless I show up with a box of See's.

Welcoming Participants

One of the ways to kick off a meeting on an up-note is to greet each person as they come into the room. I have used this for teams that are coming together for the first time, or for teams that I am working with for the first time. Make a point to greet each person individually and shake hands as they enter the meeting room. This establishes a connection with participants in a way that a command-and-control environment or a teaching environment does not. It also lays a foundation that you believe in the team's ownership of the meeting; you honor the expertise and wisdom that they are bringing into the room.

Greeting people at the door sets a tone of your service to the team. You move to them to help them know immediately that they will be the ones making the decisions and driving the work forward. This also helps break the mental barrier they may have about their work in the meeting. Regardless of where they sit in the meeting, they have already been invited into the space of collaboration by being greeted. They are not expected to just watch, listen, and then heed commands.

Kicking Off the Meeting

When it is time to start the meeting, your first order of business is to ask the team if they are ready to start. What a shock this is to lots of teams! They are not used to owning the very first decision of a meeting; that is, should we start now or should we wait? Ask a team at the posted start time if they are ready to start. If there are several people still missing from the list of participants, make a suggestion about whether to wait for them or to start. (In over 90% of all the meetings I have ever run, the immediate and happy response is "Let's start!")

Asking a group for their decision about when to start is an early, easy validation that they are in the driver's seat; they own the meeting; and they will drive the other decisions that move the meeting through to its purpose.

Introducing the Purpose and Agenda

Once you have welcomed the entire group to the meeting, your first work is to remind them of the posted Purpose and Agenda for the meeting. Having brought the group's attention to the posted Purpose, walk through the posted Agenda with them, reminding them that the role of the agenda is to help the team achieve the purpose of the meeting. Touch each agenda item as you present it to the team; this helps create focus about the flow of the posted Agenda. Then ask the team if the posted Agenda looks like the right set of items that will help the team meet the posted Purpose. If you have done your homework in surveying participants prior to the meeting, this should not be an issue.

But if that work hasn't taken place, this is a critical moment in how the meeting moves forward. You may discover that someone has some expert information they feel needs to be introduced into the meeting at a certain point. Or, you may find out that the agenda makes an assumption about a certain decision that hasn't really been resolved. Now is the time to ask the group for their recommendations on how to make the agenda work for them. Note all recommended changes on the posted Agenda.

The WIIFM and Scope of Authority

Very often when team members step into a meeting, if they have not gathered wholly as a team before, they may not yet understand or believe in "What's in it for me?" or WIIFM. During the kickoff of the meeting, take time to explicitly delineate what's in it for the participants, either as a whole, or by role. Think about what is in it for the testers in an iteration planning meeting. What's in it for the stakeholders in a pre-Release Planning meeting? Why should a developer care about a project retrospective?

Now is the time to explicitly state these compelling reasons for their participation and to ask for their active engagement in the meeting.

In addition, you may also want to clearly outline the team's "Scope of Authority." Will the decisions they make as a team today be immediately actionable? Are there still some other groups who must meet and weigh in on the topic before the final decisions? Is this just the first in a series of meetings that will ultimately lead to an overall project plan? Is the team making a recommendation to upper management who will then make the final decision?

Now is the time to clarify all these aspects of the team's impact on what happens with the meeting's outcomes.

Review of the Organizing Tools

Prior to the meeting, you have prepared a full set of organizing tools. These wall charts and process maps guide the meeting and keep it afloat as the team moves through the agenda, accumulates information, and makes decisions. Now is the time to review these tools one by one. Clarify the role of each of the tools in the meeting and ask the team's permission to use each:

1. Ground Rules
2. Parking Lot
3. Decisions Board
4. Action Plan
5. Communications Plan
6. Other(s)
7. Consensus Definition

Remember to touch each hanging chart as you explain its role in the meeting. Physical closeness creates focus for the team and confirms your intent to use the tools in service to the team.

Explaining Logistics and Participation

When kicking off a meeting, it is important to put attendees at ease about what the meeting is about, how you will help them meet their purpose, and what tools are at their disposal as they move through the agenda items. We do all of this to create and maintain focus.

Therefore, you also need to be very clear at the start of a collaborative meeting about any nuisances related to the meeting logistics: when will the breaks be, what time will the lunch be served, how much time will we have to go get lunch if it is not served, where will we be able to hold small group discussions, who do we talk to about getting messages, what time do the doors lock, how do we sign in and out of this secure building, where are the restrooms, and so on.

In explaining the logistics and overall flow of the meeting (breaks, lunch, breakouts, etc.), also explicitly ask at this time if anyone knows at the start of the meeting whether they will have to leave the meeting at any point, either temporarily or not returning at all.

This is another point where you turn to the team to ask if that works for them. If the Product Manager is intending to leave the planning meeting after the kickoff, does the team feel it can still move forward without that person's prioritization guidance? If the head of QA has to leave early, will we still be able to create a team-wide commitment to the release? Is there some way that we can accommodate these disruptions by changing the agenda around? Or is it necessary to postpone this meeting until all participants can be fully engaged?

Gathering Personal Objectives

With new groups that have never worked together before, or with a group going through a new process they have not used before, now is the time to gather their personal objectives. Just as in the pre-meeting exercise when you survey some of the participants about their participation in the meeting, you use this time to ask all the attendees to think about why they are in the meeting and what they hope to get out of the meeting.

To keep this exercise short and to engage teams early in group work, have them gather in groups of three or four and ask one person to be the scribe using a stack of sticky notes. Ask members to ponder the question that you had used in the pre-meeting survey:

> "Imagine that the meeting has just ended."
> "You are walking out the door of the meeting, and you turn to your colleague and say, 'I am so happy I attended this meeting! I got exactly what I wanted out of it!'"
> "What was it that the meeting accomplished that made you so happy?"

Allow two to three minutes for each group's scribe to write answers to this question, one answer per sticky note. When the time is up, collect the notes, read each one aloud, and place it on a posted chart entitled "Personal Objectives."

As the planner of the meeting, you may know some of this already. But here is the team's chance to have their aspirations and goals posted for the rest of the group. Additionally, you may discover information that you did not expect.

When you have posted all of the responses, you must promise to return to the posted items at the end of the meeting to see whether the personal objectives have been met. You'll go through these items at the closing, but tell participants at the start that you will work with them to determine whether:

- The personal objective has been met.
- The personal objective hasn't been met and still needs to be addressed before ending the meeting.
- The personal objective does not need to be met in order to meet the purpose of the meeting.

"I Am Here to Serve You"

The last bit of work at the start of a collaborative meeting is to very explicitly establish your role with the team, not as a commander or disciplinarian, but as an owner of the process and a servant to the team's best wisdom. "I am here to serve you." All of the meeting kickoff activities should have established this, but this is your time to state it very explicitly. Whether you are the project manager, the business owner, the architect, the ScrumMaster, the XP Coach, or an outside facilitator, establish your intent now and what it will look like in the meeting.

Although you may be holding other roles in the meeting, such as a technical lead or a subject matter expert, when you are standing in front of the group and creating a collaborative environment, you must establish and confirm your role in servant leadership.

My Anecdote

I found out just how powerful this statement was when I was preparing for a particularly large and contentious pre-release strategy meeting with a group of combative business units. I had discerned from the pre-meeting phone calls that the general sense was that the meeting would be contentious, lacking in focus, have far too many attendees, and that "Nothing will get done; we'll just be forced into a decision and be told to make it work." I could sense also that they assumed I was being asked to facilitate in order to exert control and force them to "cooperate" and complete the strategy plan.

As I completed the kickoff of the meeting, I took the time to pause and turn to the group. "This is a large group. There is a lot of work to be done. I am here to remove impediments and to serve you. If anything is getting in your way of completing your work, please come to me, grab my sleeve, and say, 'Jean, I need you to serve me.'" People laughed at this, but it clearly got their attention.

We completed the kickoff, answered remaining questions, and then had the groups divide into the various breakout teams that would be tackling the three primary business issues. Over the next two days, I had individuals from all different roles in the teams come to me, laugh sheepishly while tugging on my sleeve, and say, "Jean, I need you to serve me." Though it became a joke, it also became the "password" for getting something they felt they needed: access to a particular subject matter expert, someplace to make more copies of their high-level requirements documents, more flipchart paper, clarification on what their team was expected to produce for the rest of the group, when and how all the team results would be pulled together, and so on.

When we did the debrief at the end of the long, hard two days, we learned that people really valued the sense that they had control of what was going on and that they always had someone to turn to immediately to help them get unstuck from a block in their work.

Chapter 11

Defining the Steps

The heart and soul of team participation begins with ensuring that decisions adequately represent all participants' views. That means that teams must learn to gather and share information effectively in order to grow collaboratively. Facilitating teams through information gathering can create great trust and energy, accomplish early wins, and inspire teams to reach solutions they couldn't have reached as individuals.

Some fundamental information-gathering techniques include brainstorming, listing, grouping, prioritizing, questioning, small group discussion, and expert input. Each of these approaches needs context and structure that envelops it in a reliable packet for bringing it into the meeting as directly relevant to the meeting agenda. So before digging into the technical details of each approach, it's worth paying attention to the set of steps that guide how to deliver any of the techniques in a reliable and sustaining way.

You can think about information gathering in terms of four basic steps:

1. **Prepare**—Provide participants with all the instructions and materials they need to complete the work.
2. **Prompt**—Deliver a concise, clear question that stimulates the information gathering.
3. **Gather**—Guide participants in creating and gathering their responses through the particular information gathering process.
4. **Process**—Lead participants in using their information to formulate knowledge and actionable decisions.

1. Prepare

Whether you are leading fifty people or five, preparation on your part in understanding how to aid them in accumulating information will go a long way. For any of the variety of information-gathering processes, the first order of business is to ensure that participants know exactly what is being asked of them:

- What information do you want?
- How do you want it captured?
- How much time do I have to give it to you?
- What do I do with it when I am done?
- How can you assure me that my input will be valued?

Lack of clarity about these facts and guidelines can frustrate participants and lead to distrust, apathy, non-participation, and even sabotage. (Sabotage lingers everywhere that you explicitly or implicitly take away the team's control of its work.) Be clear, succinct, and directive in these preparations before you proceed to the Prompt, Gather, or Process steps.

Here is a simple guide for how to prepare a team in a way that removes all doubt about what will be expected of them:

1. **WHAT**—State which item in the agenda the team has now reached and point to it as you state it. (Restating the agenda and pointing to the particular item makes sure *everyone* knows where they are, whether they have been out of the meeting briefly, have just joined the meeting, or have been distracted in the middle of the meeting. Help people stay participatory!)

   Example: "We are now at Agenda Item J: *What are all the User Stories to be considered for our August release?* I'd like us to gather this information through some brainstorming."

2. **WHEN**—Tell the team the time limit you intend to use to bound the exercise, and tell them that you are going to give them all the instructions first. This helps the team set some context for knowing what is expected of them in terms of focus and time commitment. It also makes sure that they don't start answering the agenda question until they have learned how they will do so.

   Example: "We're going to take 20 minutes to gather information about this item, and then we'll take 30 minutes to discuss the results. Before we begin, I want to explain to you how we are going to do this."

3. **WHO**—Explain how they should group themselves (or not), and whether any special role is to be designated (such as one or more scribes). Have the team complete this instruction before you continue with the remaining instructions.

    Example: "I'd like you to work in four groups to do this. Please divide into the four groups based on the compass point groupings we used for Item G earlier. Once you are in your groups, could you each make sure that you have one scribe designated per group?"

4. **HOW**—Make sure that they have all the materials they will need to complete the work. This should be completed before you allow them to move to the next step.

    Example: "Once you are in your groups, could you make sure that each person in the group has a marker and a stack of Post-it Notes?" Or, "Once you have designated the scribe, could you make sure that person has a marker and a flipchart. And could you please label your chart at the top 'RELEASES USER STORIES'?"

As part of preparation, you should also have all your own materials together to process the information once the team has done its work. Have a flipchart or some other wall chart clearly labeled with the useful title of the information it will accumulate and manage during the "Process" work.

Once you have provided all these instructions and materials, state one last time what is about to occur and ensure that everyone is ready:

5. **READY**—Explain the gist of the information gathering and then ask one last time if anyone has any questions about what is to occur before you move to the next step, the Prompt question.

    Example: "Now that you are all ready, I'm going to give you a question to help you think about your work. Once I have completed the question, you'll have 20 minutes to record your answers, one answer per Post-it Note. I'll let you know when your time is just about up. Any questions before we proceed?"

    Or, "Now that you are ready, I'm going to give you a question to help you think about your work. Once I have completed the question, your group will have 20 minutes to call out responses to your designated scribe. Please give them to the scribe one person at a time. Scribes, please record verbatim what the team tells you. Any questions before we proceed?"

Clear instructions remove frustration and create trust. When you are well prepared and clear with your instructions, you provide comfort and trust to your team about what is about to take place. Free from confusion or frustration, the team can concentrate fully on the task at hand. They aren't hampered by your lack of preparation.

2. Prompt

The Prompt should be as clear and succinct as the preparation guidance. I use a fairly strict formula that establishes a non-ambiguous scenario, some of its possibilities, and then a question that invites responses. No frills. No getting lost in the details. And no wandering off the agenda item or accidentally misleading participants to answer the wrong question.

Here's how:

> ### The Prompt Question—A Story in a Triptych
>
> **Part I**—Set the stage ("Think about our upcoming August release.")
>
> > pause
>
> **Part II**—Elaborate the scenario ("Think of all the possible functions that we have been discussing about the next version of the automated system, the user interfaces, the financial data checking, the workflow analysis, newly structured cross-unit data integrity, and our own concerns about architecture and deadlines.")
>
> > pause
>
> **Part III**—Ask the question ("Now tell me: What are all the possible User Stories for our August release?")
>
> > silence

Based on this example, think about what information is being requested. Do you know the question your responses should be answering? Can you visualize the context of the question and some ideas about it adequately to spark your responses? If so, then it is a good Prompt question.

Here are the characteristics of a good Prompt question:

- It is presented in three statements, separated by pauses.
- It first sets a general context statement (Part I) to help participants come back to the meeting agenda and settle into the exercise. This is one sentence, no more. Be concise and cut a wide enough swath in which participants can feel comfortable in a general sense about the topic.
- It elaborates on the general context to help the participants start to mentally dig around in what they may know in the context (Part II). This is no more than two sentences. Be clear and brief. Help participants start to steer their thoughts into a more focused direction.
- It asks a very clear, concise question (Part III) that directly mirrors an item from the agenda. This is one question only and is *always* directly from the agenda. Be exact. Make no mistake about what is now wanted.

Prompt questions look deceptively easy. Mastering them is a different matter. Avoid these common pitfalls:

- Part I (the stage) is either too vague or too intricate and complex; participants have no idea why they should be listening to you and may just give up before the work even begins.
- Part II (the scenario) wanders on too long; participants get lost, frustrated, or bored. They now start writing up what *they* want to answer, having given up on your ability to help them focus. Or they decide not to participate at all.
- Part III (the question) doesn't reflect a question on the agenda. Or it has too many flourishes added to it, disguising it from being recognized as pertinent to the meeting. This also annoys participants beyond distraction!
- No pauses between parts. Information about the exercise becomes too hard to follow. There is no sense of focus built into the Prompt, no focal drive. If the leader isn't able to set focus, participants may find it either hard to do or uninteresting to do.

3. Gather

Once you have prepared the team with all the instructions and have delivered a clear and concise Prompt question, it is time for the participants to create their information. As they gather data through brainstorming, listing, or other gathering techniques, your job is to "Guide from the Side"—that is, once participants are engaged in their work, leave them to it. Give them your silence.

Your role during gathering is to serve them without disruption. You do this by providing guidance when asked. You are neither a contributor nor an influencer. Your guidance and service may look like the following:

- Clarify the preparation or the Prompt question for anyone who asks for that guidance. (*Note*: only provide guidance when asked; otherwise, you run the risk of distracting participants or steering their work off point inadvertently.)
- Provide timebox warnings. ("You have about one minute left to finish up your responses.")
- Supply participants with any additional tools they may need (markers, index cards, paper, flipcharts, tape, etc.).
- Scribe responses (this should only be true in a facilitator-led exercise).
- Declare the end of the timebox.
- Gather responses (this may be part of another process, such as grouping, or part of your current process; decide in advance how you will do this).

4. Process

With the information created, your job now is to lead the team in moving their work from an array of diverse data elements into a group statement of knowledge. Doing so, you ensure that their expertise converges into a useful view of priority and value that creates action and decisions. During this step, you:

- Maintain the flow of discourse and discussion that leads to decisions.
- Steer the debate to dialogue.
- Stress the convergent attributes of the data versus the divergence.
- Help the team recognize when they have reached a decision.

- Capture the action items that emerge as a result of the work.
- Guide the team in determining that they have completed the work necessary for the agenda item.

Use this *Prepare* ➔ *Prompt* ➔ *Gather* ➔ *Process* approach for every information gathering exercise you bring into a meeting, and it will become second nature to you. Moreover, you'll begin to notice that participants are able to focus more readily, get right into the work, and create more valuable information. Unhampered by confusion or frustration about the work and how to produce their outputs, participants are liberated to just get on with their work, and that is a mighty fine thing.

My Anecdote

I had been working with a colleague in figuring out some strategies for gathering risk information in anticipation of a Product Backlog prioritization review. As we were defining the agenda, he had decided to lead the team in a brainstorming exercise about the risks, and so we outlined a Prepare, Prompt, Gather, and Process approach to support the brainstorm. On the day of the meeting when he came to this exercise, he accidentally skipped the "Prepare" step and went straight into his "Prompt." During the "Prompt," he began his own brainstorming about what the risk items might be.

This combination of mix-ups caused several problems in the exercise. Some of the participants immediately began to just write things down on their own (they hadn't been prepared for what they would be doing, how they would be doing it, and when they would start). Other participants started to look around the room and flip through other materials (they had lost interest in the brainstorm because the leader was already brainstorming his own ideas first). Frustration was really taking over for the participants and for my colleague. He was bombarded with questions and comments, so both he and the team lost the focus and intent of the exercise. Later when we debriefed the exercise, he recognized the source of all the confusion.

It was wonderful the next time we were in a meeting together. He had really taken the four steps to heart, and I could see that he was able to help the team prepare for their work and then create and maintain focus on that work.

Chapter 12

Gathering the Information— Brainstorming and Listing

One of the key propellers for helping teams move from divergence to convergence and thus into high-performance is the effective implementation of information-gathering techniques. Brainstorming and listing are the tried and true workhorses employed in these collaborative contexts. Facilitators have long been turning to these two basic techniques as their stock and trade for bringing workshop participants together to express what they know in a given domain. While the two techniques do have differences, here first are some of their common characteristics:

- They provide a speedy means for gathering large amounts of data.
- They promote productivity.
- They ensure an environment of safety for sharing information.
- Every answer is a good answer.
- All answers have equal weight (changing their weights only occurs after the information gathering has ended and only as deemed necessary by the team).
- Because all answers are good answers and no answer carries more weight than any another, they promote equality among team members.

- They provide an "early win" to the team because participants, as reinforced by the facilitator, can quickly see how much they know and how easily their knowledge can be gathered and processed for further use.
- They provide a simple, straightforward means of validating collaboration in the team, either when the team creates its responses or when the facilitator helps the team process those responses.
- They encourage preservation of the team wisdom.

Brainstorming Versus Listing

Using brainstorming and listing effectively means knowing when one approach is more beneficial than the other for helping a team gather its collective wisdom. Each serves an express purpose for managing information. Here is a simple guideline to distinguish listing from brainstorming:

- **Listing**—Document the *known set*; be correct.

  In listing, you *recollect* the "As Is" information. The time limit is more relaxed and meant to encourage thoroughness and completion.

  Example: The team needs to document all the data, attributes, functions, and algorithms used to calculate the capitalizable portion of contracted labor expense. You facilitate them in a **Listing** exercise so that they can fully define all the necessary data elements and calculations. Thoroughness counts.

- **Brainstorming**—Derive the *possibilities*; anything goes.

  In brainstorming, you *create* the "What Ifs." The time limit is tight and meant to push participants to think highly creatively without rethinking the details.

  Example: Once this information has been defined, the team now needs to think of how to provide the data and calculations to project managers, program managers, directors, and contract negotiators. You facilitate the team in a **Brainstorming** exercise so that they can freely derive an unbounded set of possible solutions. Creativity counts.

Given these guidelines, you can think of various uses of each (see Table 12.1) where each is more appropriate than the other based on the type of information being sought:

Table 12.1 Brainstorming Versus Listing

Brainstorming	Listing
Futures	Current
Solutions	Attributes
Free thinking	Documenting
Creativity	Thorough coverage
Randomness	Analysis
Reflection	Recollection
The unknown	The known
Refactoring	Process definition
Strategizing	Decisions
What ifs	As Is
Risk identification and possible resolution	Risk actions
Emotion	Fact

Meanwhile, some forms of information may lend themselves to either technique equally well. Decide which to use based on whether you are motivating your team more toward creativeness or thoroughness:

- **Storybuilding**   Sometimes teams prefer to think "out of the box" in deriving all the possibilities for stories to be considered for a release (brainstorming); they then prefer to be clear and finite in defining the stories for a given iteration (listing).
- **Team building**—Just as success breeds success, collaboration breeds collaboration. Teams value early wins in how well they collaborate. Use either technique early in the team's life to instill a sense of the ease with which they can collaboratively communicate and document. Brainstorming may be the easier task; determine this based on the team culture. Does the team need a nudge in its creativity or in its thoroughness?

- **Prioritization**—If the goal is to build a prioritized list of items, you can first accumulate the full set of non-prioritized items using either brainstorming or listing. The nature of the items may tell you which technique would be preferable. When asking, "What is the highest-priority thing we must complete for this release?" you would engage the team in listing. To answer, "How should we prioritize all the possible things we could do for this release?" you could lead the team in a brainstorming exercise.
- **Grouping**—Teams may choose to track information items in categories or groups in order to help them manage large amounts of project or product detail. Sometimes the grouping will be of all the *what ifs* that surround the project; that's your signal to implement brainstorming. Other times, the grouping will manage the *defined set* of attributes or tasks that exist in the project; turn to listing to help the team define these groups.

Whatever approach looks the most appropriate for the work you want to accomplish, use the *Prepare → Prompt → Gather → Process* formula from Chapter 11, "Defining the Steps," as the basic mapping of how to use the technique in an agenda item.

The following sections present a number of techniques for accomplishing either brainstorming or listing. Pay attention to how the "Prepare" and "Gather" steps differ from technique to technique. That is where you will make sure that the technique is applied usefully. The "Prompt" step remains the same throughout.

Techniques for Brainstorming

Although brainstorming promotes creativity and unbounded possibilities for team information gathering, this freedom of expression requires (paradoxically) some strict guidelines on your part as the coordinator and process-owner of the exercise:

- Use a short enough timebox to encourage responses but discourage analysis (use a timer to strictly manage the time).
- Tell the participants how much time will be used for the exercise before you begin the brainstorming.
- Explain exactly how you will capture information in the exercise prior to starting the exercise.

- Make sure participants have all the materials they will need to complete the exercise before starting the timer.
- Start the exercise with a "Prompt" question, then begin the timer.
- *Never* comment on the value or validity of a response or compliment a response or a respondent.
- Discourage any discussion about response; discussion can be a follow-up to the brainstorming.
- *Never* interject your own responses.
- *Never* edit a response and never reproach anyone for not responding.
- Always write exactly what was spoken.
- Always end when the time is up (when the timer has beeped).

You may have to temper this last guideline if responses are coming too fast. If you cannot keep up, ask participants to speak one at a time to allow you to complete the full response from each. Remind them to bullet their responses as best as possible.

When you engage in brainstorming, stick to these guidelines regardless of which specific approach you apply; your teams will be able to respond more creatively and openly. Here are a number of approaches that rely on these brainstorming fundamentals. Keep them in your stable of collaborative tools and interchange them for variety and applicability:

- Facilitator-led Callout
- Post-it Notes
- Round robin
- Pass the pen
- Pass the card

The guidance presented here is highly prescriptive, intended as a guide when you are first applying the technique. Think about ultimately moving into your own approach that works with your personal style within your teams. Additionally, any one of these approaches lends itself to follow-on processing such as grouping or prioritizing, described in Chapter 15, "Processing the Information."

Facilitator-Led Callout

Use this technique to encourage fast, lively information gathering. This is a good early-win device to wake up a team and energize them for the more detail-oriented, intense work that may be coming later in the meeting. But be forewarned, it has its drawbacks: One or two members may tend to dominate. Avoid eye contact with participants who begin to dominate the exercise.

Some tips: Be sure to use "What else?" as your only prompt. Do not comment on responses, and never edit any response provided.

1. Prepare:
   - Label a flipchart clearly with the topic of the brainstorm ("User Interface Considerations," "What is Working Well," "Decision Strategies," "Name the Baby").
   - Explain that you will write each response on the flipchart as the team calls it out.
2. Prompt with the brainstorm question.
3. Gather:
   - Hit the timer, *say nothing else*, and poise your pen on the flipchart to signal that you are ready to begin collecting responses.
   - Remember, your only response to any offered response is "What else?"
   - Continue until time runs out.

Post-it Notes

This is a variation on the facilitator-led callout. In this technique, participants write their responses on Post-it Notes, one response per note, rather than call them out to the facilitator to be scribed on a flipchart. Be sure to remind the group of the brainstorming, fast nature of the exercise.

1. Prepare:
   - Label a flipchart clearly with the topic of the brainstorm ("User Interface Considerations," "What is Working Well," "Decision Strategies," "Name the Baby"). This reminds participants of the brainstorming topic and is used later when processing the collected individual responses.
   - Explain that you are about to begin a brainstorming where each person will be writing their responses individually on Post-it Notes. (You may want to give some hint as to what the follow-on work will be with their responses, such as

prioritizing, greater detail through small group discussion, grouping, or pros and cons to help them keep their responses short for the brainstorming.)

- Write each of your responses on a sticky, one response per sticky: three responses equals three stickies.
- Even if the exercise is conducted in small groups, there should be no discussion during the exercise; everyone is working as an individual.

2. Prompt with the brainstorm question.
3. Gather:
   - Hit the timer, say "Begin," and *say nothing else.*
   - End when time has run out.

How you "Process" the responses after the timer beeps depends on what you intend to do with the material (prioritizing, grouping, or posting).

Small Group Post-it Notes

The usefulness of the individual Post-it Notes approach suffers if you have a very large group. You may get inundated in processing all of the individual responses and lose the focus of the meeting. To keep the group moving forward and focused, consider this small group variation.

In the "Prepare" step, divide the group into smaller groups (preferably no more than five or six total groups). Ask for a scribe volunteer from each group who will do all the writing for the group. Only the scribe has the Post-it Notes and the marker for writing responses. Remind the scribes of all the rules about brainstorming: one response per sticky; write responses as spoken; do not comment on responses.

When it is time to process the responses, the scribe will represent the sum of work from the group

Round Robin

Use this technique to draw out creativity in a fast-paced fashion that purposefully engages everyone in the room. Drawbacks to this approach: Some people may feel too pressured to respond if they have not yet felt safe and secure in the meeting. For example, a customer service representative in a group of developers and architects may still feel uncomfortable presenting non-technical ideas in such a technical environment. Allow people to pass and greet them with a smile, not disappointment, when they do.

1. Prepare:
    - Label a flipchart clearly with the topic of the brainstorm ("User Functions for the Next Iteration," "Pairing Options," "Design Strategies," "Name the Pod").
    - Be prepared to scribe all the responses on this chart.
    - Responses will be gathered "Round Robin" with each person in the group answering in turn.
    - Indicate the order of the respondents by pointing out who the first, second, and third person will be (this gives these three people some heads up that they will be the first to respond!).
    - Anyone can pass on his or her turn by just saying "Pass."
    - Keep going around the team soliciting responses either by eye contact or by calling out the next person's name until the time is up.
2. Prompt with the appropriate question.
3. Gather answers on the flipchart until all participants pass or until time has run out.

Pass the Pen

Use this technique to get participants out of their chairs and actively scribing their own responses. This is a good technique to use late in the day or immediately after lunch when lethargy or apathy can set in. Being physically in charge of the information helps participants wake up and pay attention.

The drawbacks? This technique assumes everyone has the grammar, spelling, and handwriting skills to participate. Make sure you do not have anyone in the group uncomfortable with the language in written form (such as a speaker of English as a second language or in an unskilled labor group). These language-challenged team members may not be able to participate without embarrassment.

Additionally, because this technique removes anonymity, it may adversely reinforce who has contributed which items to the brainstorming. Don't use "Pass the Pen" if the group is fearful of the sponsor, manager, or any dominating, controlling participant and his or her responses. (If you still want to use this exercise to get people moving, you can safeguard anonymity somewhat by having the flipchart turned away from the group while the exercise is being conducted.)

1. Prepare:
   - Label a flipchart clearly with the topic of the brainstorm ("User Functions for the Next Iteration," "Pairing Options," "Design Strategies," "Name the Pod").
   - Explain that you are about to begin a brainstorming where the team will be writing responses on a flipchart for the entire team and have everyone move to the flipchart to have easy access to it.
   - Participation will be performed in a circular, Round-Robin fashion with each person in the group writing their response in turn.
   - As with the "Round-Robin" approach, indicate who the first, second, and third person will be (this gives these three people some heads up that they will be the first to respond!), and anyone can pass on his or her turn.
   - Explain that each person will take a turn writing on the flipchart and that the team will continue to write answers until the time ends.
2. Prompt with the brainstorm question.
3. Gather:
   - Hit the timer and say "Go!" to the first person.
   - Your only response is "Next."
   - Continue until the time has run out or there are no more responses.

To speed things up, use two pens. One is always in the hands of the current person writing; the other is in the hands of the "on deck" person. Two pens cuts down on the fumbling when the writer passes off her pen.

Pass the Card

Use this technique when you want very large groups of people to share information without having them form small groups. Passing the card helps provoke creativity by allowing participants to see some other responses yet still think independently about any other unique responses they could add. Each shifting card invites a new look at the question. Additionally, it can be another technique that gets participants on their feet and staying physically engaged while creating the brainstorm responses; rather than having them sit and pass cards from seat to seat, have all participants move about in a "cocktail party" group to complete the exercise.

This technique has a drawback in that it may require extensive follow-up processing to remove all the duplicates and to make all the responses available to everyone else.

1. Prepare:
   - Hand out an index card to each of the participants.
   - Have each of them label the top of the card with the name of the brainstorm (example: "Virtual Team Collaboration Ideas").
   - Everyone will be able to contribute on as many cards as can be passed around during the timebox; the idea is to collect as many different responses as possible from as many people as possible.
   - Explain that each person, upon being passed a card, will have 15 seconds to write as many new responses as possible on the card they have received; there should be no talking when passing cards.
   - At the end of the 15 seconds, they will be prompted to give up their card, pass it to someone else and in turn accept a new card.
   - Only write responses on a card that are unique for that card, or that you have not written on another card.
2. Prompt with the appropriate brainstorm question.
3. Gather:
   - Hit the timer and say "Go!"
   - At the end of each 15-second time slot, say "Next."
   - Continue until the time has run out.

Applying Brainstorming Techniques for Listing

Listing prompts thoroughness of information and documentation. Therefore, you can use any of the techniques described for brainstorming by just allowing much more time for each exercise and explaining the thoroughness of data desired. Your "Prepare" work should clarify the thorough, extended sense of response gathering that comes with listing.

Some helpful techniques for managing listing differently from brainstorming are as follows:

- Work to help the group give responses instead of discussing each response in detail (this lengthy analysis and discussion can occur in a separate agenda item after the listing has ended).
- Have the team help you understand what must be captured instead of what is just information that solidifies the already captured answers (very often, the continued discussion is useful for prompting juicy contributions from other participants).

- Use encouragement for clarification by prompting participants with "follow-on" questions during the listing:
  - "Can you tell me more about that?"
  - "What does that mean to you?"
  - "How does that impact what we know so far?"
  - "I'm not sure I understand; can you help me by saying a bit more about that?"
  - "Do we need to capture this detail for our list?"

Thus, the work to "Prepare," "Prompt," and "Gather" does not differ from the brainstorming steps other than validating the appropriate use of discussion during the listing and the lengthened timebox.

Your greatest challenge in listing will be to figure out when to encourage discussion and when to discourage too much detailed problem solving during the information gathering. While brainstorming discourages discussion and detail, listing can feed off of the information shared in these discussions. Help teams learn to discuss during listing without losing the goal of gathering a thorough set of responses. Teams that veer into extensive discussion and dialogue during a listing exercise fail to gather all the data before processing it. As you use the prompting "follow-on" questions during listing, reinforce the goal to keep the detail limited and the discussions focused so that teams can continue collecting the useful, needed data for later deeper discussions.

Facilitator-Led Information Listing

Use this technique early in a team's maturity, when it is still wobbly on its collaboration legs. A full-team listing exercise led by a very facilitative leader can help a team move through its Storming and highly divergent phase into a Norming and more convergent mode of working without losing participants along the way. The team watches itself create a very detailed list of items in a far more efficient way than they had been able to do in the past.

Drawbacks to this listing: one or two members may tend to dominate. Be sure to give eye contact to everyone else in the room except the dominators as you proceed. You may also interject: "Who else can tell me something about this topic?"

Follow the guidance provided in "Facilitator-Led Callout" but provide more time than in the brainstorm approach. Additionally, apply "follow-on" questions to manage discussion and thoroughness of responses.

Post-it Notes Listing

As with brainstorming, use this listing technique to help team members begin to be more self-managing and to move to the next level of collaboration where facilitator guidance is more limited. In small groups, team members scribe their collective knowledge, each writing their own responses on separate Post-it Notes (or index cards).

The listing version differs from the brainstorming technique in that discussion is encouraged and the time frame is usually much longer. Also, though the discussion is performed in small groups, each person writes their own responses, one per Post-it Note or index card. The longer time frames and greater accumulation of individual responses create an environment for discussion and thoroughness.

The drawback to this approach when conducted in small groups is that team members may want to discard responses right away. All answers or responses should be documented and presented in an open debriefing to the entire group.

Whether in a small group or the entire group, responses are only removed or added from the list as directed by the team.

Round-Robin Listing

As with brainstorming, use this technique to help non-participatory members (shy, embarrassed, asleep, apathetic) join in the discussion without being singled out. Because each person answers singly to the rest of the group, it helps level the playing field when some members tend to dominate. In a listing exercise, it also helps to weed out valuable needed information that may be hiding in the more reticent participants with or without the dominators. Finally, in "Round-Robin Listing," the team can self-manage duplicate answers.

Chapter 13

Dialogues, Small Groups, and Expert Input Approaches

Applying the basic brainstorming and listing techniques in Chapter 12, "Gathering the Information—Brainstorming and Listing," may be like finding yourself on a reliable, sturdy two-wheeled scooter on the road of collaborative group work. You have a mode of transportation, but your variety of terrain is perforce limited by the constraints of your vehicle, and passengers on a long journey may soon get bored.

Truly facilitative leaders quickly rev up their collaboration vehicle and move to a sleeker, four-wheeled model with rack and pinion steering and seat belts. You accommodate more people, rougher terrain, longer trips, and nobody gets hurt.

In this chapter, we look beyond the information gathering fundamentals and press ourselves into the more delicate operations of dialogue and small-group work. Refining your ability to engage teams in open discussion and to lead small groups from the periphery will provide the morale boost teams seek in order to bring emergent solutions to the fore.

Team Dialogue—Next-Generation Collaboration

Any collaborative leader who, by choice or ignorance, learns only the brainstorming and listing techniques defined earlier will ultimately constrict their team's ability to grow and converge. Brainstorming and listing provide good solid fundamentals, but they don't promote the maturity in collaboration that comes when teams own more and more of their information exchange.

A team that can continue to collaboratively gather information in an open dialogue moves from a freshman level to a senior level of collaboration. They move from a handheld collaboration approach, relying on the leader to keep the process flowing, to a mode of self-reliance. In open dialogue, they can create information and share it in the most effective manner for the group. They take their sense of collaboration and bump it up a notch.

Dialogue Versus Discussion Versus Debate

You'll sometimes hear the term *small group discussion* to describe work that is less formulaic than brainstorming or listing. You'll also hear individuals stress the need for more open *debate* in order for teams to be truly collaborative. However, the goal of collaborative teams should be to engage in group *dialogue* versus discussion or debate, where dialogue emphasizes the notion of seeking meaningful information exchange without the notion of a particular outcome.

Dialogue, in contrast to discussion, guides an accumulation of pertinent information about a particular problem domain or solution domain rather than open-ended, sprawling discourse without form or structure. Dialogue strives to capture what each and every team member believes to be true about a particular topic, issue, or question; in contrast, discussion is less concerned with participation and openness.

Dialogue, in contrast to debate, stresses the team view more than any individual view. Dialogue encourages team members to seek understanding of a variety of possible solutions without the burden of confrontation or defensive argument. Any individual can be considered a valuable contributor. Experts emerge through the open dialogue rather than through one-on-one debate.

My Anecdote

I am sometimes challenged by colleagues about the pros and cons of using facilitation and information-gathering techniques for promoting collaboration in teams. I've learned that people who are leery of facilitation want to get straight into discussion and debate. They feel that having a facilitator in a meeting holds them back and that the structure imposed by facilitation is constricting. For these people, true collaboration occurs only in an open, unstructured forum; brainstorming, listing, and other techniques "get in their way."

Here is what I have observed about these concerns. It is true, open dialogue is a wonderfully collaborative mode for participatory decision making. I believe that high-performance teams work best in open dialogue; their information exchange and decision making come naturally, with little or no leader input. But I know what destruction occurs when newly forming teams insist on open dialogue from the start: It doesn't work. Teams work effectively in this mode only when they have built up their trust in one another and have acquired the skills to resolve conflict collaboratively. When newly formed teams jump straight into "discussion," I start to see nonproductive conflict modes emerge (competing, compromising, avoiding, and accommodating). I also see certain individuals start to dominate and others drop out. I watch discussions get sidetracked, information get lost, and people get frustrated.

I was asked to help a client run a Release Planning meeting for a group that was made up of five teams, each contributing some component of the overall product. We had planned to facilitate breakout sessions of each of the teams to help them complete a first pass at their team release plan before reconvening with all the teams to declare the overall release plan. Two of the team leads, however, said they didn't need any help with their breakout sessions; they would run the meetings themselves. I stepped out and left them to their work, though I checked in from time to time. In those two groups, I noticed that the team lead dominated the meeting, deciding what the stories would be, what their estimates were, and when they would be scheduled. Clearly, the team leads didn't want a coach or facilitator in the room for a reason. Unfortunately though, they were creating ill will by not using open discussion collaboratively. I could see that team members were dropping out of the discussion entirely.

Meanwhile, in the other three groups, we facilitated the teams to determine the stories, their estimates, and their schedule. When they emerged from their breakout sessions, the resulting release plans clearly reflected the wisdom of the team; through dialog that had been kept open and constructive, they had captured their best thinking about the upcoming release. Three months later, the results were amazing. The two teams that had derived their plans in "open discussion" had missed a series of critical features. Additionally, the teams had low morale from having had so many stories slip. The other three teams, in contrast, had estimated their work fairly realistically and had been able to do a fairly good job of watching the issues and concerns they had raised at the start of the release.

Before you introduce open dialogue to multiple small groups, you'll first want to hone your skills within the whole group context; that is, work with the entire team before you attempt to have small groups work independently of one another. Your proficiency in keeping dialogue open and focused for the group at large sets the pattern for subsequent small group contexts. Also, make sure you are comfortable with the fundamentals (brainstorming and listing) before you begin to apply your facilitative touch to dialogue.

The Principles of Dialogue

Because dialogues can quickly be swamped in debate, accusation, or a stream of tangents, you must be clear at the start about the intent of the dialogue: primarily, that it is truly intended to promote and capture the entire group view. Thomas Justice and David W. Jamieson have a set of "12 Principles of Effective Dialogue"[1] that represent a fine guide in how to set up the atmosphere and intent for these open and constructive discussions. You may even want to post these in the team area as a reminder of the power and usefulness of dialogue:

The 12 Principles of Dialogue

1. You become conscious of your assumptions.
2. People reward each other for searching for the meaning behind ideas.
3. People work to discern the pattern of the collective experience and learn how to think together.
4. Differences are welcomed and sought out for explanation.
5. A metaphorical container is constructed big enough to hold diverse allegiances, experiences, and opinions.
6. Previously taboo subjects can be raised in a safe and meaningful inquiry.
7. There is no agenda. Agreement unfolds as it does.

---

1. Justice and Jamieson, *Facilitator's Handbook*, 193.

8. Different reasons support the direction that emerges.
9. Fragmentary thinking becomes organized into a whole.
10. We view a complex problem with "new eyes."
11. Cross-talk is discouraged.
12. The process has a beginning, but no end. Change happens when it does. There is no "hurrying the harvest."

In addition, Justice and Jamieson suggest that small groups learn to allow the discussion to slow down so that silence and acceptance can promote listening and observation that lead to the discovery of previously hidden meanings.

Small-Group Work—Getting Started

Any of the brainstorming and listing approaches described in Chapter 12 can be conducted as an entire group, or in smaller groups in parallel to one another (as suggested in the brainstorming "Small Group Post-it Notes" section). When you choose to conduct brainstorming or listing at the local, smaller level instead of as one group, follow these guidelines:

- Make sure that teams are all using the exact same process when in their separate groups (round robin, Post-it Notes, etc.) so that, as a guide, you will be able to keep everyone engaged in the exercise.
- If each small group is to have a scribe, make sure the scribe very clearly understands his or her job before you begin the "Prompt" question.
- Reinforce to the teams that discussion should either be limited (during a listing-style approach) or not happen at all (during a brainstorming-style approach).
- Make sure you are available to answer questions should a team get confused about what they are doing.
- Try not to intervene in a team's work but monitor that they are not stuck, dominated, or abandoning the exercise.

Small-Group Scribed—Turning Over the Pen

Just as servant leaders learn to turn over control of decisions to the team, so they must also learn to turn over control of the collaborative meeting by letting go of the scribing pen. To do so, engage a volunteer who will capture the information for a group-wide exercise; in this context, you can monitor and make sure the scribe is abiding by your guidelines. Later, rely on a scribe within each team when teams capture their own work. In either case, volunteer scribes reinforce the sense that the team itself owns the creation of the work that will lead to its decisions. Also, the facilitator reinforces a role as the "Guide from the Side" rather than the owner of the meeting. Find every opportunity you can to move control to the team to own its processes, the information accumulated in the processes, and the decisions that emerge from that information.

Before you engage volunteer scribes, make sure that:

- Each scribe understands his or her role.
- Scribes recognize that they may *never* edit a response from another team member (unless the team member gives permission).
- A scribe cannot pick and choose which responses to write down and which ones to ignore.
- A scribe cannot add his or her own responses without the permission of the team and should only do so after the team has had ample time to build its own responses.

Be forewarned, small-group scribing has its drawbacks:

- A very dominant person as scribe can kill the trust of the rest of the group and quickly destroy all the Norming and Performing that has occurred in the group at large.
- Too much small-group work may create a mindset that only the small group's decisions matter and may make it difficult to engender collaboration among all members of the team.
- Small groups may miss the opportunity to learn the inner workings of other small groups.
- If you form too many small groups, it may become difficult to process all the information accumulated in each exercise.

- The group scribe may write illegibly and make it hard for his or her group as well as other groups to use the information collected.

My Anecdote

I have a colleague who shared one of her worst "volunteer scribe" incidents. At a leading conference for executives interested in bringing agile approaches into their organizations, small groups were asked to brainstorm about their major reasons for considering agile approaches. Each group was asked to pick a volunteer scribe for the group. In this particular group, though there were two certified facilitators in the group, a third person jumped up, grabbed the pen, and announced that he would be scribing. What ensued was an exercise in which he captured his own contributions and those of a subset of the rest of the group; all other contributions were either ignored or dismissed by him as not relevant. Thus, when the group had its readout of its results, only a subset of findings were presented. The exercise created frustration and distrust among those members not adequately represented.

Small Group Exercise Example—Personal Objectives

An easy exercise with which to warm up small-group scribes is the Personal Objectives Exercise. Use this technique to kick off a meeting. It provides teams a chance to learn about small-group scribing without stretching their collaboration skills too much. No one scribe should be able to dominate his or her team's responses too badly because participants should have an idea of their personal objectives based on having been interviewed prior to the meeting. Moreover, gathering and posting personal objectives right at the start of the meeting can be one of your first validations that the participants truly own the meeting, not you.

1. Prepare:
   - Label a flipchart clearly with the topic "Personal Objectives."
   - Explain that you are about to begin a short exercise to learn more about why people are attending the meeting.
   - Have the team divide into three to five groups.

- Explain that you need a volunteer scribe in each group and that the scribe needs to have a marker and a set of Post-it Notes. (Sometimes, to mix things up, we tell the person who has volunteered that they are now responsible for selecting a scribe!)
- There is a time limit (use a timer to be sure you can stick to it), usually 2-3 minutes.
- Explain that scribes should record each response verbatim, one response per sticky.

2. Prompt with a Personal Objectives question as follows:
   - "Imagine that the meeting has just ended."
   - "You are walking out and turn to the person next to you and say 'I'm so glad I attended this meeting. It really met my personal reasons for attending.'"
   - "What were those personal objectives the meeting met for you?"

3. Gather:
   - Hit the timer and *say nothing else*.
   - Try to remain on the side, but you may want to walk around to ensure that scribes are really gathering responses verbatim and recording them one per Post-it Note.
   - End when the timer beeps.

You can also run this exercise with each group standing around a flipchart. Each group's scribe captures their responses as items on the flipchart instead of on Post-it Notes, using the instructions provided in the "Facilitator-Led Callout" subsection in the Brainstorming techniques in the previous chapter. Be sure that all scribes have their materials, have labeled their flipchart, and fully understand their instructions before you begin the Prompt question.

Small-Group Dialogue—Next-Generation Collaboration

Once teams are adept at small-group brainstorming and listing, you and they are ready to move into small-group dialogue. When you are able to move teams into these small group dialogue contexts, you are in essence providing them the keys to the kingdom, the heart and soul of mature collaboration.

Small-group dialogue participants should already be practiced in their ability to self-organize and self-facilitate; that is, they are fully convergent teams that have moved from Storming and Norming into Performing. Small-group dialogue is useful for encouraging participation among members who don't contribute well in large crowds and yet can trust the members of a small group. It encourages more familiarity and bonding among team members when they completely own their discussion independently of any other groups or the meeting leader.

Small-group dialogues are also good follow-up for bringing detail and advice about information that has been gathered via a listing or brainstorming. Or they can be used to investigate the many facets of a problem domain prior to a team brainstorming about a solution strategy. In any case, ensure that the small groups are convergent enough and Performing enough to move into such an exercise with the confidence that they can fully communicate and capture the full sense of the team's views.

My Anecdote

I refer to this incident as "The Scribe That Ate New York." In one of our Release Planning meetings, we ran into two different small-group dialogues in which scribing backfired and actually eroded trust instead of building it. Here is the first incident.

A development team member had been asked to scribe the User Stories being created by the help center representatives about reducing failed or flawed orders. The scribe was creating the user stories on her own laptop in order to directly collect them online into the enterprise release management tool. As a result, none of the other members of the small group could see what she was writing as they articulated their stories. At one point, however, one of the user team members came to me and explained that the scribe was not only changing the wording of her stories about the role of the help center representative, but she was also deciding which stories should be captured and how. As a result, the help center representative was quite annoyed and threatening to no longer participate in the user story definition. Tensions were high.

During a break, I pulled the scribe aside to thank her for her hard work. I then also reminded her of the importance of taking every story as spoken, not editing stories, and not choosing which stories would be captured. When the session started again, we worked together with the help center representative to make the wording of her stories reflect what she really had intended. Smiles returned, and we were able to complete the remainder of the story definitions for the release.

Managing Small-Group Dialogue

Small-group dialogues can tend to turn into free-for-all discussions, getting off point easily unless the team has learned to be truly self-governing and is able to practice "guerilla facilitation" about the small group topic. Use the small-group dialogue approach sparingly until you feel comfortable in guiding multiple teams with respect to how to stick to the topic, the process, and the timebox defined without squelching creativity in an open forum.

Also beware: A dominating person or viewpoint can quickly take over if the team is not well schooled in the art and intent of dialogue. Be a close monitor of small-group dialogues as teams mature. And while tangential, interesting-but-not-useful discussions must be kept in check; remind teams that differing viewpoints are constantly encouraged, not judged, and are considered useful and important in crafting the group view.

My Anecdote

In another small-group exercise during the same Release Planning meeting described earlier, the lead architect did not want a facilitator managing the scribing of the future strategies discussion. Without asking the rest of the group, he grabbed the marker and began listing his own ideas for creating a new process for managing inventory loss. When he was through, he turned to the group and began to call on the other people he knew in the room, commenting while people gave their ideas, and picking which ideas he would write down. Very soon, at least 50% of the group gave up trying to provide input. When it was time to prioritize the suggestions, he did so by himself with one other person standing with him at the board, not asking for feedback from anyone else in the group. When done, he declared the discussion over, and the group disbanded with a good number of the "participants" never having provided their input.

The following exercise, the Small-Group Problem Probing, provides a good starting point for helping teams understand the inner workings of a truly effective dialogue. While working in a small group and self-governing, they learn to simultaneously keep open-minded and on-topic.

Small-Group Problem Probing

Use this technique to help a team fully investigate a problem domain prior to brainstorming solutions for it. Probing the problem in a non-judgmental, objective dialogue promotes a collaborative convergence on what is believed to be factually true about the problem domain. When groups are able to maneuver the problem waters successfully in small group settings through open dialogue, they create a sense of confidence in their ability to then tackle what might be most true about the solution set.

Note: Because this exercise emphasizes problem investigation, make sure teams understand that they are not to delve into problem resolution or solution definition. Software teams are often very challenged to stay in the problem space without delving into the solution, so this exercise affords technical teams the opportunity to create self-discipline with respect to their problem identification work.

The directions here are highly prescriptive; refer to this detailed set of instructions as a guide for how to kick off any small-group dialogue.

1. Prepare:
   - Prior to conducting the exercise, have a flipchart labeled "Problem Definition Questions" and list some of the following bullet points on it that seem to address useful observations in your problem domain:
     - Where does this problem occur?
     - When does it occur?
     - What does it cost us (in sales, time, money, jobs, etc.)?
     - What are some of the root causes of the problem?
     - Who is most affected by the problem (users, stakeholders, roles, organizations)?
     - What systems, processes, or procedures are most impacted by the problem?
     - What event caused this problem to become a priority for us to investigate?
     - Who has the authority to correct or control this problem?
     - How did we work before we had this problem?
   - Explain that you are about start the team on an exercise in which small teams will work to investigate the problem domain fully through open dialogue.
   - Have the team divide into three to five groups.
   - Explain that each group will use the "Problem Definition Questions" as listed on the flipchart as their guide for dialogue. Teams are to stick to problem definition *only;* no solution definition.
   - Explain that you need a volunteer scribe in each group and that the scribe needs to have a marker and a flipchart pad.
   - The scribe should label the top sheet of the flipchart pad with the first question. As the team tackles other questions, the scribe should prepare a labeled flipchart upon which to capture team observations.

- Remind scribes to contribute only when they feel that other members have had a chance to present information.
- Remind groups that they should self-govern the participation of both themselves and the scribe.
- There is a time limit; use a timer to be sure you can stick to it. (For a time limit, start with 45-60 minutes to see how your groups work; adjust the timebox as you learn more about their dialogue abilities and their specific problem domains.)
- Remind groups that the goal is to capture a *group* viewpoint, so everyone needs to be encouraged to contribute to the dialogue. Groups should self-govern to make sure no one dominates and no one drops out.
- Explain that groups should evaluate the problem set openly and factually, reserving their assumptions and judgments as much as possible. The idea is to get as much information about the problem domain as possible from every person in the group versus having one defined viewpoint.

2. Prompt with the problem domain question:
   1. "Consider the following problem (state the problem)."
   2. "Think of all the possible contributory factors that we currently know about the problem: when it occurs, how it occurs, what are its impacts, why is it important to us now, and so forth."
   3. "Now, using the 'Problem Definition Questions' provided on this flipchart, discuss: 'What are all the attributes of our current problem?'"

3. Gather:
   - Hit the timer and *say nothing else.*
   - Remain physically on the side and outside of teams, but you may want to walk around to ensure that teams are truly engaging in dialogue and that scribes are able to capture the observations from every team member.
   - Call the group work to an end when the timer beeps.

Once teams have completed their work, you can invite one member from each group to debrief their collected findings to the rest of the team. Conduct each debrief in a timebox of 5-15 minutes, depending on the complexity of the topic. Chapter 15, "Processing the Information," covers how to then process the accumulated information into a more organized form for further use in the meeting.

Individual and Dyad Scribed Work

Sometimes, when a group is still in distrust, or when it has moved from a Performing mode back into a Forming mode (such as when someone has just joined the team, or one or more members have left the team), you can simply have members perform their brainstorming or listing on their own or in a dyad with one other team member. This gives members a bit of breathing space by creating a safe place in which to build their responses. Individual and dyad work reestablishes each person's identity even in large group venues.

For instance, individual brainstorming can work well when you are kicking off a timeline for a project retrospective; each person works alone collecting memories and impressions of events and milestones within the project timeline. Such an approach encourages quiet introspection and reflection that can benefit the group-wide retrospective. Or you can use dyad brainstorming (where two people interview one another for information) in order to gather personal objectives at the start of a meeting if you know that there is a problem of distrust in the group.

Using an individual mode or dyad mode too often for information gathering, however, has its drawbacks:

1. Members don't learn to work with a view into the entire team to build creativity.
2. When someone gets stuck thinking of ideas or contributions, it can be harder to dig out without hearing or seeing what others are contributing.

When you choose to apply an individual or dyad approach, refer to any of the group-wide approaches (brainstorming, listing, etc.) for the overall *Prepare* → *Prompt* → *Gather* guidance. Once the timebox for gathering data has completed, you should collect the items from all participants so that you can lead the "Process" approach that best safeguards the responses. Because the members may still be in a Forming or Storming mode, you need to be the owner of how the information is brought out to the group at large.

Sharing Individual and Dyad Work

Here are some ideas for moving from individual work to a larger group collaborative setting that allows all participants to have access to the individual data:

1. Have individuals complete their work on either a sheet of paper, individual index cards, or Post-it Notes. Once the timebox has ended, have them form pairs/dyads to exchange their responses and discuss them. Have them think about the trends that are emerging. Now have each dyad join with another dyad to share responses among the four members. In this way, the information gathering can move from the individual level to the group level, preserving a variety of responses while converging on the group viewpoints.

2. Have the group divide into dyads (pairs) at the start of the information gathering exercise. Instruct each member to act as scribe to the other member of the dyad for collecting his or her responses. Make sure both members have a chance to have their responses recorded, first one person responding and then the other person responding in turn. Allow a certain period of time for the pair to compare their responses. You can then use this approach to have the dyad select the top three or four responses from among their collected work to share with the rest of the group.

3. Have a box in the center of the room and have participants toss their responses into the box as they complete them. Paper airplanes are one way to launch items into the pile. This provides target practice for later uses (!) and preserves anonymity. The facilitator can then collect the box and read all the responses.

4. As the leader of the exercise, walk around and collect the individual responses without looking at them. Wait until you are back at the head of group to then read responses out loud and invite observations.

5. Ask participants to pass all their responses forward and ask for a volunteer to read each of the responses.

6. Provide a large wall chart upon which participants can post their own responses. This is useful if the group is either building a timeline or has already determined some useful categories of responses into which responses can be divided.

Sequential Questioning

This exercise, nicely outlined by Ingrid Bens in her book *Facilitating With Ease!*,[2] provides an alternative approach to the Small-Group Problem Probing exercise. In this approach, small groups are presented with a series of Yes/No statements or questions that lead them to test their assumptions and reveal their observations and reactions. Like the problem probing exercise, it strives to bring forward the group's wealth of data about, for example, an issue, a risk, a dependency, a function, or a process. However, this approach may require a bit more advanced or in-depth knowledge of the problem domain by the leader. The sequence of questions prepared in advance by you has to make sense in the particular realm within which the group is working. As a result, it is a fine exercise for team leads and lead architects to master.

To conduct this exercise, you must first analyze the particular issue and create a series of questions that can lead your team to move from a high-level, non-granular view of the topic to a more focused micro-view of it. Your goal is to create detailed information about assumptions and viewpoints that will help the team formulate its solution. Within the exercise, work with the entire group. For each question you've formulated, you'll ask for a response (yes or no) from one participant. (You can also use questions that request a rating of 1 to 5 versus just a Yes/No response.) You'll then record subsequent reactions by others to the response: assumptions, concerns, reasons, and so on.

Use this exercise to delve into a problem set in anticipation of then moving into small-group dialogue around problem solving, or brainstorming around potential solutions.

Note: Because this exercise strives to provoke team members to challenge existing assumptions and conventions, you should be prepared to introduce conflict resolution techniques (outlined and discussed in Chapter 17, "Managing the Meeting Participants").

Sequential Questioning Exercise Example

1. Prepare:
   - Prior to the meeting, gather information about the particular issue or item to be investigated. Your pre-work should reveal particularly contentious or sensitive aspects of the issue. Examples of statements about software development approaches that could evoke a Yes or No response:

---

2. Bens, *Facilitating With Ease!*, 153.

We have a mature software development methodology.

We consistently gather information about our projects with regard to what worked well and what could use improvement.

We know what metrics to track to evaluate project success.

We really understand how to adapt our methodology based on our past project successes.

We are flexible in how our development teams define their roles and responsibilities.

We pick and choose from agile software development practices based on our team experience.

- For each statement (up to 10) that you identify, create a flipchart with the statement labeled at the top of the chart. Show only the first question.
- Explain to the entire group that you are about to engage in a Sequential Questioning exercise that will consist of evaluating several statements about a particular topic and then gathering further observations and concerns.
- Explain that you will lead the exercise and that it will be timeboxed. An extensive, in-depth exercise can take at least an hour, with a timebox of 5-10 minutes for each statement/question. You will have to learn over time from your teams how they engage in exchanging their assumptions and challenges.
- Ask that all team members participate in the exercise to ensure the greatest amount of information and feedback about the topic.

2. Prompt the group with a guiding question. Here is an example based on the software development methodology statements accumulated earlier:

   1. "Think about how we have been applying our software development methodology in the past 12 months."
   2. "Consider what statements may or may not be true in declaring our experience in this realm."
   3. "Now, as we move through each of these statements, what assumptions and challenges do we see about our application of the software development methodology?"

3. Gather:

   - Start the timer.
   - Read the first statement and ask someone to provide a Yes or a No response; record this on the sheet.

- Now ask for reactions to this response. Collect all responses on the sheet. Encourage challenges to assumptions and ask for guidance from participants in capturing the responses correctly (in paraphrased or bullet form).
- Hang the collected assumptions and reactions on the wall and proceed with the next statement/question, again requesting a Yes/No response and subsequent reactions.
- Continue to accumulate reactions to each statement until the team has finished or until the timebox has ended.

Expert Input

Inevitably, in our software development project collaborations, we need space to learn either some pre-existing information (for example, the corporate-wide .NET defined architecture) or some new information (the proposed IT Financials intake process) from an organization or person that holds that data. In these cases, we aren't relying on team collaboration techniques to gather information. Instead, we turn to expert input that can prepare the team to move into its next phase of collaborative work. As straightforward as this may appear, expert input is potentially one of the most damaging tools for information gathering in software development teams. Here are some warning signs that the use of expert input in a team is going awry:

- The expert does not have useful reference material available to the team in advance of the meeting.
- The expert concentrates more on opinion showering than information exchange.
- The expert is unmindful of the expertise of the team and assumes that only he (the expert) has all the answers.
- The team is not afforded an opportunity to react to the information provided by the expert.
- The expert input takes up the majority of the team meeting, allowing for no collaboration on the material.

In short: Never engage expert input in your agenda without an explicit exercise to gather team reaction to the information afterward.

Expert Input Exercise

1. Prepare:
   - Identify in advance of the meeting what the information is that can only be gathered from an expert; that is, there is a clear bound around what is to be presented as useful for the team versus what is interesting to the expert.
   - Confirm that the only way to provide the information to the team is during the meeting through expert input (not as prior reading or as another meeting).
   - Explain that the information is being offered as expert input to the team database. With this in mind, team members should allow the presenter to provide as much information as possible within the timebox.
   - Assure the team that, during the presentation, they are encouraged to ask clarifying questions. The idea in expert input is to get as much of the expert's information as possible, so questions should focus on clarity, not opinion. (The team will be able to exchange opinions after the presentation in an open forum.)

2. Prompt:
   - At the proper point in the agenda, introduce the presenter of the expert input and explain which agenda question their presentation will help answer.
   - Set the timebox for the expert input. Be clear with the person or organization providing the expert input about their time constraints.
   - Encourage the team to help the presenter stick to an information exchange versus opinion exchange.

3. Gather:
   - Begin the timer and ask the presenter to proceed.
   - When the presentation has completed, or when the timebox has ended, ask if there are any additional questions before the team captures its reactions to the information.
   - Using a flipchart page, create two columns in which to capture reactions: Likes/Dislikes or Concerns/Suggestions, for example.
   - Conduct a timeboxed exercise of brainstorming around the Likes/Dislikes for the team. This should be at least 15 minutes.
   - Be sure to capture responses faithfully.

To help the expert manage her time with the team, you should also check in with her when she has only 10 minutes and then 5 minutes remaining in her time slot.

Chapter 14

Team Estimating Approaches

In agile software development projects, we inevitably come to a point where we as a team need to derive estimates for our work. This information-gathering exercise builds on the fundamentals described thus far (brainstorming, round robin, expert input) and applies some guidance specific to the information being gathered and massaged, namely estimates. Choose from the various exercises described here based on your team's preferences with regard to:

- What measurement to use in estimating
- How to gather expert information about estimates
- How to converge on a final estimate

Wideband Delphi Estimating

Mike Cohn gives a wonderful explanation of the Wideband Delphi approach to estimating in his *User Stories Applied*[1] (you'll also find useful guidance in Craig Larman's *Agile & Iterative Development*[2]). Mike's approach combines individual brainstorming, round-robin information gathering, and multi-voting to create estimates that reflect the full-participation of the team. Here's a straightforward exercise for delivering these estimates:

---

1. Cohn, *User Stories Applied,* 88.

2. Larman, *Agile & Iterative Development,* 261.

Wideband Delphi Estimate Exercise

1. Prepare:
   - Prior to the meeting or as a previous agenda item in the meeting, determine which stories, requirements, or use cases will be estimated during the exercise; this may be for a Sprint, an iteration, a timebox, a feature set, or an operational sub-system. (In this exercise, I'll refer to "stories" for a Sprint.)
   - Prior to the exercise, the team should have already determined what the estimate measurement will be (ideal hours, ideal days, points, etc.).
   - Explain that the exercise will involve story input from the customers and estimate feedback from developers. The work will be completed as an entire group (versus in parallel small groups).
   - Label a flipchart "Story Estimates."
   - Distribute index cards and markers to all developers.
   - Provide full explanation of all the steps that will be used in the "Gather" work.
2. Prompt:
   - Introduce the agenda item with an appropriate "Prompt" question that leads to:
     - "What are all our Sprint's estimated stories?"
3. Gather:
   - For each story to be estimated, a customer will read the story. (The facilitator documents the story title or description on the "Story Estimates" flipchart.)
   - Developers can then ask any clarifying questions about the story. If the customers cannot answer the questions adequately, the team may choose to defer its estimate and ask to track it as an Action Item in the "Action Plan." (Remember, this is always the team election, not yours, though you may work to help them see when they appear to be bogging down.)
   - Once all questions are answered, each developer then "brainstorms" an estimate and writes that value on a single card.
   - In a round-robin fashion, all developers' estimates will be declared.
   - The developer with the highest estimate describes the thinking behind his or her estimate, followed by a description from the developer with the lowest estimate. (For complex stories, the facilitator tracks these points as in a small-group dialogue exercise described earlier.)
   - Dialogue concerning the estimates is timeboxed, and then another sweep of estimates is gathered (each developer records his or her estimate on a card and reveals it in a round robin).

- A final estimate is reached when, in a consensus check, the developers agree that they have reached a value that all can live with and support.
- This is recorded on the flipchart next to the story description, and the exercise proceeds to the next story.

Note: Start with a large timebox for the overall exercise and be prepared to be counseled by the team about how to manage any necessary increase in time. Remember, your role is to help them complete their work; using a timebox helps them learn about how they will complete estimates the next time. Additionally, it helps them make decisions about how they are using their time so that they can ask you to help them use it differently. For each individual story estimate, start with a seven-minute timebox (between 5 and 10 minutes). Be prepared to learn from the team if the timebox is not sufficient to keep them on task and focused.

Velocity Estimates

You can think of velocity-based estimates as a congruence of expert input (a report from the tracker regarding the last iteration's/Sprint's estimates on story points) and listing (defining all the tasks that can impact the estimate of the current overall story) followed by brainstorming (what the possible overall estimate might be) that leads to a consensus check on what the final estimate should be. For further guidance on defining points and velocity, consult Martin Fowler and Kent Beck's *Planning Extreme Programming* and Mike Cohn's book *Agile Estimating and Planning*.

Velocity-Based Estimate Exercise

1. Prepare:
   - Prior to the meeting or as a previous agenda item in the meeting, determine which stories, requirements, or use cases will be estimated during the exercise; this may be for a Sprint, an iteration, a timebox, or an operational subset. (In this exercise, I'll refer to stories in an iteration.)
   - Label a flipchart "Story Estimates" and divide it into three columns:

Story	Estimate	Total

- ◆ Explain that the exercise will be conducted in a timebox (see advice in "Wideband Delphi Estimate Exercise" for defining the overall timebox and the individual timeboxes).

2. Prompt the team with the agenda item:

   1. "What are all the estimated stories for this iteration?"

3. Gather:

   - Introduce the Tracker and explain that the purpose of this expert input is to learn about what we estimated in the previous iteration (what value, how many stories, total estimate, actuals, etc.).
   - Timebox the Tracker's input (use guidelines from the "Expert Input Exercise" in the previous chapter).
   - Conduct a timeboxed "Concerns/Suggestions" brainstorming afterward for the entire team, developers, and customers. This is where the team can learn about exceptions or dependencies that may have abnormally impacted the estimates, the delivered, and the actuals.
   - Capture the velocity value on the top of the "Story Estimates" flipchart.
   - Start the timer.
   - For each of the stories to be estimated:
     1. Record the story title/description on the "Story Estimates" flipchart.
     2. The developers are invited to ask questions of the customers to clarify any needed detail about the story in order to complete the estimate. Testers may also provide any clarity about the story that could impact the estimate.
     3. The developers may also ask the Tracker for any estimate from the previous iteration that closely resembles the current story.
     4. The developers then engage in discussion to determine an estimate.
     5. In a consensus check, the final estimate is recorded on the flipchart and the "Total" column incremented by the estimate amount.
   - Perform a time check to see how the group is doing with the timebox. If estimates and discussions are taking longer than anticipated, seek group suggestions on whether to speed up the process or add more time to the timebox.

T-Shirt Sizing

T-shirt size estimates (i.e., Small, Medium, Large, Extra-Large) help a team conduct parallel, quick small group estimates early in a project (or multiple projects) without bogging down concerning points or exact numbers. This approach works well for large, complex program teams involving multiple technical organizations and user groups attempting to estimate multiple, overlaying projects for a coordinated release. T-shirt sizing helps such teams to estimate by:

1. Providing a high-level abstraction language that specifically steers technical teams away from low-level technical detail in very early estimating efforts.
2. Allowing large teams to confidently break up the estimating work into parallel small group efforts.
3. Helping customers recognize early in a complex multi-project development definition what the gross efforts may entail.
4. Keeping the estimate exercise collaborative and focused through a simple language that customers and developers can share without extended explanation or validation.
5. Creating a placeholder, like a story card, for further discussion about the estimate when more detail can be discerned.

In T-Shirt Estimating, as in story points, estimators work with a simple assumption to guide their estimating, for instance: Small (S) is probably half as big as Medium (M), which is half as big as Large (L). Prior to the estimating exercise, teams should agree on a rough standard for their use of the terms (some teams have the sizes increase more rapidly and on a sliding scale; other teams have the sizes represent much smaller increments in effort). Capture these assumptions clearly on a flipchart and make sure that all small groups working in parallel during the estimating exercise have access to the same set of assumptions.

Note: When teams feel a need to go beyond Extra Large (XL) to XXL or XXXL, have them check in with one another about their estimation assumptions with regard to size increments. Very large, unwieldy estimates may need to reside in a Parking Lot for later review or be defined in a follow-on meeting as captured in the Action Plan. Let your team tell you.

T-Shirt Sizing Exercise

1. Prepare:
   - Prior to the meeting or as a previous agenda item in the meeting, determine which stories, requirements, or use cases will be estimated during the exercise. Also determine what the criteria should be for defining how small groups need to be working in parallel to complete the estimating.
   - Explain that the team will first resolve the assumptions about how to interpret the sizes for all of the subsequent small group work.
   - Ask for a volunteer from each small group to act as scribe for their group.
   - Have each scribe create a flipchart labeled "T-Shirt Sizes" and create a chart at the top for the size assumptions:

Size	Assumptions
S	
M	
L	
XL	

   - Also ask each scribe to create another flipchart labeled "Story Estimates" and divide it into two columns:

Story	Estimate

   - Explain that, for the remainder of the exercise, each of the groups will work independently to complete their estimates in t-shirt sizes.

- Lead the entire team in a dialogue about the assumptions for sizing. Perform a consensus check about the accumulated assumptions and have the scribes record the final guidance for each size on the chart.
- Be sure to timebox this work.

2. Prompt:
   - Introduce the agenda item that the team will be completing: "What are all the t-shirt estimated stories?"

3. Gather:
   - Begin the timer for the timebox.
   - For each story to be estimated:
     1. Record the story title/description on the "Story Estimates" flipchart.
     2. The developers then ask questions of the customers to clarify any needed information about the story in order to complete the estimate. Testers may also provide any clarity about the story that may impact the estimate.
     3. The developers engage in discussion to determine an estimate: S, M, L, or XL.
     4. In a consensus check, the final estimate is recorded on the flipchart and the "Total" column incremented by the estimate amount.
   - Perform a time check to see how the group is doing with the timebox. If estimates and discussions are taking longer than anticipated timebox, seek group suggestions on whether to speed up the process or add more time to the timebox.

Triangulate Estimating

Triangulating on an estimate is a useful approach that can be applied in support of other estimating exercise. For any new story, requirement, or use case being estimated, the team reviews their previous assumptions about estimate size. As Mike Cohn suggests in *User Stories Applied*, if the current story is smaller than a story that had been estimated at 4 points yet larger than another story that had been estimated at 2 points, the triangulation approach guides the team to apply an estimate of 3.[3]

Supply triangulation guidance as a Prompt question when teams continue to struggle with their estimates. This helps team members clear the cobwebs and focus more directly on what the story entails in comparison to other stories.

---

3. Cohn, *User Stories Applied*, 90.

Triangulating Estimate Exercise

1. Prompt:
   - Explain that the team is going to use triangulating to converge on an estimate for the story.
   - Have the customer read the story.
   - Guide developers in asking clarifying questions about the story.
2. Prompt:
   - Introduce the agenda item that the team will be completing:

   > "Think about some of the other stories that we have estimated so far."
   >
   > "Consider which stories have seemed smaller in effort and what value we applied to those stories. Also, consider stories that were heftier in effort and think about the estimates we applied."
   >
   > "Now, what is a close triangulation of an estimate for this story based on these other stories?"

3. Gather:
   - Guide developers' dialogue toward the stories that could be used for triangulation.
   - Review each story's recorded estimate on the "Story Estimates" chart.
   - Ask for a suggestion from one of the team members about what the triangulated estimate might be.

Perform a consensus check among the developers and record the final answer.

Chapter 15

Processing the Information

Once teams have collaboratively gathered information to help them define and run their projects, whether it is stories, risks, plans, acceptance tests, or design alternatives, they very often still need some further processing to turn the information into actions and decisions. For the "Process" step of the *Prepare* ➔ *Prompt* ➔ *Gather* ➔ *Process* equation, I often rely on *grouping* and *prioritizing* as two useful next steps to move team data along this continuum. In effect, these two techniques help teams create parcels of value that apply useful focus to their depth and breadth of knowledge.

To complete the transformation of data into actions and decisions, we process by applying a subset of the step, either *Prepare* ➔ *Prompt* ➔ *Gather* or *Prepare* ➔ *Process*, in a cycle until the useful knowledge emerges.

Grouping and Categorizing

Teams group and categorize information when, on its own, the data doesn't clearly reveal what we need to know. Groupings help us move from the need to consider 100 distinct items to instead, say, 7 categories of items. Grouped, we may discover that one category has caught the overwhelming attention of the team. Or we may learn that we lack clear understanding of another category as evidenced by the sparse number of responses in it. Grouping can also help clear priorities emerge, such as when we decide to parse items into pre-defined groups. Items that are grouped into Iteration 1 for work hold a higher priority for the team than items placed into Iteration 5. Items grouped into various levels of effort (low, medium, high) may also reveal implicit priorities.

When a team completes a grouping, they have actually applied valuable mental muscle around two very useful information calisthenics:

- Defining what the categories are
- Deciding which items belong in each of the categories

When you are leading a grouping exercise, be clear and explicit from the start about how the categories are to be defined. You'll have to plan your exercise to do one of the following:

- Have the team define the category names in advance.
- Learn the category names from an expert outside source in advance.
- Have the category names emerge during the grouping.
- Name the categories after the grouping has completed.

For example, a team may know that there are seven main subsystems into which the features may be grouped. These categories are known in advance and can be set up in anticipation of the grouping. They need not be defined again in order to complete the grouping. Or, in brainstorming about risks, a team may want to allow the categories of risk to emerge during the grouping (cost, time, team makeup, experience, etc.) but then have well-defined subcategories (highly probable, probable, low probability, unknown). Finally, as described by Ellen Gottesdiener, teams may want to perform a little of both, in what is referred to as a *middle-out* approach in which teams create responses in brainstorming or listing, define useful categories, and then create more responses once the categories have been defined.[1]

Facilitator-Led Categories

Use this technique when you want to guide the team in both the placement of items into groups as well as the emergence of group names based on which items come together in groups. This method is a good exercise to use early in a team's collaborative maturity. As

---

1. Gottesdiener, *Requirements by Collaboration*, 201.

you facilitate the grouping, you can ensure equal footing in both naming and placement and validate that the team owns the final naming and placement of responses.

Warning: This is one of those exercises that can truly test your ability to remain neutral and non-possessive of the results. What may seem like either a natural name of a grouping or a natural placement of an item to you ends up not even being considered by the team. Follow these instructions carefully, or you may be accused of commandeering the exercise to reflect your natural groupings.

1. Prepare:
   - Before starting this exercise, the team should have completed one of the information gathering techniques that leaves them with numerous responses, either captured as individuals or in small groups. (The responses need to be on individual Post-it Notes, one response per Post-it.)
   - Prior to the grouping, label a flipchart or wall chart (depending on the number of responses) with the title of the items to be grouped ("Risks," "User Stories," "Concerns," "Benefits").
   - Draw lines on the chart to divide it into six to eight areas (with most exercises in brainstorming, you'll discover a natural tendency for the data to fall into seven general categories).
   - Explain that you now want to help the team learn about the primary groupings of their information. (This may be an agenda item such as "What are the primary categories of risks with this project?")
   - Invite someone to come forward (going round robin around the team or small groups is an easy way to move through the team) to read his or her responses out loud.
2. Process:
   - For the first response, after the participant has read the response, simply place it in one of the boxes on the chart.
   - Have the same or next participant read the next response. Now, ask the team "Does this look similar to or different from the first response?" If similar, place it in the same box as the first response; if different, place it in a different box.
   - Continue having the participants read the responses one at a time and asking the team whether it is similar to or different from any of the other already posted responses.
   - Once there are at least three responses in a box, you now ask the team: "Given the items we have in this box, what might the name of this group be?" If there is more than one suggestion for the label, ask for a third suggestion that might

express the combined intent of the other two labels. Write the agreed-upon label name in the box.

■ Continue processing all the remaining responses, either from each individual, or by small group representative, posting items as directed and labeling boxes as directed.

A few helpful guidelines to complete the grouping:

• You should have an extra flipchart of boxes already drawn up in case the group identifies more than the six or eight you have drawn on your original chart.

• Often, teams will decide that they have mislabeled a box and want to change the label to be more appropriate for its contents; don't be afraid to re-label boxes as guided by the team!

• Sometimes, teams watch groupings emerge as they move through their response; don't be afraid to combine groups and provide the newly formed category with a new name as directed by the team.

• Teams may discover that with further reflection, some items might reside more appropriately in another box; make sure that the team has consensus before moving an item from one box to another, but be sure to reflect their emerging sense of their data.

• If participants can't agree whether an item should be placed in one box or another, simply write up a duplicate item and place it in both.

Silent Grouping

Use this technique to encourage participants to get on their feet and own the entire exercise of placing items without worrying about how many categories there are or what their names are. It is particularly useful for grouping a very large number of items (60 or more).

1. Prepare:
   ■ Before starting this exercise, the team should have completed one of the information gathering techniques that leaves them with numerous responses, either captured as individuals or in small groups. (The responses need to be on individual Post-it Notes, one response per Post-it.)

- Prior to the grouping, label a large wall chart with the title of the items to be grouped ("Strategic Actions," "Budget Items," "User Stories," "Nonfunctional Requirements").
- Explain to the team that in the next 20 minutes, they will be invited to bring their responses forward to post on the wall chart.

2. Process:
   - As items are posted, each participant is invited to start to group items as appropriate. Anyone can move any item to begin to form groups.
   - There are no pre-defined divisions; there are no pre-defined categories; there are no labels.
   - All participants are welcome to move posted responses around to form groups until the timebox is over.
   - Allow 20-40 minutes for this exercise, depending on the number of participants and the number of responses.
   - Once the timebox ends, or when there are no more changes in groupings, you can use the labeling approach described in the "Facilitator-Led Labeling" section of this chapter.

Timeline Creation

A timeline is simply a grouping based on a chronology or sequence of actions, deadlines, timeboxes, or milestones.

Follow the directions for the "Silent Grouping" technique to take all items and place them across a large wall chart that represents the timeline. Decide in advance what the useful markings along the timeline should be (weeks, months, seasons, releases).

Similarly, you can set up the timeline as in the "Silent Grouping" but have the teams also engage in small-group dialogue in order to declare placement of items on the timeline, such as determining which stories of a release should be planned into each of the release's iterations.

Facilitator-Led Labeling

Use this technique after a silent grouping to help a team evaluate their natural groupings and what appropriate labels can be applied.

1. Prepare:
   - Explain to the team that with the already grouped items posted in the wall chart, we now need to find useful labels to help evaluate the groupings.
2. Process:
   - Select one of the groups on the chart and read each item in the grouping.
   - Ask the team for a recommendation for a label for the grouping.
   - Be sure that there is consensus about the label before you apply it to the group.
   - If there are several suggestions about which the team is struggling to decide, ask for a suggested third label that could combine the meanings of the other labels.
   - Continue through the remainder of the wall chart groupings in the same manner until all boxes have been labeled.

Group Brainstorming of Labels

Use this technique when the team has widely varying views about what may be a useful delineation of the data. This approach encourages an assimilation of many possible category names by reviewing all participants' ideas, and then combining and deleting possibilities until the team has defined a set of labels that appropriately reflects their combined knowledge. Perform this exercise either before or after the brainstorming or listing of the items to be grouped.

1. Prepare:
   - Explain that the team is going to perform an individual brainstorm in a five-minute timebox. Each participant should create his or her own responses, one response per Post-it.
   - Ensure that everyone has materials (Post-its, markers) to complete their brainstorm.

2. Prompt:
   - Prepare the team to brainstorm categories by providing a Prompt question:

   > "We are now considering all of the possible kinds of features to be delivered in this project."
   >
   > "To help us think about the many features, envision some useful ways of grouping or categories of the features we might include, such as functionality, or system, or distributed team, or user group."
   >
   > "Now, what are all the categories of features we should define for our system?"

3. Process:
   - Start the timer and allow the individual work to proceed until the time ends.
   - Ask someone to volunteer to read their list of category labels for the team and post their items on the "Feature Categories" flipchart.
   - Ask someone else to volunteer to read and post their labels, eliminating any duplicates.
   - After three people have read and posted their responses, ask the team to see if there is a combination of labels that forms a useful grouping scheme.
   - Now ask for any remaining recommendations to massage the labeling scheme until the team has converged on a scheme that has their consensus.

Impact/Effort Grid Definition

Use this technique to help a team identify easy wins versus the big, more complex items of work. It is used after teams have completed either a brainstorming or a listing exercise and items have been captured as separate responses, one per sticky.

An Impact/Effort Grid (see Table 15.1) is a great example of the use of predefined categories, in this case arranged by impact (minor or major) and effort (difficult or easy). I use the grid format outlined by Ingrid Bens:[2]

---

2. Bens, *Facilitating with Ease!*, 163.

Table 15.1   Impact/Effort Grid

Effort/Impact	Difficult to Do	Easy to Do
Major Improvement	3.	1.
Minor Improvement	4.	2.

where each box in the grid represents the following categories:

1. Easy to do and yields a major improvement.
2. Easy to do but yields a minor improvement.
3. Difficult to do but yields a major improvement.
4. Difficult to do and yields a minor improvement.

When you are preparing to conduct this exercise:

- Create a large enough grid in a wall chart to hold all of your items, whether using multiple flipcharts or using a large sheet of butcher paper.
- Write the four explanations on a separate flipchart as a reference for the significance of each block in the grid.

Before beginning the exercise, you may additionally choose to lead the team in 5-10 minutes of dialogue to explicitly declare their interpretations of the terms, such as "What does 'Easy to do' mean to us?" Capture this on a separate flipchart and make it visible for the exercise.

1. Prepare:
   - Explain that the team is going to perform a grouping of items based on their impact and effort.
   - Review each of the four squares on the chart of the grid and also their definitions (by pointing to the definitions as listed on the flipchart).
   - Explain that this will be a group-wide grouping exercise where you will place each item in the block chosen by the group.
   - Any items that cannot be easily placed will be placed in a Parking Lot to be addressed once all other items have been placed.
   - Ask if there are any questions about how the exercise will proceed.

2. Process:
   - Depending on how the brainstorm or listing has been conducted, begin to process the items one by one, reading the item aloud to the team and then asking for their recommendation for where to place it.
   - For any item that takes over 30 seconds to place, ask for permission to place it in the Parking Lot to be processed at the end of the exercise.
   - Proceed through all the items until every response has been placed in the grid.
   - If any items have been placed in the Parking Lot, address these items one by one:
     - Ask for a volunteer to provide a recommendation for its placement and a two-minute explanation for that placement.
     - Ask for another volunteer to provide an alternative recommendation and a two-minute explanation.
     - Ask for consensus concerning the first recommendation ("Knowing what you know now, can you live with and support the first alternative?").
     - Ask for a consensus check about the second recommendation as previously shown.
   - If consensus cannot be reached, ask for an alternative decision (vote, expert decision, more discussion) and resolve as recommended.
   - Once all items have been processed, ask the team to provide their observations about their groupings (five minutes).

As an alternative grouping approach, allow the team to reflect individually about what each of the four grid squares means to them. Then conduct a silent grouping as described earlier where team members place the items in the grid without talking. In this case, make sure there is ample room, such as at a large sheet of butcher paper, for all to participate.

Prioritizing and Weighting

Teams prioritize and weight information when, on its own, the collected data does not naturally reveal what can guide us to make decisions. Decisions may best be made when clumped around factors such as time, cost, impact, desirability, significance to the business, or some other factor that could impact team work. For instance, when there are 100 item requests in a Product Backlog, the customer or product manager applies a hierarchy of importance or a system of urgency to the items in order to guide a team with respect to where to concentrate its actions, resources, or planning.

Technical teams rely on prioritization for a number of data items that move the project forward. As Craig Larman points out, teams can create quick, effective project focus when they collaboratively apply prioritizing to such items as:[3]

- User Stories
- Features
- Defects
- Risks
- Benefits
- Concerns
- Nonfunctional requirements
- Use case scenarios

Prioritization plays a particularly hefty role in agile software development teams as a means to set the scope and course for a team's timebox. In the XP Planning Game, the customer owns the prioritization of User Stories, though they can be guided in that prioritization by input from the technical team members. Similarly, in Scrum, the Product Manager owns both the Product Backlog and the Sprint Backlog, both of which are prioritized lists of items to be deployed. Feature-Driven Development teams must prioritize the client-valued functions (a.k.a. features) to plan their work. And DSDM (Dynamic Systems Development Methodology) teams maintain a Prioritized Requirements List (PRL) to guide what must be delivered within a timebox.

With this in mind, servant leaders do well to keep a few prioritization schemes in their collaboration toolbox for quickly and effectively guiding a team to learn its priorities:

- **MoSCoW**—Hierarchical prioritization (also "1, 2, 3," "High, Medium, Low," etc.).
- **Multi-Voting**—Public or private prioritization of votes spread across the total constellation of items.
- **"Pass the Card"**—Large group negotiated multi-voting.
- **Priority/Weighting Grid**—Applying priorities across a set of criteria averaging the values applied by each participant.

---

3. Craig Larman, *Agile & Iterative Development*, 264.

In any of these prioritization schemes, you can apply some useful guidance to ensure that the team's best decisions guide the rankings:

1. **Tie-break mechanism decision**—Decide in advance how the team will deal with any ties in the voting:
   - An expert individual tiebreaker is assigned.
   - A 2/3's majority vote breaks the tie.
   - A consensus dialogue breaks all ties, etc.
2. **Influence Peddling**—Prior to the exercise, any individual can plead the case for their particular priority in a two-minute or less acclamation of their stance. Ask all "peddlers" to identify themselves prior to beginning the prioritization. Be clear that no one under any circumstance can exceed the two-minute limit. Additionally, explain that this is not a Q&A forum, just the presentation of one viewpoint. Facilitate the two-minute intervals until all peddlers have presented their case.

   (I've used this very successfully in a number of collaboration scenarios: deciding how to proceed with the agenda; determining what risks should be investigated in greater detail within the meeting; how the multiple customer voices will be heard for prioritizing User Stories).

MoSCoW—Prioritized Requirements List (PRL)

While MoSCoW comes to us via the DSDM approach around its Prioritized Requirements List (PRL), I use this approach across multiple methodologies. All items to be prioritized are maintained in a ranked list according to how urgently they are needed. "MoSCoW" represents the four possible values any item in the list may have:

- M—A MUST HAVE, this is the highest priority an item can receive.
- S—A SHOULD HAVE, second in priority, this item is highly desirable.
- C—A COULD HAVE, the item is a nice-to-have, third in priority.
- W—A WON'T HAVE, this item is clearly out of the scope of the current release but is tracked for future priority considerations.

MoSCoW is attractive in helping teams learn a simple language about their sense of necessity. Stating priorities in chunks of the MUST HAVEs versus the SHOULD HAVEs and COULD HAVEs may be more meaningful to customers initially in requirements management than listing items in a numeric serial ranking system 1 to N (more useful later when work decisions must be made).

The danger of using MoSCoW for your rankings is a young (a.k.a. "Forming") team's tendency to value too many items as MUST HAVE. This can negatively alter the team's sense of scope management ("How can we cut back the scope; all of these stories are MUST HAVEs?") Balancing MoSCoW by the Product Owner or customer with technical estimates that clearly bound a timebox scope may help a team better grade its stories or requirements.

MoSCoW prioritization should be preceded by either a brainstorming or a listing exercise to accumulate the items to be ranked.

MoSCoW Exercise

1. Prepare:
   - Prepare a flipchart with the four priority definitions associated with the MoSCoW approach:

> **MoSCoW Priorities**
> M—MUST HAVE, the highest priority
> S—SHOULD HAVE, desirable to have
> C—COULD HAVE, nice-to-have
> W—WON'T HAVE, out of scope

   - Explain to the team that we are now going to engage in a prioritization of the accumulated items. Go through the MoSCoW flipchart verbatim to remind them what each ranking represents.
   - Explain that this will be a group-wide exercise where you grade each item M, S, C, or W, as decided by the group.

- If any item takes longer than two minutes to rank, you will ask the group's permission to place it in the Parking Lot to be ranked at the end of the exercise.
- Ask if there are any questions about how the exercise will proceed.

2. Process:
   - For each item to be prioritized, read the item aloud verbatim from its Post-it or index card, and ask for a recommendation on the ranking: M, S, C, or W.
   - Ask for consensus or discussion around the recommendation.
   - If agreed to, mark the item with the rank and place on the flipchart labeled "Prioritized Stories (Features/Requirements)." (If items were written directly on a flipchart, as in some brainstorming exercises, and not on a moveable medium such as a Post-it, simply create a column down the left side of the flipchart to hold all MoSCoW values.)
   - Once all items have been graded, review the list with the team, evaluating the ratio of MUST HAVEs to SHOULD HAVEs and COULD HAVEs, and ask for observations so that the team can (now or later) make decisions about the scope of their work.

Multi-Voting/Dot Voting

Multi-voting creates a forum in which the team's wisdom about its priorities emerges through the individual priorities of each team member. It is sometimes referred to as "dot-voting" when each vote is represented by a dot sticker. Every member is allowed a certain number of votes/dots to apply across the total number of items. The leader sums the votes for each item, which then creates the rankings of the items from highest to lowest based on the greatest to least number of votes per item.

Multi-voting differs from the MoSCoW approach in that:

- The team does not make agreements as a group.
- Individuals vote independent of one another.
- The number of urgency values in voting is binary (you either vote for an item, or you don't).

You can conduct multi-voting either in a public forum, where everyone can see how everyone else has voted, or in a private approach, where all votes are completely anonymous and tallied offline. The public exercise is a good way to energize a team, having the team move along a wall with all the items posted in order to mark their votes themselves. If your team is not yet out of its Forming or Storming mode, and you are aware of some power struggles or other group issues, avoid using the public voting exercise. Allow members to privately cast their votes and then move offline to sum the values for them without revealing how specific votes were cast.

What number of votes should you assign to each participant in multi-voting? A good guide to follow is 20% of the total number of items. So, in the case of 30 risks being prioritized, each voting team member would receive 6 votes to assign across the population of risks.

Although multi-voting is easy to conduct, it is best used when only the top priorities are needed ("What is the most important thing we should do next?") because it may not provide granular enough guidance for items less than the most important. For example, imagine a prioritization exercise in which a team needs to evaluate 20 features; each participant has 4 votes. It soon emerges that everyone seems to feel that deploying dynamically configurable rate tables is an absolute necessity, along with email notification of any table updates and an audit trail of the requestor, the date, and the time. So these three features receive a vote/dot from nearly everyone on the team. With only two votes/dots remaining for evaluating the remaining 17 items, the team may find it hard to learn any useful priority information for any more than one or two more features.

A few other considerations when leading your teams in multi-voting:

- Any stumping for a particular item (influence peddling) should be conducted prior to the multi-voting.
- Participants cannot place more than one vote on any given item.
- Voting, whether public or private, should be conducted in silence without discussion.
- You may place the flipchart with the posted items facing away from the group so that no one can see the voting as it takes place.

Public Multi-Voting Exercise

In a public multi-voting exercise, each participant gets a number of sticky dots, stars, hand votes, or marks to place as "votes" across all the items. A few guidelines for public multi-voting:

- Decide in advance how many votes each person will receive and how they will be noted (dots, raised hands, check marks, etc.).
- Decide in advance whether everyone will vote at once or one by one.
- Decide in advance if the posted items will be facing toward the group or away from the group (for instance on easels) during the voting.
- If public voting is being conducted one by one, as in a round robin, the team lead or other participants of high influence should always vote last.

Once everyone has voted, either circle the top N items (for instance, the top five items) that have the greatest number of votes, or rewrite the top items on a separate labeled flipchart. In multi-voting, as mentioned earlier, there may be a severe dropoff of votes from a certain pack of items at the top of the list; let that number emerge from the geography of the cast votes.

Private Voting Exercise

Private multi voting is useful in teams where trust may still be an issue. All items under consideration are assigned a numeric or letter value. Prior to conducting the exercise, allow the team to silently review the items for their priority or significance. Each person then privately writes down the numbers of their priority items on a piece of paper. All other rules still apply:

- No discussion during voting.
- All votes must be distributed across the items, one vote per item.

Once everyone has had a chance to write down their choices, collect all the papers yourself, making sure that no one can see any of the responses. Your job is to then tally the votes and provide the final results to the team. You can do this by simply marking the posted items with the total number of votes each received.

Pass the Cards

This is a great exercise to use with a very large group to help them conduct modified multi-voting across a set of items not yet revealed openly to the group. It combines a brainstorm exercise with a voting process in that individuals each brainstorm one idea and then, in the course of the exercise, share the idea with one other person and negotiate a priority between their two items. "Pass the cards" is very interactive and, unlike MoSCoW or multi-voting, actually encourages dialogue during the voting. But like multi-voting, "Pass the Cards" usually only reveals the very top items of priority as votes tend to quickly fall off.

1. Prepare:
   - Prior to conducting the exercise, write the brainstorm question on a flipchart; for example, "What was the biggest problem our team faced in this last iteration?"
   - Make sure each participant has an index card and a pen for the brainstorming.
   - Explain that each person will be writing one response on the index card in response to a brainstorm question. Then there will be five cycles of prioritization that will occur among all the cards, but only in dyads (pairs), to provide points to each card. In each cycle, the pair will be asked to divide a total of 7 points between their two cards. The cards with the highest number of points at the end of the five cycles of prioritization will be the top-priority items.
   - Explain that each participant will have 30 seconds to respond to the brainstorm, and that each of the prioritization cycles will be two minutes long.
   - Ask everyone to get on their feet.
2. Provide the Prompt question for the brainstorm.
3. Process:
   - After 30 seconds, ask everyone to find one other person in the group and in the next two minutes, share each other's responses and allocate 7 points between the two cards (if one card is awarded 5 points, the other card can only be awarded 2 points; if one card is awarded 7 points, the other card receives a 0) and write the value on the cards.
   - Direct the two participants in each pair to exchange cards once the point allocation has been recorded.
   - Start the next 30-second cycle, again directing everyone to find one other person with which to share cards and discuss their merits. Again, direct each dyad to allocate 7 points between the two cards, write the numbers down, and exchange cards.
   - Perform this "discuss, prioritize, exchange" cycle three more times. At this point, each card should have five numbers written on it, one for each prioritization cycle.

- Ask everyone to return to their seats and sum up the points on the card they currently hold. Ask for a show of hands of anyone who has a card that has 35 points on it (the highest possible accumulation of points in the five cycles). Keep asking for the next highest values and write down the brainstorm responses and their values on a labeled flipchart.
- Lead the team in 10 minutes of discussion about the results of their brainstorm and prioritization exercise.

Priority/Weighting Grid

A weighting or priority grid provides the team with a more detailed tool for capturing their priorities as a team, allowing the highest priority items to emerge across a set of criteria selected by the team, either weighted or not. Compare this to multi-voting, which tends to reveal the highest priorities but not all the priorities. Multi-voting is faster but less granular. The priority grid is very detailed but takes more time and preparation.

Prior to the weighting, the team brainstorms a set of useful criteria for evaluating their priorities, preferably between three and five total criteria. Each eligible team member then provides a value or priority against each of the criteria in the grid. In our example, where User Stories are being prioritized, this might only represent the values of the customer team members; in other exercises, all team members may be supplying values.

The criteria values can represent priorities as follows:

- 1 = Low priority, does not meet criterion.
- 2 = Medium priority, somewhat meets criterion.
- 3 = High priority, meets criterion.

For each item, the priority is determined by summing the average value in each category (the sum of member values divided by the number of members) to produce a total score for that item. I use a grid recommended by Ingrid Bens (see Table 15.2):[4]

---

4. Bens, *Facilitating with Ease!*, 163.

Table 15.2 Priority/Weighting Grid

Item/ Criterion	Presents Low Risk	Delivers High Business Value	Imple- ments Easily	Creates Team Good Will	Total Score	Rank
User Story 1	3, 2, 2, 1 = 2	3, 3, 3, 1= 2.5	1, 2, 2, 1 = 1.5	3, 2, 2, 2 = 2.25	8.25	4
User Story 2	3, 3, 3, 3= 3	2, 2, 2, 1 = 1.75	3, 2, 2, 1 = 2	3, 3, 3, 3= 3	9.75	2
User Story 3	2, 1, 1, 1 = 1.25	3, 3, 3, 3 = 3	1, 1, 1, 1= 1	1, 2, 1, 2 = 1.5	6.75	6
User Story 4	3, 2, 2, 2 = 2.25	3, 3, 2, 1 = 2.25	1, 1, 1, 1= 1	3, 3, 3, 2 = 2.75	8.25	3
User Story 5	3, 3, 3, 3 = 3	2, 1, 1, 1 = 1.25	3, 3, 3, 3 = 3	3, 3, 2, 2 = 2.5	9.75	1
User Story 6	3, 1, 1, 3 = 2	2, 1, 1, 1= 1.25	3, 3, 3, 3 = 3	1, 1, 1, 2 = 1.25	7.5	5

You can also apply weights to each of the categories (see Table 15.3). For instance, in the previous example, if "Delivers High Business Value" is weighted at three times the value of the other criteria, the priorities shift as follows:

Table 15.3 Priority/Weighting Grid Weighted by Category

Item/ Criterion	Presents Low Risk	Delivers High Business Value (* 3)	Imple- ments Easily	Creates Team Good Will	Total Score	Rank
User Story 1	3, 2, 2, 1 = 2	3, 3, 3, 1= 2.5 * 3	1, 2, 2, 1 = 1.5	3, 2, 2, 2 = 2.25	13.25	1
User Story 2	3, 3, 3, 3= 3	2, 2, 2, 1 = 1.75 * 3	3, 2, 2, 1 = 2	3, 3, 3, 3= 3	13.25	2
User Story 3	2, 1, 1, 1 = 1.25	3, 3, 3, 3 = 3 * 3	1, 1, 1, 1= 1	1, 2, 1, 2 = 1.5	12.75	3

Item/ Criterion	Presents Low Risk	Delivers High Business Value (* 3)	Imple- ments Easily	Creates Team Good Will	Total Score	Rank
User Story 4	3, 2, 2, 2 = 2.25	3, 3, 2, 1 = 2.25 * 3	1, 1, 1, 1= 1	3, 3, 3, 2 = 2.75	12.75	4
User Story 5	3, 3, 3, 3 = 3	2, 2, 1, 2 = 1.25 * 3	3, 3, 3, 3 = 3	3, 3, 2, 2 = 2.5	12.25	5
User Story 6	3, 1, 1, 3 = 2	2, 1, 1, 1= 1.25 * 3	3, 3, 3, 3 = 3	1, 1, 1, 2 = 1.25	10.00	6

Use a Priority/Weighting Grid when there are clear, multiple criteria to apply to the items; otherwise, stick with simple multi-voting or MoSCoW to derive priorities.

Chapter 16

Visioning, Retrospection, and Other Approaches

Project Visioning

Visioning is a great technique that helps a group believe in its ownership of the project and what the outcome of the project will be.

Project visioning prompts participants to think through what they believe will be true about the project so that they can create their own destiny about the project. They do this by answering questions around some future vision of the project, discussing their responses with each other, and then finding common, prioritized themes among the responses.

Use this technique to help a team at the start of a project to envision the work, the deliverables, the accomplishments, the way the team will communicate, and so on. (You can also use visioning at the start of a project release, gaining insight into similar aspects of the release.) As the facilitator of this project kickoff exercise, your goal is to stay out of the way and allow members of the team to communicate among themselves as they answer questions about the future.

Visioning at the start of a project is particularly powerful when the team has already conducted a reflection or retrospective at the end of another project or at the end of a release. Visioning may be less useful for well-formed teams that are already in a high-performance mode, very comfortable with how they work, and able to consistently accomplish their goals collaboratively.

To ensure the success of any visioning exercise:

1. Always use a timer to timebox the various steps of the exercise.
2. Plan your questions in advance to ensure that they provide useful vision information (such as material that could be reviewed during a retrospective).
3. Be sure to explain the purpose of creating vision for the project: "To create our own destiny for the project outcome."
4. Only provide guidance at the beginning, at each time interval, and then in processing the information at the end; you do not provide any vision input.

Project Visioning Exercise

I use an approach outlined by Ingrid Bens that combines brainstorming, dyad exchanges, and dialogue as well as prioritizing, all of which are techniques that were described earlier.[1]

1. Prepare:
   - Prior to beginning the visioning exercise, label a flipchart with "Imagine it is exactly 90 days from today..."
   - Now list the following items in large bold letters:

> - What specific work have we accomplished?
> - What problems have we been able to solve?
> - What are people saying about our team and how it works?
> - What do we tell others about our team?
> - How have we changed the way we work from our previous project?
> - How do we celebrate success?
> - How do we manage conflict?

---

1. Bens, *Facilitating with Ease!*, 151.

- Label another flipchart "Our Project Vision."
- Explain that the group is about to complete some project visioning: "The purpose is to create our own destiny about the project and how we will work in it."
- Provide each participant with a chart pen and Post-it Notes.
- Provide clear instructions to everyone at the same time about how the exercise will proceed (one response per Post-it, time limit, individual work to start, then participants will share responses in subsequent pairs).
- For each response that a participant has for one of the questions, they should use a separate Post-it. For instance: "We successfully engaged in problem solving without getting bogged down in politics."
- Then provide instructions about the "Gather" steps listed in the following.

2. Prompt with the visioning question:

> - "Imagine it is exactly 90 days from today..."
> - "Think about all the practices we engaged and all the successes we enjoyed."
> - "What are all the practices and successes of our project?"

3. Gather:
- In the first timebox, 5 minutes, individuals should provide as many responses as they can to any or all of the posted questions.
- In the next timebox, 6 minutes, each participant pairs with one other participant. Each will take 3 minutes to give an overview of their responses to the other. Note which responses are considered key to the project vision.
- In the next timebox, 6 minutes, each participant switches partners and repeats their overview of their responses to one another. Again, note which responses are considered key to the project vision.
- (You can now end the paired-information exchange or conduct one more timebox, this one only 4 minutes long where pairs take turns exchanging ideas for 2 minutes each and noting their key responses.)
- Now take 10 minutes to bring forward all of the primary responses and place them on the "Our Project Vision" flipchart.

"Giving an A" Exercise

I borrowed this idea from the book *The Art of Possibility* by Rosamund Stone Zander and Benjamin Zander, in which they describe a technique to help students at the beginning of a semester set goals for themselves about the end of the semester. Working with Pam Rostal and Tim Bacon at a Retrospectives Gathering in February of 2005, we were able to shift the story enough to make it work for our "futurspectives."

In a software project team, each participant is asked to think into the future about the end of the project and how they had excelled ("got an A") in the course of the project. Prompted with this question, they are then asked to individually write three letters of explanation about their "A" as follows:

- "Dear Customer, as a team we are proud of the work we did on this project because…"
- "Dear Manager, we are proud of how we engaged as a collaborative team on this project because…"
- "Dear Team, I am proud of how I contributed on this project because…"

"Picture This" Exercise

One way to help a team retrospect a Sprint, an iteration, a release, or an entire project is to apply a visioning exercise called "Picture This." Again, this exercise came out of work at the Retrospectives Gathering in February 2005, with many thanks to Debra Schratz and Ainsley Nies.

1. Prepare:
   - Prior to beginning the visioning exercise, make sure you have paper, pencils, and markers available for the drawing.
   - Explain that the group is about to engage in a sort of art project: "The purpose is to picture what we felt the iteration/Sprint/release/project looked like."
   - Have the group subdivide into groups of two or three, depending on the size of the group.
   - Provide each sub-group with a set of supplies.
   - Provide clear instructions to everyone at the same time about how the exercise will proceed (complete a drawing on the sheet of paper that represents the group's vision of what the time period felt like).

- Then provide instructions about the "Gather" steps listed in the following.
- Tell them that they will have five minutes to complete their picture and that each team will be asked to explain their picture to the rest of the group.

2. Prompt with the visioning question:

> - "Think about this last iteration/Sprint/release/ project time period."
> - "Think about what that period felt like in terms of an image or picture, whether in terms of mythology, weather, actions, etc."
> - "What is your picture of this time?"

3. Gather:
- For each sub-group, ask a team member to present the picture to the rest of the group, explaining what influenced their picture.
- Find out what particularly drove any strong positive or strong negative images.
- Once all teams have debriefed, hang each of the pictures on the wall and ask the group as a whole to sum up the results. In particular, guide the group in discovering how these pictures might help them learn something that could impact how they conduct their next time period.

Timelining

Timelining is an excellent companion exercise for the Project Visioning exercise. Used either as a guide for what shall be or as a reflection for what has been, timelining helps teams record a common sense of their movement through time as a team:

- What will we strive to do; what are we capable of accomplishing over time?
- What were we successful in delivering over the course of the release/iteration/ Sprint?
- What trends emerge over time about how we work jointly to deliver value?

Timelines reinforce a team's sense of owning the project and its stalwart march through corporate calendars. In a way, facilitating a team through a timelining exercise invites them to take over the project plan and be responsible for either what occurred or what can occur. The large colorful team-produced responses hanging in their self-defined timeline hands them the power over the project's definition. It invites their ownership, their scrutiny, and their support.

Norm Kerth's *Project Retrospectives: A Handbook for Team Members* is an enlightened source for how to effectively apply timelines (and other reflective exercises) to retrospective workshops. Using his timeline guidance can then expand beyond retrospectives to:

- Release plans
- Strategy action plans
- Dependency analysis
- Release retrospectives

For any timeline exercise, I recommend the use of bright white butcher paper (found at art supply shops in ample quantity) to cover a wall in a unifying, long material. Butcher paper comes in 3- to 4-feet-wide rolls to accommodate any length you may need. Don't be skimpy. Creating a large banner across a wall is visually stimulating to participants; that long, blank sheet of paper signals to them that their contributions are eagerly awaited. In lieu of butcher paper, you can also use several parachute cloths treated with self-adhesive spray. Or you can line up multiple flipchart pages to create the length you need.

As with any flipchart you use in an exercise, label your timeline wall with large, dark block letters. Big is beautiful. In addition, think about what natural sections should be applied to the timeline vertically across the wall (weeks, months, quarters, releases, iterations, milestones, deadlines) and horizontally down the paper (deliverables, life events, project events, celebrations, stresses, other). You can even ask the team to decide at the start of the exercise, in a brief brainstorm, what the natural sections should be, if any (some teams prefer completely free-flowing timelines that act more like self-grouping calendars, letting the sections naturally emerge as the responses are filled in).

As you conduct the timeline exercise, you may want to encourage the team to think about a variety of items that could be captured in the timeline:

- Milestones
- Risks
- Impacts
- Market events

- Vacations/holidays
- Other deadlines/dependencies
- Birthdays/anniversaries (March 26th is the anniversary of my first paying job as an IT professional. I always celebrate it with whatever team I am working, so it is on any first-quarter timeline to which I have access ☺.)

Each of these categories of response can be captured on different colored Post-its or index cards, or you can select a different color of ink for each major type of response. The idea is to have the timeline graphically represent useful data other than just the text. (In one timeline for a technical strategy plan, each technical group used a different color of Post-it to capture their stories and milestones. In another exercise, the team chose to capture major milestones and dependencies in one color and all stories in another color.)

Timelining Exercise

1. Prepare:
    - Create a large wall chart with the timeline label and any useful sections delineated (horizontal and vertical) based on feedback from the team.
    - Label a flipchart "Timeline Response Types" and list the categories of entries being tracked on this timeline (stories, milestones, vacations, dependencies, celebrations, stresses, etc.). This should be driven both by the purpose of the timeline (reflection or planning) and what could best serve the team.
    - Explain to the participants that you are about to engage in a timelining exercise. Use the agenda item question as a prompt for the purpose of the timeline.
    - Explain that while everyone will be writing their own individual responses, the team is encouraged to form, as Norm Keith calls them, natural affinity groups; that is, groupings of people with whom you can brainstorm ideas and responses to provoke more ideas. (If you can arrange it, have groups form around a large table to encourage this natural interchange, particularly if different types of responses are being captured on different color Post-its/cards.)
    - Make sure all participants have plenty of Post-its or index cards as well as pens. (If using cards, make sure all participants or groups of participants have a supply of tape for posting their responses.) For an exercise where each type of response is written in a different color or captured on a different color of card, be sure all

participants have access to ample supplies of both (see earlier suggestion about using a cluster of large tables to hold all supplies).

- Explain that participants will be invited to write their responses, one per sticky, in response to the Prompt question you are going to provide. When useful, they may also include the date at the top of the response, particularly for well-known past events or future milestones.

- Explain that when they feel that they have exhausted their wealth of knowledge about the timeline in their responses, they should individually move to the timeline chart and begin to post their responses. If the timeline has any vertical or horizontal sections, they should pay attention to these as they post.

- Explain what the timebox for the listing/posting part of the exercise will be. Norm Kerth suggests 1-2 hours for a reflective timeline used in a project retrospective.

2. Prompt:

   - Provide the "Prompt" question. For a strategic planning timeline, consider a Prompt as follows:

   > "Think about all our goals for the next six months in strategic planning."
   >
   > "Consider all the work we must complete in our systems development projects, what the market pressures are, any predefined milestones. Think about all the types of events we may want to track as defined by our list."
   >
   > "Now, what are all your timeline events for our strategic plan?"

   - For a reflection or retrospective timeline, you can use the following:

   > "Take a moment now and think about all the work that we have accomplished in the last six months (or "over the course of the release/project/etc.")."

> "We have come through many events, milestones, stresses, and celebrations, some of them personal, some of them very project-specific. Review our list of response types posted here on the flipchart."
>
> "Now, what are all your timeline events for the past six months (or the project/release/etc.)?"

3. Gather:
   - Start the timer and *say nothing else.*
   - Once the timebox has ended for completing responses, ask participants to finish posting their work on the timeline.
   - Now, invite everyone to take the next 10 minutes to review the work the team has posted in silence. Ask them to think about the impact that it has on them.

Once the reflection timebox has ended, you can conduct a 20-minute brainstorm around the trends or striking information the team sees emerging from the timeline. For a project retrospective, I stick with the five flipcharts that Norm Kerth recommends posting for responses:[2]

"What worked well that we don't want to forget."

"What we learned."

"What we should do differently next time."

"What still puzzles us."

"What we need to discuss in greater detail."

I apply similar "gold-mining" when I have a very large planning timeline:

"What we see that worries us."

"What we need to discuss in greater detail."

"What may still be missing."

"What dependencies seemed to emerge."

---

2. Kerth, *Project Retrospectives*, 125.

Other Information-Gathering Techniques

Beyond brainstorming, listing, and these additional techniques, you can decide to expand your information-gathering repertoire by bringing in additional styles. When you apply other information-gathering techniques, you keep your participants motivated by moving away from the same box of tools. The suggestions listed here still require that you have mastered the basics:

- Be a servant.
- Ask questions.
- Use timeboxes.
- Record the team information and make it highly visible.

Open Space Technology

When I have large groups of people wanting to exchange a variety of information where no roles or topics have been predefined, an Open Space is a phenomenal approach to allow the topics and roles and information to emerge. In sum, open space technology, as defined by Harrison Owen, is a great way to help a large group to think innovatively, depart from their norm, and learn what they would like to learn from one another around a particular theme and then "just do it": who has a problem that they would like to investigate with others; who has a theory about a brand-new strategy they'd like to discuss; what contradictory plans, work efforts, or practices are taking place and how can we deal with them?[3]

Open Space Technology is founded on four principles and one law that govern the leader's behavior and the participants' behaviors throughout the duration of the exercise or meeting.

The Four Principles of Open Space Technology:

1. Whoever comes is the right people.
2. Whatever happens is the only thing that could have.
3. Whenever it starts is the right time.
4. When it is over, it is over.

---

3. Owen, *A Brief User's Guide to Open Space Technology.*

The one law of Open Space Technology:

The Law of Two Feet

Summarized, these four principles and the supporting law validate the very open, innovative, and highly creative nature of this sort of information-gathering technique. Whatever topics or issues emerge will be discussed by whoever shows up (the Law of Two Feet) and who chooses to stay to participate in the information gathering. Anyone can choose to leave any discussion any time they feel that they are no longer contributory (the Law of Two Feet), and all discussions begin and end based on the behavior of the group.

Open Space Technology is deceptive in its simplicity. In truth, it requires your expert engagement as a servant leader with the innate facilitation skills to set information gathering in motion and then step aside. Through a careful sense of framework and servitude, you ensure that the open space does not just equate to chaos or zero organization despite its leaderless sense. In the proper setting, a loose and collaborative framework, teams, and topics are encouraged to be far more fluid than the normal meeting agenda.

As the leader/initiator in an Open Space Technology, you provide:

- **The theme**—This must be the unifying, compelling subject around which all the discussion topics revolve.
- **The meeting space**—A large room or rooms with ample chairs to encourage movement from group to group for all participants. This is often referred to as the Market Place as it becomes the "mission control" of the meeting where information is shared and revisited and teams reconvene at the end of the exercise or meeting.
- **The supplies**—Flipcharts and easels, markers, Post-it Notes, index cards, and tape.
- **The timeboxes**—A time slot and location for each of the topics to emerge from the group.
- **The basic instructions**—You help participants understand their role in defining and running the open space:
  - If you have a topic you'd like to open up to the group, nominate it at the start of the exercise.
  - Once all the nominated topics have been identified, a time and location in a timebox (usually groups start with a 1-2 hour timebox) is appointed to each.
  - Find a topic that interests you and sign up for it.
  - "Vote with your feet"—whoever shows up to discuss a topic are the right people to be there; however, the discussion progresses is the right way.

- Participate until you feel your participation is no longer needed (the topic doesn't interest you, it is not the discussion you thought it would be, no one else showed up for the discussion, or it is not a collaborative investigation of the topic). Politely indicate that you are exiting the group, and leave.
- **The collaborative encouragement**—You can still be a servant to a group by encouraging all participants to engage in open dialogue in their individual topic areas, without attack or judgment, seeking all opinions and all information about a topic through participation by all attendees about the topic Remind people of the "Law of Two Feet," which they can use if one person is dominating a topic (everyone else can just get up and leave!).
- **The ongoing guidance**—Make sure participants know how to find topics, how to capture their documentation, and how to update their timeslots and locations. You are the person responsible for helping with all of these process guidelines.
- **The documentation**—Information radiators about the timeslots and locations for topic discussions; posting of each groups results; information about any follow-on documentation or action items; an opportunity for participants to voice their comments about how the open space exercise worked for them.
- **The accumulation of all groups' final reports**—A compendium of each final report submitted for each topic discussed.

Appreciative Inquiry

When organizations believe they are ready to make a major change in how they work, Appreciative Inquiry (AI) may be the approach to use in evaluating a team's or set of teams' current viewpoints and how these might evolve to a more positive future. AI builds on the brainstorming, listing, and small-group dialogue exercises defined earlier and puts them in this context of "study and exploration of what gives life to human systems when they function at their best."[4]

Appreciative Inquiry is a very prescriptive information gathering approach as documented by Whitney and Trosten-Bloom, and it requires training and mentoring to learn it and conduct it well. Consider using this valuable series of exercises when you have been well schooled and when significant, far-reaching organizational change is sought.

---

4. Whitney, *The Power of Appreciative Inquiry*, 1.

As the words suggest, AI emphasizes a positive, appreciative view of what has been true in the past for an organization (its successes, assets, etc.) as a means to initiate fundamental change through careful, detailed, open inquiry and exploration of what could be true for the organization, free of judgment or prejudice. Our interest in AI in the context of technical organizations springs from this basic belief in a positive, explicit approach to organizational change, using the power of the people and their knowledge as a means to move away from command-and-control cultures to the collaboration cultures necessary to support emerging technical solutions.

Appreciative Inquiry workshops can span anywhere from a single workshop over two days to a series of meetings that span weeks or months. Although AI workshops are made up of the basic collaboration exercises defined here, you should use a professional facilitator who specializes in Appreciative Inquiry for your first offering. Or seek a mentor with whom you can conduct your first workshop to ensure that you can keep the workshop flow positive and on-track over the course of the days or meetings.

To read further about Appreciative Inquiry and how it could help your organization, look to *The Power of Appreciative Inquiry: A Practical Guide to Positive Change*, by Diana Whitney and Amanda Trosten-Bloom, and *Appreciative Inquiry: Change at the Speed of Imagination,* by Jane Magruder Watkins and Bernard J. Mohr.

Chapter 17

Managing the Meeting Participants

Groups attain their maximum performance when they have successfully moved from Forming, through Storming, into Norming, and then on to Performing. Guiding the team as it maneuvers its way through these four stages of development requires your conviction in their ability to achieve true performance velocity. And that means paying attention to what level of interpersonal intervention on your part is appropriate.

A team that is still in Forming requires your keen eye as an outside observer to see what roles are falling out, who the Drivers of the DISC model are versus the Sympathizers. A team that is in Storming requires your strong intervention in helping the group manage its inevitable one-on-one conflicts during the necessary divergence. A team that is Norming relies on your clear and continuous affirmation that they now know how to pay attention to the hazards of conflict and can remain productive. And a team that is Performing needs you primarily as a process servant and then as a conflict referee on an as-needed basis.

So, in terms of being an effective guide through the individual conflicts that define teams in Forming, Storming, and Norming, you'll need to rely not only on the information gathering and processing techniques we've reviewed, but also on practices and techniques in the interpersonal work of:

- Planning problems away
- Maintaining composure
- Maintaining participation
- Encouraging conflict
- Resolving conflict
- Managing dysfunction

When you couple the collaborative approaches for information accumulation with these conflict management skills, you clearly establish a team's ownership of its success both inside and outside meetings.

Planning Problems Away

Chapter 7, "Preparing Participants for Collaboration," covered the work you need to complete in order to prepare participants to be collaborative in their meetings. As you provide information to them about the meeting and their roles in the meeting, you also accumulate information from them and about their interest in the meeting. This is the start of your detective work in the interpersonal landscape of the team with which you are working. Whether this is a new team or a team with which you have been working for a year, it is worth paying attention to the dysfunctional behaviors that may arise in a meeting due to a simple case of bad history.

When I teach facilitation techniques in our classes, one of the mantras I impress upon the participants is:

"Most meetings fail before the meeting has ever begun."

I say this to stress the need for very good planning prior to *any* meeting, including "planning problems away" about the team's questionable (and seemingly entrenched) behaviors. So, as you design a purpose and agenda, create the processes that can best gather the information, and interview the participants, pay attention to other situations that can destroy a meeting before it begins:

- **Is there a history of conflict between two participants in particular?**—In this case, you can help them contribute better and behave more rationally by keeping them away from each other's line of sight. I take advantage of U-shaped rooms and place each of the disgruntled parties in opposite corners of the U so that they are blocked from seeing one another.

My Anecdote

This may seem incredibly simplistic, but it works! I had a situation in one group with a tester and a customer who simply could not get along on any issue, even if it had nothing to do with the project stories and the testing around them. When one said "Black," the other said "White."

I decided to invoke the U-shaped meeting chart and always place them in the corners of the U. This allowed both of them some breathing space to be contributory without being continually visually riled by the other participant. As a result, it also calmed the rest of the group and helped the entire team to work more productively without the tension that had once been ever present. The two still had their issues, and other interpersonal work still had to come into play, but at least the U-shape intervention provided us all some respite from that tension.

- **Does someone have something to lose?**—Pay attention to whose job is on the line in this project, whether due to performance concerns or just the reality of the economy. In such situations, be particularly mindful to not embarrass the individual in public.

My Anecdote

In the large telecom company where I worked, I was once helping to facilitate a Release Planning meeting for an updated call center initiative. I found out just prior to the meeting that the customer representatives in the room were probably going to lose their jobs very soon after the project was over. In essence, the software they were helping to define would eventually replace them. Though a formal announcement had not been made with regard to the layoffs, there was clearly a sense that changes were coming and that jobs were at stake. In this situation, I had been specifically brought in to facilitate so that I could be attentive to their situation in guiding the discussions of the story creation and prioritization. That meant allowing them a bit more voice and sense of pride about their work than I normally would have included in the meeting.

- **Does the group as a whole have a history of conflict and non-productivity?**—In these cases, where a team can't move out of Forming and Storming, you may need to be a bit more directive in how the Ground Rules are determined and pay much closer attention to the processes you use to help the team achieve actionable decisions. Teams stuck in the low tide of Forming and Storming are typically suffering from an accumulation of bad behaviors due to scrambling for power and control of the meeting or group.
  - Find out in advance what Ground Rules participants would like to have in place as norms prior to the meeting.
  - Learn when certain topics or discussions need to be "off-limits" (such as revisiting work that has already been completed).

- Exert more process controls than you would for a team that is already well into Norming and Performing. As you become more and more adept at understanding the best way to guide a team through Forming and Storming, you'll understand that exerting more process control at the start with such groups ultimately liberates them to require less and less process guidance as a Performing team.

My Anecdote

When I was preparing to facilitate one team in their retrospective, I discovered after a few phone calls that there were two people in particular who seemed to dominate most of the team meetings. Phone call after phone call, I was asked to "Please! Do something about these people; they are driving me crazy!" I then knew that to move this team through to Performing and make them truly productive, I had to first gain the team's trust as their guide: I had to bring the two "Dominators" under control. This wasn't just about saving the agenda; this was about saving the team. This information helped me plan in advance how I would work with these two people in the meeting. I focused on processes that created full participation, and I used body language and verbal cues with these individuals that helped them step back from needing to continuously give their feedback. (You'll see how I did this in the "Managing Dysfunction" section later.)

- **Has the team suffered at the hands of a bad facilitation experience in the past?**— Often, when I interview participants prior to a meeting, I learn that they have a predisposition against facilitation due to a bad experience in the past. This usually involved facilitation as "controlling" or "strong-arming" the team and its agenda. It may have also included facilitation through attack or embarrassment of participants. That is neither facilitation nor collaboration! If your team has suffered a similar fate, several important techniques are at your disposal:
  - Be sure to get this information from them prior to the meeting and be grateful for it! It is far better to know about this situation than to come into your meeting and have a subversive plot in place to destroy the meeting despite your best intentions to be truly collaborative.
  - Have a trusted team member introduce you into the team, assuring them of your intentions and your collaborative approach.
  - Be sure to stress at the start of the meeting that the team owns the meeting and its outcomes and that you are just their servant in getting to that purpose via the agenda.

- Plan to gather "Personal Objectives" at the start of the meeting so that each participant can be clear about their goals for the meeting. Refer to these personal objectives frequently throughout the meeting to continually reaffirm their ownership of the meeting.
- Plan a quick brainstorm about what has not worked well in the past in their meetings. Then invite suggestions of "Ground Rules" that could help forestall such problems in this meeting.

- **Do the technical team members tend to suffer from "TDC" or "Thinly Disguised Contempt" about contributions from the non-technical participants?**—Overt or thinly disguised contempt about the contributions of the customer or support staff will either cause these members to drop out completely or create their own level of contempt about the technical team contributions.[1] You can help teams move through this by doing the following:
  - Plan to engage the team early in brainstorming what the team has accomplished to date, capturing all its achievements. You can do this either as a whole team exercise where you act as the scribe, or you can move the team into dyads where members are paired off randomly and each must tell the other about the work the other has done that has been helpful to the team. Each dyad then reports what the two of them have contributed to the success of the team.
  - Plan an early brainstorming around "What Works Well" to emphasize the ways that the group does function well. Then lead the team in a brainstorm around "What Could Be Improved," which then leads to a dialogue about suggestions for implementing improvements while maintaining "What Works Well."
  - Plan an early brainstorming with role-play where technical team members have to perform the role of the customer or support staff, and the customers have to play the role of the technical staff. I like to use the exercises such as the "house of cards" and "balloon blowing" stories created for the XP Game by the Benelux XP group: www.xpgame.be/xpgame/.

When you purposefully plan these exercises into an agenda, you help a team to reexamine its prejudices while removing emotion about those prejudices so that they can proceed as a team with a better understanding about how the "other half" really does contribute to the success of the team.

---

1. Brad Feld blog, http://www.feld.com/blog/archives/2004/05/tdc_thinly_disg.html, May 6, 2004.

Maintaining Composure

Once you've done your planning to manage dysfunctional behaviors before they happen, your next service to your team is to maintain your composure.

The greatest test of your resolve around collaboration very often lies in the "goo" of conflict and the questionable behaviors that arise in it. How do you approach conflict and guide it to resolution constructively without getting mixed up in it yourself? Or, if you find yourself in potentially destructive conflict with one of the team members, what can you do to keep the discussion useful and non-damaging in its resolution?

How Do I React to Conflict?

Chapter 4, "What Are Collaborative Teams?," described the Thomas-Kilmann conflict mode instrument (TKI) as a model for thinking about individual and team conflict styles. How a leader deals with conflict creates a mold of sorts for the team. Teams seem to fall either into the same mode (leader avoids, therefore we avoid) or into a mode that is a violent opposite reaction (leader competes, therefore we avoid).

This gets into some of that "fluffy" stuff about leadership. That is, to learn about how to positively manage team conflict, we first have to ask ourselves:

"What is my natural tendency in conflict?"

Do you tend to avoid conflict at all costs? Do you engage in conflict in order to win? Do you tend to shut down in conflict and become blameful? Do you become defensive and aggressively confront those who disagree with you? When you look at your conflict tendency, you can then learn to recognize it and manage it constructively. Being cognizant, you can then maintain composure when helping teams manage their conflicts. In short, if conflict naturally causes you to lose your cool, all bets are off on the meeting having any shred of hope in attaining its purpose. In one fell swoop, collaboration is tossed out the window, and the group is left in upheaval.

Lack of composure comes in a variety of unpleasant forms. Have you resorted to any of the following behaviors in meetings? If so, you may need to revisit your personal conflict style and give it a good wash, rinse, and polish.

- You take over meeting decisions out of your frustration with the team.
- You publicly ridicule the person who has "touched your nerve."

- You publicly mock the whole team for their disruptive behaviors.
- You stop listening to the team's requests to change the agenda or make a certain decision.
- You blame the team when your meetings don't meet their purpose.
- You manipulate the team to agree to come to the decision that you personally want.
- You attack people personally because you disagree with their stance.
- You leave the meeting because you aren't getting what you want from the participants.

My Anecdote

I have witnessed these behaviors among my colleagues, and I have watched myself resort to unattractive behaviors in meetings where I felt my knowledge or expertise was not just being challenged—it was (to my way of thinking) being completely ignored. When I feel attacked or feel that the meeting is not going the way that *I* want it to go, I know that my tendency has been to mentally abandon the meeting. Rather than compete, I shut down and move into an uber-avoidance mode. I can also feel my resentments rise. Of course the person I perceive at the core of my pain may not even know about this conflict that I perceive! I have had to recognize this weakness of mine and then apply techniques to keep myself in the meeting without going to the opposite extreme of controlling the group in revenge. This is hard stuff! For me as a participant, the personal lesson has been to show up, find something that has meaning to me, tell my truth about it, and then let it go. Applying that as a collaborative leader has been a bit trickier. For me as leader, showing up, finding passion, and telling the truth has been about my conviction about process, the power of collaboration, and the wisdom of each and every team.

Your first order of business in your own behavioral "goo" is to recognize it and then seek some personal composure about it. Recognize that when your emotion about the meeting outcomes gets high, you've made the meeting about you and not about the team. Remove your emotion by relying on your organizing tools and on the team members to bring the team through very simple behavior or participation issues.

Turn to the Ground Rules

Help the team self-govern through their posted "Ground Rules," "Purpose," and "Agenda." When they do so, you take your emotion out of their Storming stage and encourage their ability to move into a Norming mode of organization. When you don't do this, you actually impede their ability to move out of Storming.

You may find yourself losing your composure because you feel the meeting is getting out of your control. Actually, that may be a sign that it is getting out of the *team's* control: the team is bored, the team is annoyed, the team is tired, the team feels herded or controlled. Rule #1: Don't ignore all the messages the team is sending you. You need to do something about this; that is your job. As you pull your own emotion out of the issue, turn to the organizing tools as the team's guide. Here are some ways to maintain your composure while addressing the situation first via the team's Ground Rules:

- "These are the Ground Rules you agreed to at the beginning of the meeting. I'm concerned that these are not helping the team toward its purpose. Should we review the Ground Rules for their usefulness?"
- "I'd like to check in with you about how we are progressing on meeting our goal. Are there any additional Ground Rules that could help you meet the purpose more effectively?"
- "We seem to be ignoring this particular Ground Rule, and I am fearful of the damage it may be causing to participation. Could you tell me what might be useful for proceeding?" (I covered these earlier in Chapter 9, "The Organizing Tools.")

My Anecdote

When I first began to apply these collaboration techniques in my own software teams, my greatest challenge lay in the interpersonal bumps and squeaks we would encounter in our planning meetings. Getting to decisions that the entire team could support inevitably raised hackles. In particular, I discovered that some of the large planning teams that I supported in IT had an unattractive history of dysfunction. Technical people were dismissive of the customers. And the customers were very distrustful of the technical folks. Lots of ugly behaviors tended to come out very quickly in their meetings. And I discovered that their less-than-attractive behaviors were having a negative impact on me.

In these murky waters, I learned to frequently swim to the surface and bring the team back to the group's Agenda and Ground Rules as my first means to get back to my own composure with respect to their behaviors. I kept the team working as one large group until I was assured that they believed in the power of these tools and in my trust of their ability to work productively.

Turning to the posted guidelines for participation wasn't just for them, as it turns out. It reminded me that I didn't own the meeting, they did. And, indeed, it removed my emotion from their Forming and Storming so that I could return to being a useful guide.

Reflect on the Framework

In addition to reapplying the posted "Ground Rules," consider reevaluating your processes for decision making. When you see your own composure slipping, it may be because you have misread what the team really needs. Take a break. Pause. Reflect. Think about how you might run the meeting differently: what processes might work better, what agenda items might be moved around, how the purpose might be massaged slightly to be more meaningful. Then decide if it is time to turn to the group with recommendations about the meeting and how to make it work better for them.

Two important notes to consider as you help a team through its Storming stage:

1. If a team is stuck in the Storming stage, it is probably because they haven't had the time or guidance to work effectively through their Forming stage. This can result either because you were unable to maintain your composure around that work or because they had been forced into a Norming mode of work without sufficient information and interaction to ferry them effectively through their Storming. In these circumstances, avoid small group work and turn frequently to the organizing tools to help the team reform and thus navigate their Storming more constructively. Bring in lots of brainstorming work that reminds the team of their ability to create information and draw useful guidance from it.

2. Any time you add a new person to the mix, or if a team member leaves the team, you need to bring the team back to a Forming mode of working. The team must once again go through divergence modes of work and that Groan Zone of finding its collective footing. Turn once again to a very process-driven mode of working to help the team members learn about how they will work with one another and who will play what roles. Keep your composure about team churn by addressing it head-on in refacilitating the team as one large group needing to reestablish roles.

Take Time and Space

Sometimes, the troubles you are experiencing may not be at the team level. They may be with a particular individual. This may include personal attack by someone in the meeting. Never under any circumstances address someone in public about their disruptive or bad behaviors, even if they are directed at you. When you feel yourself losing your composure or feel yourself under personal attack, you have several useful facilitation tools to guide you.

Find out who you are today—Call a 10-minute break and take some private time to find out why you are reacting the way you are. Make sure that it isn't just about you having a bad day. My colleague Bob Moir calls this "Who showed up wearing my clothes today?" None of us is in stellar form 100% of the time (though I certainly have colleagues who think that they are!). That means we need to take a step back and admit to our own "bad hair days" around our collaborative misbehaviors. Feeling attacked or needing to control what is occurring may have everything to do with your own "goo" and nothing more. Take the time to accept that about yourself and rejoin the group with a plan for engaging the team in work that will ensure that the meeting is about them (such as small group discussions) and not about you.

Find out who someone else is today—If you are troubled with a particular person's behavior in the meeting, call a 10-minute break. During that time, ask the person to speak with you privately outside the room away from the others. Find out what is happening with him and help him understand the impact it is having on the meeting. Ask what you can do to change the tense atmosphere. In short, try to work through this in your role as a servant to the team by dealing directly with the impact it is having on you. Make every attempt to bring this person back into a productive role in the meeting and to keep yourself fully engaged in the meeting.

If you continue to feel ill at ease after checking with yourself and with the other person, you may have to consult with someone higher up (the Executive Sponsor, the next level manager) to help the behavior be resolved. Or, you may have to ask the person to leave the meeting. Finally, you may have to excuse yourself as the meeting leader and bring someone else in who doesn't have the same clash.

In any of these situations, your goal is always to maintain composure and to learn what is best for the team. If you continually feel under attack, you are doing the team no good by staying in the meeting.

My Anecdote

During an Iteration Planning meeting I was facilitating for an offshore team just learning about agile software development approaches, I found that I kept being distracted by two testers who were not contributing to the meeting. Instead, they were distancing themselves from the rest of the group, snickering at the work of the group, and playing with a Blackberry pager/phone. At one point, I stopped the meeting and, to the group in general, suggested that there were some people not engaging in the meeting who were also creating distractions. I admitted that the distractions were hard for me to work through. I asked them to think about the importance of the meeting and the need to stay engaged.

Unfortunately, it felt as though my suggestion fell on deaf ears, and I could feel my ire growing. After another 20 minutes, where they were still not participating and just creating disruptions, I called a break and asked everyone to make sure that they got up, left the room, and stretched their legs before coming back. I then approached the two testers in the hallway and asked them what their purpose for being in the meeting was, and how I could help them meet that purpose. I could see their discomfort, but I worked to make it my problem, not theirs. I wanted them to be able to be open with me and not defensive. They admitted that they just didn't trust the process of using a timebox and doing testing within the timebox. I asked for their trust in moving through the process a bit longer and also committed to bringing up their concerns with the rest of the group (the developers and the customer) before we proceeded with any further planning. I received their apologies and their promise to engage more actively when the group returned.

As you become more and more skilled at maintaining your composure, you help the team through its next collaboration hurdle: maintaining participation.

Maintaining Participation

Truly collaborative teams in the Performing mode of working hold the conviction that the best decisions and work can only occur with the full participation of each member of the team. Period. As the team guide, you need to watch the early stages of a team to help ensure that they learn to get everything they can out of each and every participant. In any collaboration, you must guide the team by the rule: "In order for this work to proceed, I need the full participation of everyone in this meeting."

Maintaining full-group participation during the many team interactions requires your keen eye to watch how the group as a whole is working:

- Have they become disinterested?
- Are they frequently going off topic?
- Are there lots of interruptions when someone is speaking?
- Are some people not contributing at all?
- Are a few people doing all the talking and decision making?

When you see these imbalanced participation modes begin to become the team norm, you can help the team members evaluate their own participation effectiveness by having them fill out a "World Impact" chart as recommended by Justice and Jamieson:[2]

On a flipchart, draw a set of three concentric circles. Explain that the innermost circle represents the placement of people who are participating a lot and have a high impact on the decisions in the meeting, whereas the outermost circle represents the placement of people who participate little and have little impact on the decision. The intermediate circle represents those who feel they have average participation and impact.

Ask each person to think about where their participation is and to place an X on the chart where they feel they are currently in the meeting. Then explain that meetings that produce the best results and the most intelligent decisions have a norm state where all participants tend to gravitate to the second circle.

Continue working with the team about their collaboration and participation using some of the techniques described in the next section. Check in with them again after an hour or two to see if they have been able to self-organize into a more balanced participation mode.

Symptoms and Cures

To maintain team-level participation, here are a few tricks of the trade to keep in your hip pocket:

1. **Disinterest in the meeting**—When two or more people lose interest in the meeting, you've lost the collective wisdom of the team. To help solve the problem, you can:
   - Review the "What's In It For Me" value of the meeting, making sure that there really is a reason for each person to be there. Perhaps some people were only invited for political reasons.
   - Create a small group (dyads, triads, or quads) exercise to make sure everyone is engaged. Continually doing work with the entire group may become too monotonous and allow too much drifting from real work.
   - Review the posted "Purpose" of the meeting and ask the group for a 15-minute "Agenda Check" to make sure that the agenda is really getting them what they want or need out of the meeting. Sometimes groups are too reticent to speak up about an agenda that just is not helping them get what they need out of

---

2. Justice and Jamieson, *The Facilitator's Fieldbook*, 128.

a meeting. You'll need to actively gauge this yourself and explicitly raise the topic for them.

- Find out if different groups within the meeting play very different roles. Do they tend to divide up work to be completed in parallel, where each group is working within its realm of expertise? If so, don't force whole groups of people to sit, watch, and wait while a small group is solving a problem peculiar to their group. Either have the sub-group solving the problem form a separate meeting, or have them take an Action Item to address their issue after the general meeting.

2. **Off-topic or ill-focused discussions**—This is a problem in particular when you are trying to help a team engage in open dialogue. You can help them track their topics while gaining their trust simply by being their ears and tracker:

   - When you hear a discussion moving from one topic to another, and members seem to be reacting to both topics, step in and alert the team to what you hear: "I hear us moving away from Tim's original scenario onto another one raised by Claire. I'd like us to stop and take a few more comments on Tim's scenario first before we come back to the next scenario introduced by Claire."

   - When you hear more than one person talking at once, step in and alert the team to what you hear: "I hear three different use case scenarios being discussed right now. Did I capture all of them?" This will allow anyone to correct you or add his or her topic as well. Or, "I am having trouble tracking the various discussions going on right now, but this is what I think I hear (and list all the topics)." Then, let the team tell you what they want to do with the topics: focus on one topic, combine them into a more useful single topic, or talk about them one at a time in order. Never tell the team what to do with their discussion! Just give them the information to make their decision.

   - When you hear one topic raised and then another one takes over, you can help the team get back on track by giving them some focus guidance: "I hear us now talking about this feature, but I thought Sean had begun the discussion around another feature. Are we through discussing the other feature, or does someone have additional comments for Sean?"

   - When several people have been talking about a topic, you can ask the team for reactions or questions to what the speakers have been saying. "We've just heard some feedback from Brian, Susan, and Lauren about the release. Does anyone have any specific questions for them about what they have just heard? Do we need to stay in this topic to draw out more information from others?" This will in effect allow the team to determine what the primary topic should be and bring the whole team either into the discussion or back to the original discussion.

3. **Lots of interruptions and speaking over one another**—When multiple opinions or recommendations are being made at the same time, teams can lose the flow of the conversation and find themselves mired in tangents.

   - Keep team members on track by helping them to "stack" their responses, asking them to first raise their hands before responding. You can then help them know that they are going to have a chance to speak by indicating: "These are the hands I see: Richard, Seth, and Jeff. Richard please go first, then Seth, then Jeff. If anyone else has an idea, raise your hand and I'll make sure you can speak in order." This confirms to the team that you truly want each of them to be heard and understood. If many people want to speak, you may need to either apply time limits on each person's contribution, or do a "process check" with the team about how to proceed.

My Anecdote

When I use this approach, it is apparent that the team immediately appreciates that someone is ensuring that they will each have a chance to respond, versus only the most insistent talkers or the loudest talkers. I watch people start to focus on me to get into the queue of discussion, and I see their sense of relief that they really will be able to contribute. Additionally, a discussion that brings up this dynamic usually indicates that the team needs time to just wade through it for a while. I very often stay with a team in this stacking mode for a while until there is a sense of full disclosure and understanding among all the team members. At that point, we revisit the posted "Agenda," and I ask for a recommendation about the outcome of the discussion and how to use it in moving through the agenda and converging on the meeting purpose.

   - Return to the team's Ground Rules and ask for any recommendation about how to ensure that each person is heard in the discussions. "One conversation at a time" is one good way to capture this. Ask the team to self-govern around the Ground Rule so that everyone can be heard.

4. **Non-participating members**—This is usually a sign that there are some people who always dominate the meetings, so the other participants have given up trying to contribute. They see the competition as just too stiff, or they are too shy to try to contribute, even in open forums.

   - Put the team into dyads for information gathering. Some people need an opportunity to express themselves in a smaller venue before they have the courage to contribute in front of the entire team.

My Anecdote

I've seen this happen many times both in technical people as well as non-technical customer representatives or other ancillary team members (technical publications, usability, product packaging, etc.). Some of the most valuable people on the team, the ones with true expertise around a particular feature or design solution, are too used to deferring to one or two more vocal, more forceful team members. Placing them in one-on-one dialogues for problem solving brings out bright, brave contributions from them that then encourage them to contribute more in the larger group setting.

- Ask for feedback in a Round Robin format so that the reticent members have a chance to contribute without competition. In any Round Robin, do not force members to offer a response. Anyone during their turn can simply respond, "Pass."
- Provide good eye contact and "space" (silence) to people who aren't contributing so that they feel there is an opportunity to contribute if they want it. Silence is an amazing gift to provide a group for reflection and consideration about additional contributions.
- Ask the group "We've heard from a number of you on this topic; is there anyone else who has some ideas to offer in the remaining five minutes we have?" This alerts the other speakers that they need to cede the floor to members who haven't spoken. It also establishes that the group is wrapping up the discussion so that they can make a choice to either participate or not participate.

5. **A few people are doing all the talking and decision making**—Some members of the team may be in lead or management positions. In a command-and-control environment, the team may be used to deferring to these managers' opinions. Collaboration in these situations needs coaxing

- Help the rest of the team feel welcome to contribute as well by saying, "We've now heard from Kelly and Bob on this topic; do we have other ideas we want to bring forward from some of the other team members?"
- If the primary contributor is the manager or boss, suggest that she refrain from responding until a few other team members have brought their ideas forward.

Managing Dysfunction

Sometimes, despite your best efforts to plan for a team's participation and to encourage and maintain participation during meetings and workshops, you will run into a beehive of bad behavior in one or more individuals. To help keep some perspective about the challenges in this work, here are some simple truths to consider:

- People are not dysfunctional; their behaviors are.
- Often, a bad behavior by someone in your team is a reflection of bad planning or behavior on your part.
- Or, it may not be about you or the meeting at all.

To encourage collaboration, your job as a facilitative leader is to help eliminate the bad behaviors while saving the person. If you sacrifice the person in order to eliminate the behavior, you risk losing that person as a contributory participant in your meeting. Moreover, you may incur the resentment of the rest of the team and lose their participation as well.

Managing dysfunction requires your total neutrality and your belief in the team. For that reason, there are some simple rules to apply when you are confronted with dysfunctional behaviors:

1. **Never use anger to confront the person exhibiting the dysfunctional behavior—** The person may have resorted to a dysfunctional behavior because of a dysfunction on your part. Resorting to anger only encourages the rest of the team to join that person in bad behaviors. Your anger indicates that you have lost neutrality in the situation. It may also signal to the team that you have lost confidence in their ability to be collaborative. Finally, it may unintentionally confirm to the team that you can't help them be collaborative, even if they want to be. They've lost confidence in your ability to be their guide.

2. **Never use embarrassment to resolve dysfunction**—When you embarrass someone on your team, you are telling others on the team that they run the same risk of embarrassment. At this point, you have lost the trust of the team, and you may have lost their respect.

3. **Always strive to bring the person back into the meeting**—Dysfunctional behaviors have a way of capsizing your resolve around the team's ability to do its work. When you sense that occurring, remember that as the lead example of collaboration for the team and as a servant to the team, your job is to help the team help the person reengage. You need each member of the team engaged in order to have the team truly reach collaborative, participatory decisions, the kinds of decisions that stick and motivate a team to perform.

4. **Stay mindful of your own dysfunctions**—Just as other team members may use bad behavior to gain attention (or control), so must you recognize your own tendency to do so. When other bad behaviors pop up in an environment in which you are trying to instill collaboration, you'll discover that disagreement and conflict can move you into bad instinctual behaviors that have saved you in the past. This in turn can destroy any trust you have accumulated with the team. Know what brings out your bad behaviors, admit it, and face it.

These general rules can keep you on an even keel for the overall management of crumbling behaviors. However, sometimes there are specific personalities that cause problems peculiar to their role or dysfunction. In these cases, you can turn to more specific advice on how to maintain team participation while squelching individual disruptions.

Managing the Sponsor/Manager

Sometimes when a higher-level manager or project executive is in the room, you'll find that a team, while posing as a collaborative, self-organizing team, may not really be at all. You may watch them consistently defer to the manager's opinions and decisions. Very often, they won't express an opinion until the manager has stated an opinion first.

In these cases, you have a couple of options:

- Offline, ask the manager to provide his or her feedback last on any issue.
- Collect responses anonymously from each person and then read them aloud so that the manager's voice is leveled out among all member voices.
- If the behavior is extremely controlling, call a break in the meeting and speak with the manager about the goal of the team's participation in a sustainable solution. If the manager can't pay attention to the team's needs, ask the manager to leave the meeting.

I usually observe this problem with teams that are still in Forming and Storming. If a higher-level manager is too controlling, the group never moves into Norming and Performing because they never engage in the healthy constructive conflict needed to get out of Storming. So, besides paying specific attention to the manager, also think about applying some of the general guidelines about how to engage teams when they are stuck in Storming.

Managing the Observer

The biggest problem with managing observers is that they aren't. Observers have a hard time just observing. Here are some typical unhealthy behaviors you may encounter with observers in your meetings:

- They begin to talk among themselves and so distract the team.
- They are "in" the meeting but not really "in" the meeting, answering emails, doing their own work, taking phone calls, and so are becoming a distraction.
- They believe that their behaviors do not need to abide by the Ground Rules laid out by the team: answering the phone, ignoring the speaker, etc.
- They decide to voice their observations and so become non-observers.
- Just by their presence, they influence how the team expresses its opinions and suggestions, especially if the observer is someone in a position of power.

If your meeting has a need to accommodate observers (such as in the Daily Scrum meeting where the observers are known as "Chickens" while the active committed participants are the "Pigs"), be sure to guide the team in setting Ground Rules specifically around observer decorum. If you have a choice, discourage the attendance of observers in your team meetings. Make the meetings about the team and its successes and decisions. In compensation, be sure that the team agrees on an action item to communicate pertinent meeting information to those who would have been observing (stakeholders, ancillary teams, etc.).

If any observer is not abiding by the guidelines set forth by the team either verbally at the start of the meeting or in its Ground Rules, you can:

- Address the entire group about the need to pay attention to the posted "Ground Rules," even the observers, so that the team can meet its purpose.
- Call a quick break and speak to the observer personally about their disruption and ask them to either abide by the "Ground Rules" or discontinue attending the meeting.
- Ask the team to revisit the "Ground Rules" about observers and ask for recommendations that could help the team stay focused without disruptions from any observers.

"Give Me the Bullet Points"—Managing Someone Who Rambles

A rambler can single-handedly kill collaboration in a meeting by taking over all discussions and not letting go. Other members give up trying to interject. They become exhausted and resentful of both the rambler for dominating as well as the meeting leader for not wresting the meeting away from the rambler.

You have a few useful tactics to apply to this loquacious individual:

- When the rambler wants to speak, explain, "Jill, the team has enjoyed a number of excellent recommendations from you already today. Let's get some ideas from some of the other participants first."
- Ask the rambler to provide information in three or four bullets or points.
- Ask the rambler to cut to the final point: "I'm having trouble following your thought. Could you cut to your final point for me, please?"
- Move to a position standing near or behind the person so that he can't get your attention but can see everyone else's focus shifting away from him. This helps him understand that he needs to wrap up. Additionally, because he can't get your eye contact, you can easily shift the discussion to someone else.
- Start to apply a time limit to all responses, not just the rambler's responses.

Finally, managing a rambler is a good job to turn over to the team. When you are opening the meeting and explaining the use of the Ground Rules and the Parking Lot, use this opportunity to remind the team that they need to be owners of the flow of their meeting. Therefore, if they determine that someone is rambling and that the discussion is not serving the Purpose and Agenda of the meeting, they need to be the ones to ask that the discussion be curtailed or the item put in the Parking Lot.

My Anecdote

When I open meetings and am introducing the Parking Lot, I use "The Rambler" as my example of how the team owns their meeting and therefore the posted "Parking Lot." I explain that the team members are the experts of their material, and so as experts, only they can know if what someone ("The Rambler") is providing is necessary for the success of the meeting, or if the topic has gone too far afield to be of use. If the team believes that the content is not getting to a useful point, they have the right to stop the person and ask that the topic be placed in the Parking Lot.

For one of the offshore teams I was working with, I showed the group the hand signal for "TIME!" by making a big "T" with my hands, and asked if that was a signal they used in their culture as well to mean "Stop!" They said, "Yes!" And so we agreed that we had an International Symbol for Stopping Ramblers. I told them that they were responsible for calling "TIME!" on anyone who they felt was not getting to a point that would be useful in the meeting. This was a great way to engage them at the very beginning of the meeting about how to own their meeting and how to do it in a fun, non-hurtful way.

"The Third Man"—Managing Someone Who Dominates

This may be either the well-acknowledged expert or the self-appointed expert in the room. In either case, they are the person who seems to control any discussion or decision. If one person is making all the decisions, a meeting wasn't needed, and collaboration wasn't called for by the team. Or, the team simply has not been provided a safe environment in which to express differing opinions.

You can handle this in several ways:

- Don't give the dominating person eye contact.
- Give eye contact to the other team members, and ask for contributions or responses from the other team members first before addressing the dominator.

- In private, specifically ask this person to go third or last in order to encourage others to participate more.

You may also find yourself with another type of dominating expert: the self-appointed facilitator. This person may consider herself a facilitator because of her ability to "control" a group. Such a person may, if dissatisfied with your approach at having the team make its decisions, jump up, grab your pen and take over the meeting. In such a situation:

1. Call an immediate break in order to speak with the person privately.
2. Explain that, while you value her expertise, she needs to continue to work with the rest of the team as a team member to collaboratively bring about decisions.
3. Also remind her that at the beginning of the meeting, you received the buy-in from the team to guide them through to their Purpose via the posted Agenda.
4. Also remind her of the Ground Rules around participation.

"You May Be Right"—Managing the Naysayer

The Naysayer is someone who seems to always be ready to put down any idea before it has been discussed or investigated. Think of the old cartoon with Rocky the Squirrel and his old pal Bullwinkle Moose who prides himself as an amateur magician. Rocky always tries to stop anything Bullwinkle is about to perform by quickly declaring, "But that trick *never* works!" Like Rocky, the Naysayers always have a score of reasons why some idea won't work. What's worse, they have an ability to kill any creative energy any other participants may have with their bottomless negativity.

In agile software development methodologies, we very often talk about "the art of the possible"—helping teams move out of a "We can't possibly do that" mode to one of "Let's try it and learn from it." We move teams away from a fear of failing to one of an eagerness to learn. For that reason, it is all the more important to quickly identify Naysayers and manage them in collaborative meetings.

Here are some ways to help Naysayers curb their enthusiasm for killing change:

- Thank the person for her insights and ask others for recommendations about how the idea *could* work.
- Admit to the person, "You may be right," and then ask for other comments on the topic from other members of the team.

"You may be right" may be one of the most powerful phrases in the English language for squashing the arguments that come about in teams just because of someone's argumentative nature. This phrase, along with the phrase "I can live with that and support it," are powerful tools to introduce into the lexicon of teams troubled by Naysayers and by members who dominate. Because of their power to create breathing space in teams, they have become major themes in any number of teams in which I have worked. By using the phrases frequently, we constantly check in with ourselves about:

- How much am I striving to allow another viewpoint to be "good enough?"
- How much can I hear the validity of the other point while still holding on to my own viewpoint?
- How well am I letting go of "winning" and instead focusing on what can work as a sustainable agreement?

Each of these checks and balances helps curb the dysfunctions around dominating and naysaying behaviors.

"We're Headed Your Way"—Managing Someone Who Drops Out

There are any number of reasons someone may be dropping out of your attempts to engage a team collaboratively:

- The person has felt "beat up" before by someone in the team and so no longer attempts to offer responses or solutions.
- The person has problems in his personal life that are causing distraction or pain that have nothing to do with the meeting.
- The person does not feel heard or understood by you as the meeting leader and so has given up responding.
- The person is shy and has a difficult time warming up to speaking in a large group.

You can help this person reengage in the meeting participation through a number of techniques:

- Conduct a simple Round-Robin exercise to get some quick feedback that starts two people before the person in question. "Let's do a quick check on where we are with the various attributes of our user actor in this use case. Can we start with Dean, then Monica, then Mary, and so on to get feedback?" (In this case, Mary is the one who has dropped out of the discussion or is asleep.) When you give participants such as Mary advance warning that they are going to be participating, you help nudge them back into the meeting without embarrassing them.

- Tell the group that they are all looking a bit tired, and ask everyone to stand up for 30 seconds and stretch before resuming the discussion. Or, keep them in their seats and ask them to do "The Wave" either by throwing their arms in the air one-by-one or kicking a leg out one-by-one. Blood flow does wonders for dropouts.

- Take a quick five-minute break and ask the person in private if there is anything you can do to help her reengage in the meeting.

"I'm in Your Corner"—Managing Side Conversations and Continuous Talking

Usually, ongoing side conversations indicate that the two people engaged in the conversations have lost interest in the meeting or have simply forgotten that their participation is needed. This is not your time to play elementary school teacher and openly confront them by saying, "Do you have something to share with everyone else? I'm sure we would all want to know what is so important to you." (I have actually seen a manager do this in a room full of coworkers on the same project!)

Take their lack of participation as a sign that you are not helping them stay active in the meeting. You can:

- Simply stand near them but give them no eye contact. Moving your body near their location is usually enough presence to help them refocus without having any attention being brought to them. In a U-shaped meeting configuration, you can move within the U-shape to where they are located and just continue talking with your back to them. (Remember, you are not providing eye contact or overt admonishments.) Or, you can move outside the U-shape and stand behind them with similar impact.

- If you have a ground rule about "Respect the speaker" or "One conversation at a time," return to the posted "Ground Rules" and ask if the team is still self-governing around its participation and respect for others in the meeting. Ask the team for any recommendations about what would make the "Ground Rules" more useful with respect to their participation.

- Recheck your homework on the team and their roles and ensure that there is work for everyone to do in each of the agenda items. You may need to rework your agenda to initiate some parallel small group activities to help everyone stay engaged.

"Elvis Has Left the Building"—Managing the Bolter

Sometimes, you may be in a meeting and suddenly hear a door slam, and someone is no longer in the meeting. Or, you watch a participant get up and charge aggressively out of the room. Because such actions typically create a lot of discomfort for the team, you have a few responsibilities in order to help the team stay engaged and collaborative:

1. Don't ignore it when someone leaves the meeting unannounced. It may have jolted more participants than just you, and you need to help the other members figure out what the departure means to their work.
2. Take a quick break to see if you can find the person and ask him what has happened. Find out if there was something in how you were managing the meeting or the group that caused the person to leave. Take in his information and seek to find a solution to the problem.
3. If you can't locate the person, find out from the group if anyone knows why the person left. It may be that he suddenly remembered an appointment, or received a sudden urgent message. Help the others know that the departure had nothing to do with either the topic that was being discussed or the decisions that were being made.
4. If it turns out that there had been emotion around the departure (door slamming, yelling, chair flinging), ask the group:
   a. "What could I have done to have prevented this from occurring?"
   b. "What recommendations do you have for the meeting moving forward in a way that we can prevent this from happening again?"

Additionally, ask the group how they will handle discussion of the incident outside of the team. If a team does not want ill will about the team or the individual to fester as a result of the incident, help them formulate their team story about what occurred such that no injury occurs.

"Stop the Violence"—Managing Personal Attacks

Sometimes, bad behaviors reach such a level of dysfunction that it leads to personal attacks by one or more people. It is your job to manage this as soon as possible.

1. Immediately place yourself between the eye contact of the attacker and the person being attacked. This is where a U-shaped meeting space really works for you. Within the center of the U-shape, you can position yourself to act as the physical barrier to the attacks. Your goal is to break their eye contact and redirect the discussion.
2. Ask for other members to provide feedback on the topic, reminding them to keep to facts and non-personal opinions.
3. Remind the team of any Ground Rules around non-attacking behavior. Or, ask the team for some guidance around Ground Rules that could curtail any future personal attacks.
4. Also help participants rephrase such attacks as information, not attacks: "Steve's architecture work is too shoddy for me to use for my designs. He always does a lousy job," can be rephrased with "I have trouble with the architecture deliverables. They are not in a form that I can use. I need further detail about the clustering environment in particular." Stay away from using names and stick to what is useful information about the work or deliverables or timelines.
5. This may also be a good time to invoke the "Take the blame away" rule for collaborative leadership. Pull attention from the attacks by bringing the team back to taking blame yourself, not allowing any blame to be assigned to anyone else.

If the attacks continue, immediately call a break and speak to the attacker directly in private. If he cannot stop attacking, explain that he will not be allowed to continue to participate in the meeting.

Chapter 18

Managing Conflict

Shepherding a team from divergence through that nasty Groan Zone into convergence requires the work of a highly collaborative leader, adept at engaging constructive conflict among team members. Leaders intimidated by conflict very often press their teams to avoid it. They may encourage members to compromise or even abandon their expert opinions. These leaders would rather accept a potentially ill-defined, uninformed solution for the sake of "keeping the peace." Or, they may be motivated by time pressures to quell conflicts in order to keep moving through the meeting agenda. Finally, leaders may use signs of conflict within the team as an excuse to usurp the team's collective power and take over any subsequent decisions as a means to "save the team."

Encouraging Conflict

To encourage and manage team conflict, learn to discern the difference between useful, constructive conflict and its counterpart, destructive argument. Well-engaged conflict leads to better team decision making; argument exhausts and potentially unhinges a team. Table 18.1 lists some common characteristics of both and how they contrast from one another.

Table 18.1   Constructive Conflict versus Destructive Argument

Constructive Conflict	Destructive Argument
The team is collectively engaged in finding a variety of possibilities.	Individuals are more interested in winning the argument.
Everyone is engaged in the discussion.	A few people dominate while others just drop out.
Discussions focus on facts: who, what, when, why, how, where.	Conversation is fraught with opinions and personal attacks.
The discussion stays focused on the issue being investigated.	The discussion continually devolves from the original topic.
Members encourage each other's input.	Members fight for control and discourage others from speaking.
People ask for further detail on each other's feedback.	People ignore what has been said for the sake of presenting their own view.
Members provide encouragement for each other's ideas, regardless of whether they agree or not.	Members encourage people who agree with them and find fault with any other stated viewpoints.

You can encourage the sort of conflict described in the left side of this table versus being destroyed by the arguments outlined on the right by turning to that basic guidance from Chapter 6, "Preparing Yourself as the Process Owner," for maintaining your role as the owner of the process, not the content:

- Stay neutral.
- Ask questions.
- Encourage information sharing.
- Make information and decisions highly accessible.
- Take away the blame.
- Drive to consensus.
- Help team members feel heard and understood.

As discussed in Chapter 6, these guidelines help you and your team sit in the discomfort and edginess of the Groan Zone without fear of collapse from absorbing various perspectives and ideas. Along with this guidance, apply a few additional tactical skills:

1. Do not ignore conflict; be ready early in a discussion to help diverse ideas emerge in a structured, non-destructive manner. Jump in.

2. Stay in the middle of the discussion. Don't back down. Insist on helping the team discover the useful bits of their conversation. (This is a tough part of conflict management: When should I jump in to make observations or recommendations, and how much should I stand "in the middle" with the heat the group needs to navigate?)

3. Stay calm. When you apply neutrality and calm to a potentially explosive topic, you help the team believe that they can engage in conflict and can reach a useful resolution.

4. Document the facts. Go to a whiteboard or flipchart and start writing down the facts as spoken and ask for guidance from the team about how exactly to state the issue, recommendation, concern, disagreement, and so on.

5. Apply this structure and documentation as a means to help the group slow down, hear one another, and stay focused on one topic at a time. You do this when you are writing the responses as well as when you go back and reread the accumulated information.

6. To further slow down the influx of heat, ask participants to paraphrase the previous member's feedback before providing their own. This reflective listening technique helps the conversation stay focused and slow down enough for everyone to be heard and understood. You can start this by being the first to paraphrase input as it occurs. ("Mike, I hear you saying that the portal server component is currently in need of a more robust automated testing harness. Is this correct? Who else has additional information about this issue?")

7. Challenge the team about whether they are making progress on the problem/topic. Ask them for recommendations on how they can move from where they are to a next step in defining the problem.

8. Apply your "Dysfunctional Behavior" management skills when people begin to behave badly. Remember, bad behaviors usually occur when people don't feel heard and understood. So, for instance, if personal attacks start, stop the attacks immediately. Refer to Ground Rules and group norms around dialogue and conversation. If the attacks continue, promptly call a break.

You don't need to wait for a full-blown confrontation to apply these techniques. Begin to apply conflict resolution techniques informally when a small group dialogue starts to get heated or when you sense frustration rising. In essence, take control of the dialogue before confrontation sets in or positions are set in stone. Use skills one through eight bit by bit in less heated situations in order to acquire experience with them. When very heated discussions flare from smoke to flame, you will be ready and more confident about your prowess to manage the muck of it.

My Anecdote

Sometimes you find yourself in a situation where a number of facilitation techniques come together in helping a group move through turmoil into consensus. I was working with a group of three project teams in Release Planning, facilitating them through their first planning session as an entire group. First decision: How long should the release be (should there be more than one?) and how many iterations should there be? This led to another decision: How long should each iteration be? There were three decisions running in parallel and up to 20 voices coming in on all three. Because the group was new, I had to watch who was trying to take control and who was shutting down. Divergence was definitely in the air, and I wanted to make sure that the conflict that ensued stayed healthy.

First, I used the stacking method to stack decisions. ("Let's deal with the iteration length decision first, and then move on to the release length, and then we'll discuss the number of iterations in each release. Will that work for everyone?") Then, with many voices popping up around each issue, I again applied stacking to create an order for who would speak when. ("I see three people with ideas: Let's take Joel first, then Ann, then Paresh.") The combination of these techniques kept the group on topic and ensured that all voices were heard. As conflict arose, the stacking method helped manage the conversation to ensure that all sides of the debate could be heard. The debate was instead a dialogue about sharing solutions from all team members.

When it seemed the same people were dominating with their opinions (one person was adamant that the iterations be four weeks in length), I asked for other voices that had not yet been heard from.

When the conversation started to sound circular, it was time to call for a recommendation. We got three. This led to more discussion. Because the group had already been used to "Fist of Five" consensus checking, I was able to then quickly call for a consensus check. Two participants were still disgruntled. We concentrated on their issues, came up with one more recommendation, and finally had a full consensus decision. This led to the same work on the other two decisions, but discussion moved much more rapidly and with less confrontation. Ultimately, the group came to a decision to have two-week iterations, two releases, and five iterations in each release.

When you work with teams in this way, you help them maintain their "central selves" in the discussion versus reverting to their "calculating selves." These terms, from Rosamund Stone Zander and Benjamin Zander in *The Art of Possibility*, describe the confident, grounded side of ourselves that can engage, hear, and discuss openly versus the calculating personality that listens defensively, needs control, and may even seek to hurt through insult or revenge. Staying centered and sticking right in the middle of the conflict with the team can help each individual maintain their "central self" that then helps the group maintain its own "central self."

Sometimes, however, even with these eight techniques masterfully applied, you'll find members deadlocked in an issue, not making progress, and moving into destruction out of pure annoyance, or frustration, or just plain ignorance about what is really going on in the decision. This is where you move to very explicitly guide them to resolve the conflict.

Resolving Conflict

If you find that dialogue has brought your team into deep conflict, you need to be well-schooled in the non-destructive, effective technique of helping them resolve head-on conflict. So, if a consensus check reveals any votes of "one" (completely disagree) or "two" (have reservations about the recommendation), you have the responsibility to address the disagreement and concerns constructively. And yes, there really are specific tools you can employ to guide a team's ability to resolve their conflicts in a useful constructive manner. In a healthy conflict resolution mode, teams learn more about the strength of its members and their collective wisdom and thus move into the much-desired state of high performance.

Your first step is to help a team decide how important the resolution of the conflict is in terms of its impact. The group may decide that the conflict is not really relevant to their work and decide to drop the topic entirely. Or, they may decide that a simple majority vote will do for resolving the impasse. But find this out and have the team tell you where the conflict sits in terms of its relevancy. When figuring out what to do with conflict, Ingrid Bens offers guidance about the five Thomas-Kilmann conflict modes (see Table 18.2) and how we might use these effectively with conflict resolution in meetings:[1]

---

1. Ingrid Bens, *Facilitating with Ease!*, pg. 91.

Table 18.2 Conflict Resolution Modes and their Uses

Conflict Resolution Mode	Usage
Avoidance—This doesn't really deal with the conflict.	Used when an issue simply can't be resolved profitably and is holding the team back from its real work. Turn to this method only 10% of the time, and only when the team chooses to avoid, not when you choose to avoid the conflict. At the very least, prompt the team to define an Action Item to address the issue at some point in the near future.
Accommodation—One step up from avoidance; you guide the team to just accept.	Used when keeping the peace is more important than finding a solution, you should only rely on this resolution style 5% of the time. Like avoidance, you should only apply this approach through assessment from the team that the conflict is not worth the time it would take to build consensus.
Competition—Your worst possible solution to a conflict is to put yourself in the middle and create win/lose stances.	Never rely on this one!
Compromise—You try to help a team seek a middle ground.	Used when you can't take the time to engender consensus but the choices are very polarized, it has 20% applicability.
Collaboration—A team works through the many facets of the viewpoints to create a new solution they can all live with and support.	This creates the most sustainable agreements but takes time. Strive for collaborative conflict resolution 65% of the time, particularly on your meatiest issues.

Collaborative Conflict Resolution

To engage in collaborative conflict resolution, your work largely focuses on helping the various viewpoints be clarified, heard, dissected, and evaluated for their viability. You do this by guiding a team to sift out the noise, pay singular attention to each viewpoint, learn the separate facets of each viewpoint, and combine value from each to create a new vision.

You can do this by following these simple but hard steps:

1. Ask the group to help you move back to the point in the discussion where there was still agreement and consensus. This ensures that everyone understands that agreement is possible, we've been working from agreement, and we won't be rehashing materials that were already discussed and accepted.

2. Determine the number of clear and opposing recommendations that occur around the issue of discord.

3. Ask for a champion to represent each recommendation (only one champion is allowed per recommendation).

4. Ask for permission from all of the group members to engage each champion one at a time to document the *facts* about their position. The goal is to allow each person to have a clear, uninterrupted voice to provide useful information about their recommendation.

5. For each champion presenting their solution, guide them with factual questions that can be used to objectively learn the benefits and potential downsides of their solution. Guide them as carefully as possible to speak factually about the solutions. Use questions such as:

    Who does this involve?
    What are its benefits (ROI, time savings, cost savings, reduced workload, increased coding efficiency, streamlined architecture, wider market appeal)?
    What are the costs?
    What are the time constraints?
    What skills are needed?
    What other resources might be needed?
    What are the risks?
    What is the projected ROI?
    What are the time savings?

6. Document the information for each viewpoint, either on flipcharts or a whiteboard, where all responses can be visible. This allows the group to consider all the information and perform their own compare and contrast. Allow time for the entire group to consider all recommendations and their merits. You may want to do this by having everyone get up from their chairs and "walk the walls" in silence to absorb all the information.

7. Turn to the rest of the group and ask for any new recommendation that emerges by combining features of the championed recommendations. Guide the entire group in dialogue around the new recommendation.

---

8. Determine if you see the group converging on or diverging from the new recommendation. In particular, pay attention to how the champions are engaged. Make sure they are participating. Ask questions and provide observations that can prompt creative consideration of the emergent view.

9. Perform a consensus check about this recommendation.

10. If consensus still cannot be reached (in the "Fist of Five," all votes are a "three" or above), go back to finding out what agreement *does* exist and again ask for the recommendations that should move forward. Apply the same steps as before.

This process continues until either the group converges on a solution around which it can come to consensus, or the group determines that it cannot reach consensus in the time constraints of the meeting. At that point, they may choose to either take an Action Item to meet on the topic again later (this can allow them to gather more expert input to guide the discussion and decisions). Or, they may choose to have an expert take the decision for them. Or, they may choose to have a sub-group of people (such as the champions) meet to come to a decision for the rest of the group.

My Anecdote

Early in my work with XP teams, I had been asked to act as neutral facilitator for a large Release Planning meeting that would bring together 3 different business groups and 11 different application representatives from IT. I had worked diligently with the IT sponsor of the event to ensure that the two-day meeting would collaboratively produce the release's User Stories, their priorities and estimates, as well as a cut at the plan for the first iteration. The sponsor had assured me that the business partners were in sync and ready to attend. She also assured me that both groups had been working well together and were ready for the Release Planning meeting to take place. I took her at her word.

Within the first two hours of the meeting, however, a mini-revolt emerged. The business representatives had felt railroaded into building stories that didn't reflect real business functions. And the IT representatives were upset that the business representatives hadn't really defined one clear scope from all concerns. Massive finger pointing ensued, and I quickly realized that everyone was actually still in very strong divergence. No one had felt that they had truly been consulted about the decisions that had led up to the meeting, despite the meetings that had occurred in anticipation of and in preparation for the Release Planning meeting.

To help the group refocus, I began a group discussion, a divergence exercise, managing fair use of "the floor," making sure that no one became too attacking and that each speaker could express their concern and recommendation without dominating the meeting. I kept repeating to the group what I was hearing from each speaker, guiding them into seeing any possible solutions. From all the proposed solutions, two solutions eventually emerged that the group felt adequately addressed the various concerns voiced. I then asked for speakers from each "camp" to come forward to the front of the room and gave them two minutes each to describe their desired solution to the scope and User Story impasse. When the speakers from each group had finished, I then called for a show of hands for one solution versus the other.

One solution definitely had more hands, but I could still see some steam emitting from some of the other camp. I then asked the group for a recommendation on *one* change in the winning decision that would help all the people in the group feel that they could move forward. A useful "good enough" alteration was suggested, the group accepted it, and we were finally ready to move forward with the meeting.

This exercise had taken an hour. The sponsors were not happy; they had seen the hour as wasted time. They had wanted to simply take control of the group, telling them what to do in no uncertain terms. I refused to let them and received some criticism for that. However, over the course of the next two days, the small groups that moved through the work were collaborative, engaged, and eager to complete the planning work.

Chapter 19

Guerilla Collaboration

As a servant to your team, you may not always be the person leading a meeting: A group of developers may have gathered to make refactoring decisions, an architect may want to share a vision for how the team should proceed within a defined framework, or the customer may want to hold a meeting to voice concerns about the project, for example.

These other meeting organizers (developers, architects, customers) may only be holding the meeting to force the group into agreeing with a decision they have already made. Or, they may simply not have the skills to ensure that the meeting is productive, focused, and inclusive of all attendees. They also may not think to track decisions of the team or collect actions that they owe the team after the meeting is over. In these meetings, whether you are a participating developer, tester, or project manager who has been invited to attend, you still have an important role in helping a group work collaboratively.

In such instances, you have a golden opportunity to apply the "Guerilla Facilitator" or "Guerilla Collaborator" role. Don't confuse "guerilla" with "gorilla" (as one of my colleagues does in jest!). This is not about strong-arming a meeting through simian brawn. Nor does guerilla here mean subversive or destructive. Rather, it suggests a constructive, gentle prodding to help the meeting organizer and the group achieve their purpose through a collaborative approach that might otherwise not be obvious or attainable to them.

There are some very simple techniques guerilla facilitators use to serve the team while sitting as a participant.

Questions for Guerilla Facilitation and Collaboration

Guerilla facilitation largely relies on your ability to assess the timbre of a meeting and to know when to ask useful guiding questions. Some very basic questions can prod a team to stop, evaluate, and potentially change how they are communicating and creating decisions.

- **"Is there an agenda?"**—Prior to the team meeting, as soon as you see the meeting invitation in your Outlook Calendar, you have an opportunity to determine if the person calling for the meeting has a plan for what they want to accomplish, by asking, "Is there an agenda?" While a very formally documented agenda may not be necessary, zero hint of a plan is a bad sign. Contact the developer, architect, or customer and ask:

  "Are there any items I need to read or prepare prior to the meeting in order to be prepared?"

  "Do we have an idea of all the things we plan to do in the meeting?"

  (I've learned of one company that became so emphatic about this concept of an agenda or plan for every meeting that over the door of each meeting room in the company hung a sign that read, "If you do not have an agenda for this meeting, turn around and go back to your desk.")

  This insistence on an agenda is not born of a need to control. Rather, it is a desire to ensure that:

  - The people entering the room are the right people for the meeting.
  - The meeting organizer hasn't failed to invite other important attendees.
  - Attendees aren't going to spend the majority of their time groping for what they should be doing and how they should be doing it.

- **"What's the purpose of this meeting?"**—This is my classic haunting refrain any time someone even sits down at my desk to talk to me, not to mention if they call me into a one- or two-hour meeting. If they haven't told me in advance the specific goal for our meeting, even in as informal a setting as one-on-one at my desk, I ask them, "What is the purpose of this meeting?" This ensures that whoever is leading the meeting has taken the time to consider why they have invited everyone. If they haven't resolved that, I don't want to be there. It also ensures that the other attendees and I agree that we are in the right meeting and that we can be contributory...no small beans.

- **"Can we maintain a Parking Lot? I'd like to stay on course with our purpose, and this could help."**—Very often, meeting leaders don't even really know that they are holding or leading a meeting. So they may not understand that it is their job to provide tools to support and guide the meeting. Moreover, some meeting leaders believe that unbridled communication is the only way to "get to the truth" that will cause a useful decision to emerge. Without some gentle guerilla facilitation, such meetings tend to move from one tangent to another before returning to the main topic, if at all.

- **"I'm not sure I agree that this topic should be put in the Parking Lot; can we find out any other opinions on that?"**—This tactic is coupled with the one suggesting the use of a Parking Lot. A facilitator or meeting leader should *never* be the lone person who decides what goes into a Parking Lot, so applying this tactic is critical for proper implementation of the Parking Lot. As the guerilla of collaboration, you'll need to help the meeting leader as well as the team understand that only the team has the authority to place any item there.

- **"Is this discussion still around the purpose of the meeting?"**—This is a great way to help the meeting leader and attendees check in with how they are using their time. Even when you are not in charge of the meeting, you can help them know that you are specifically attending the meeting for the specified end. Don't be too dogmatic in this, however; sometimes the group has implicitly altered the purpose for which it has come together. Your question can simply help the group explicitly evaluate its course and make a team decision to alter the purpose.

- **"Can we track what we need to be doing after the meeting?"**—This is your request to the group and meeting leader for an Action Item list to help attendees really know what they are signing up for when they make commitments or decisions in the meeting. Nudging a team from the side to track the meeting actions and decisions will help the team grow to appreciate its meetings over time.

- **"I see commonality in both these views. Is there some way we can combine these thoughts?"**—The guerilla collaborator actually watches how the team is interacting and helps conflicting members step out of conflict and consider what their viewpoints have in common. As you become better and better at this as a meeting participant, you'll learn to be more and more open to other viewpoints as a means to augment your own suggestion, opinion, or stance. This is true collaboration: working through constructive divergence to collaborative convergence on the best decision of the team, believing that the group wisdom is always better than any one individual's wisdom.

My Anecdote

This happened to me recently in a design meeting about a conceptual class model proposed by the lead data architect. The architect was looking for suggestions to help solve some of the potential pitfalls of the relationships and classes he had modeled. We had a second person present an alternative model, a bit more complex than the proposed model but definitely solving one of the major concerns of the model. We then had a third person present a dramatically different alternative, stressing the need for a far more simplistic view of the objects and a sense of data transformation. A fourth person jumped in to argue against the second view and the third view (he had been one of the visionaries of the initial model).

I wasn't the meeting facilitator, but I saw the complexity mounting and no goal in sight. Plus, it was just getting confusing to follow who was advocating what; the topics kept flipping and the focus kept moving. I asked if we could start tracking the various pros and cons of each model on a flipchart. After 10 minutes of back and forth discussion about all three models, mainly stressing the cons of each model, we then were able to take a step back and recognize the pros that could lead us to yet another alternative. Specifically, that:

- The second model truly solved a *major* design problem in the first model.

- The third model presented a higher-level, even more conceptual view of the second model that gave the second model strength and flow without all the detail.

- A fourth suggestion, layered on the second and third models, strengthened the flow and intent even more while maintaining the underlying complexity necessary to implement the model.

Soon, we moved out of disagreement into all the ways that the models actually worked well with one another to solve the design problem first presented. We had accomplished true collaborative success: The team's solution was better than any one of the individual solutions.

- **"Could we do a time check? I'm worried that we are running out of time."**—When you say this, you are helping the meeting organizer and the other attendees pay attention to how they are using the time (are they being productive, are they working toward the purpose, have they moved into inertia, have they met any of their goals?).

Other Guerilla Collaborator Considerations

In general, the guerilla collaborator can use her own behavior in a collaborative way to set a tone for other participants. When you keep your emotions in check, as you have learned as a facilitator, you become a more valuable participant. And you allow others to keep their emotions steady as well.

Use questions to seek clarification. Engage in dialogue versus argument to encourage information. Seek out the opinions of others in the meeting, particularly those people who may not be participating because of having lost a sense of being heard and understood. Pay attention to the mood in the room and the mood of individuals as well as your reaction to them. And turn to your sense of the strength of collaborative participatory decision making in each of your interactions.

In short, be a collaborator who encourages collaboration through example.

Chapter 20

Closing the Collaborative Meeting

Just as a servant leader guides a team in participatory decision making throughout the meeting, so must the leader guide the team in collaboratively Closing the meeting. The Closing plays a remarkably key role in how a collaborative meeting's work and decisions weave back into the work of the group. It sews together all the pieces of convergence and divergence accumulated during the meeting to create a sturdy fabric of consensus and action. Therefore, it is worth your time to become an adept meeting closer. Some simple steps outlined here will be your guide.

Take the Time to Close

A sure sign of a poorly planned, poorly managed meeting is the two minute close: You've run out of time and the team is ready to go, so with two minutes remaining, you simply thank everyone for attending and you end the meeting. The team and you have no time at the end to really absorb the full impact of the meeting before disbanding.

So first things first: Always leave yourself enough time to close the meeting appropriately. A simple approach for planning the length of the Closing is to assume that 10% of the total meeting time should be devoted to the close. A four-hour meeting should reserve 15 to 30 minutes just for the Closing. The less gelled the team is, the more time you should reserve. Although 10% may seem like a rather long Closing, you'll soon learn that your most effective meetings are those that hold that 10% slot sacred. You'll find that through a well-timed Closing, you are able to build that all-important bridge from the meeting back to each person's desk.

Secondly, use the Organizing Tools that helped you run the meeting to help you now close the meeting effectively. In particular, use the Parking Lot and Action Items throughout the Closing to ensure that you stick to what emerges out of the information you accumulate as you end the meeting.

So, now that you have given the team and yourself adequate time to pause and reflect upon the meeting, this is what you want to accomplish in that time:

1. Review the Purpose and Agenda.
2. Celebrate the work.
3. Review the Personal Objectives.
4. Clear the Parking Lot.
5. Complete the Action Plan.
6. Complete the Communications Plan.
7. Reflect on the meeting.

Review the Purpose and Agenda

Closing the meeting begins with explicitly bringing the team full circle through its purpose for meeting. To accomplish this, you ask the team to ask itself "Have we met the posted Purpose of this meeting?" Create evidence around the answer to this question by reviewing the posted Agenda item-by-item with the team. Remind them of the work they accomplished and the outputs or decisions that they created as a result of that work. To do this effectively, follow these steps:

1. Walk through each posted Agenda item one-by-one.
2. Reflect on how the team answered each question, what decisions were made, and what new information emerged.
3. Ask for a consensus check on whether the team believes they have met the posted Purpose of the meeting.
4. If anyone does not believe the posted Purpose has been met, capture their concern as an item for the Parking Lot; the team will need to figure out what to do with this item before adjourning the meeting.

Note: In each step of Closing the meeting, you will continue to check the team's consensus about the meeting: do you believe in the work of this agenda item; do you believe in the decisions made; do you believe in the purpose?

Celebrate the Work

"We've met our goal!" Teams plagued with a history of ill-defined, non-collaborative, long drawn-out meetings deserve a moment to pause, believe in themselves, and enjoy their accomplishments. Celebrating the difference between a non-collaborative, non-productive meeting and a collaborative, highly productive meeting allows the team time to absorb what it has done. With their work done, they can think about the impact their work will have on the project, the organization, or the company.

Take time to celebrate now so that the team can take this breath before going back into their work, before other work and distractions have a chance to diminish their sense of accomplishment.

Review the Personal Objectives

Even when the team agrees that the meeting has met the posted Purpose and Agenda, they still need to have a chance to reflect on their own purposes for attending. If you have collected and posted Personal Objectives at the start of the meeting, the Closing is when you should review them one-by-one with the team. You are closing the loop on your commitment to be a servant to the team in working collaboratively with them.

To answer the question, "Have we met your personal objectives for attending this meeting," use these steps with regard to the collected Personal Objectives:

1. Take each item in the posted Personal Objectives list one-by-one and read it aloud to the entire team.
2. Ask the team if it feels that the objective has been met (sometimes the specific individual that had the request may speak up here; other times, they may want to maintain anonymity about the objective).

---

3. If any objective has not been met, ask if it still needs to be met in order to meet the purpose of the meeting. If not, it can be discarded. Otherwise, place it in the Parking Lot to be discussed further once all the other objectives have been reviewed.

Never leave posted Personal Objectives unaccounted for at the end of the meeting.

Clear the Parking Lot

In reviewing the posted Purpose, Agenda, and Personal Objectives of the meeting, you may have accumulated items in the Parking Lot, indicators that there is some leftover business. Or, items may have been placed in the Parking Lot during the course of the meeting as a result of the team paying attention to its purpose and agenda. The Closing is the time to pay explicit attention to every item that has found its way into this space, no matter the reason. If you don't return to the Parking Lot at the end of a meeting, you lose credibility as a guardian of the team's decisions and the process that leads them to those decisions. So take the time to manage the Parking Lot with the team in the following fashion:

1. Read each item one-by-one from the posted Parking Lot items.
2. Find out from the team, "Have we addressed this item?" If so, you can discard it.
3. If not, ask the team, "Does this item still need to be addressed in order for this meeting to have met its purpose?"
4. If the answer is "Yes," you must address this item right now. Do not go any further with closing the meeting until you have asked the team what must be done in the meeting to address the item: further discussion, further clarification, a recommendation, a decision, an action item, etc.
5. If the item does not need to be addressed in the meeting, ask, "Does this need to be addressed after this meeting?"
6. If so, this becomes an item for the Action Plan (covered as the next step in Closing).
7. Otherwise, the item is no longer considered necessary for the meeting's success or for follow-up from the meeting; you have the team's permission to put it aside for them.

Complete the Action Plan

Either through the course of the meeting, or as a result of clearing the Parking Lot, you may have items in the Action Plan. These items indicate that work from the meeting has fed directly into the participants' work after the meeting, either as decisions that must be acted upon, or as work that has emerged as a result of new information revealed in the meeting.

To ensure that this work really occurs, each item in the Action Plan must have a description, an owner, and a due date. The owner of any item *must* be in the meeting to accept ownership of it; an owner cannot be named who is not present to accept ownership. If no one in the meeting can take ownership of the item, it is considered non-actionable and is dropped from the list. Similarly, if an Action Item cannot have a due date set, it is not truly an action that can be tracked. Either ask for a recommendation on how to restate the action so that it can be expressed with a due date, or drop the item from the list.

Any item that cannot be assigned to an owner or cannot be given a due date is dropped by the group as an action.

To document the actions in the list, ask these three questions of each:

- "What needs to be done to complete this item?"
- "Who is prepared to own the completion of this item?"
- "When does this item need to be completed?"

Once the Action Plan is completed, the team should come up with a plan for how to follow up. Either someone is appointed to track items daily, or each owner reports back to the entire team daily. Make sure this is decided before you move on to the next step in closing the meeting.

Complete the Communications Plan

Very often, teams make decisions about project or organizational strategies that may impact people not attending the meeting. As servants to their organizations, teams have a duty to communicate their work in a useful and timely manner. As stated in Chapter 9, "The Organizing Tools," the Communications Plan guides a team in doing just that; it guides a group to make decisions and actions about what must be communicated, how, and to whom. For very informal communications, the team may agree that a quick conversation or email may suffice. A wiki entry may also be needed. Or, a detailed announcement about the agreed-upon design, architecture, or plan may be in order.

To help a team create or review its Communications Plan, ask these questions:

- "Who needs to know what we have done here?"
- "What form should the communication take to tell them?"
- "Who will be responsible for completing the communication?"
- "When does this need to be completed?"
- Other(s)

Reflect on the Meeting

Although you can hold an entire meeting known as a Retrospective, each meeting you hold that has led a team through work, decisions, and consensus should have its own mini-reflection or retrospective. To finish the Closing of a meeting, ask the participants to take a moment to reflect with you about their meeting and all that they did throughout the meeting.

Ask the team to provide you information about "What Worked Well" for them with regard to how the meeting was run. Collect these items on a flipchart. Then ask them to provide you guidance on "What We Would Change" and collect these items on a flipchart as well. In this way, you ask for their help in improving your role as a their process owner and servant leader.

Finally, once the team reflection is done, create your own reflection about the meeting. Offer thanks to the participants for their work and their accomplishments. Provide them with positive guidance about their ability to collaborate: what you saw that worked well, what you experienced in witnessing their convergence on decisions, and what you observed in their ability to perform constructively with their conflicts and resolutions.

You can now call for an end to the meeting.

After the Meeting—A Bridge to Each Desk

Closing the meeting doesn't end your work for the team. To sustain the collaboration, you have to build the bridge from the meeting back to each participant's desk. The Action Plan is one way that the bridge is built. It carries decisions and teamwork out of the meeting into the workplace as a traceable flow of tasks, deliverables, follow-on meetings, or conversations. Your job as the team's servant is to ensure that this flow really occurs. An Agile Project Manager, ScrumMaster, or XP Coach wears the mantle of ensuring that the work of a meeting doesn't end when the meeting is over. Rather, the work of the team continues to flow as a result of the meeting.

To do this, you take on a pledge of documentation and follow-up.

Documentation

Highly collaborative meetings create lots of materials as evidence of the work and decisions formulated by the team. You need to ensure that this documentation is appropriately documented and distributed. Make sure that this task is assigned to one of the meeting participants as an item for the Action Plan. Or, make a commitment yourself as the owner of the documentation to deliver the information by a specific due date. Have the team guide you in the most appropriate form to document their work. Additionally, seek recommendations about exactly which work they want to capture (they may not be interested in the "Personal Objectives" they listed but may want to see all the "Concerns" they had accumulated around the schedule).

Make all these decisions and commitments before you end the meeting.

Follow-up

Before the team leaves the meeting, someone will have made a commitment to own the Action Plan. Make your own commitment to follow up with this person (if it is not you) to see how the meeting's work is progressing. If you have taken the commitment to manage the follow-up to the Action Plan, report back to the team on a regular basis about the current state of each item. Additionally, for any recurring meetings, bring a status report back to any subsequent meetings about any Action Plan from the previous meeting. In short, make the Action Plan follow-up one of the first articles of clothing you put on each morning before you head to work!

Extending Collaboration

Section II, "Applying Collaboration," offered a cookbook of practices for the meetings that buoy software teams as they navigate the many decision points in a project. This collaboration guidance purposefully targeted leaders of co-located medium to large teams on a path through divergence to convergence based on creating a context for building sustainable decisions. Still, collaborative techniques need to benefit us in other project contexts as well: the very nascence of a team with a small group of visionaries, one-on-one team discussions, and larger, distributed teams.

Extending collaboration involves expanding both the contexts (when, where, and for whom) for collaboration as well as the practices (what and how) for these contexts. This section suggests variations for applying the prescribed collaboration practices in small contexts, in distributed contexts, and in organizational initiatives. Finally, it provides suggestions on how to extend your own collaboration skills to move from being an apprentice of specific practices to a master of principles and approaches.

Chapter 21

Collaboration Practices
for Small Teams

Peering into the breadth and detail of practices captured in Section II, you may question the validity of this guidance when engaged in small team collaboration: two, three, or four people coming together to make decisions about their work in the project. The formality or ceremony of the techniques may ebb and flow, but shifting your perspective from the weight of the prescription to the discipline of the approach can reveal useful techniques worth absorbing.

Planning for Two

Pregnant women talk about "eating for two" when they seek to satisfy cravings and vitamin intake. When you want to act collaboratively in one-on-one, face-to-face communication, you can think about "planning for two." To ensure that you and your colleague act and decide collaboratively, follow the fundamentals from the team-level meetings:

- Make sure you both agree that you have something to talk about.
- State your purpose explicitly at the start so that you agree on the intent of your talk.
- Set a time limit to the discussion and find out if either of you has a specific need to end earlier than originally planned.
- Take Action Items seriously and follow up on them with one another.

My Anecdote

I am notorious for how I tend to start a conversation with my colleagues at work, particularly if they come to talk with me at my desk. After "Hey!," the first thing out of my mouth is "What is the purpose of our meeting?" At one company where I had just started, I wanted to bring this practice with me, trying not to be too obnoxious, but fairly explicit nonetheless. By the end of the first week, it had already become a team joke that if anyone wanted to talk to me, they better first be ready with an answer to my question. Before I could even say "Hello," my colleagues would say "I know, I know, 'What is the purpose of this meeting?!'" Although it was initially a joke, they later admitted that it had become a useful tool in managing their time and work, particularly in the large open area in which we all sat. (And by the way, sometimes the purpose of the talk was clearly to have no purpose. And that was okay!)

Ready to Rumble

I find that people can get sloppy about acting collaboratively when they are engaged in one-on-one discourse. Discussions may wander, one person may tend to dominate, one person may feel personally attacked, neither may pay attention to the decisions that are being made, and no one may be tracking any actions that, as a result, should be taken. Collaboration requires discipline even in these one-on-one contexts. If you have a need to work together, and you have stated your purpose explicitly toward that end, you owe each other the privilege of meeting that purpose and enjoying the sense of accomplishment through collaboration.

Keep each other focused. Technical discussions can quickly wander into non-productive conjecture, even with just two or three people engaged. As one colleague would admonish, "That may be more interesting than useful." Check in with one another about the interesting versus useful ratio in your discussion. If you see the focus shift, call this out explicitly, just as we do in large meetings. Ask, "Is the discussion we are having helping us meet the purpose of our meeting?" If not, guide each other back to the last discussion point that was still on target. Or, agree together that the new focus is more important and move on.

Track your decisions. If your one-on-one work doesn't lead to decisions or actions, you may not be meeting for the appropriate purpose. Or, you may be wasting your time. For problem-solving, work-focused conversations, pay attention to what you produce.

Even one-on-one, consider the advice Mary and Tom Poppendieck offer in *Lean Software Development* about how to apply the tenets of "Lean Thinking": "Eliminate waste."[1]

Maintain your sense of collaboration, even in conversation. Diana Larsen's advice in Chapter 9 about organizing tools for large planning meetings and retrospectives is just as valuable in two-person or three-person interactions:[2]

Focus On	Don't Focus On
Inquiry	Advocacy
Discussion	Debate
Convergence	Argument
Understanding	Defending

Encourage your own brainstorming. Part of maintaining discussion versus debate is the ability to keep each other from narrowing the discussion before having expanded the possibilities. You can keep discussion and possibilities alive and yet bounded to the purpose if you direct your thinking through brainstorming questions: "Let's think about that," "What are some of your ideas around that?," "What have you observed in the past?", and "What are your possible recommendations?"

Use the "Fist of Five" terminology (described in Chapter 6)—establishing that you are both able to "live with and support" a possible solution in a problem-solving discussion is some of the most powerful work a dyad or triad can do in a small one-on-one meeting. Being able to "throw down a *three!*" on a topic has an amazingly powerful impact on a team of two people working to resolve a situation. Using small but powerful consensus statements explicitly clarifies where each of you is in your discussion.

Figure out if others need to be engaged for expert input and call another meeting at that point. Teams, even small ones, that are eager to come to an action or decision that they can "live with and support" are ready to call in experts as useful (not just interesting!) to further enlighten their decision. In one-on-one discourse, be sure to watch for implicit invitations for outside input. Manage the addition of someone new into your discussion just as you manage new participants in a meeting: review the purpose of the meeting and

1. Poppendieck and Poppendieck, *Lean Software Development*, 1.

2. Diana Larsen, Retrospectives Gathering, February 2005.

the purpose of their contribution. Keep all your other practices on track with the new participant as well.

My Anecdote

As goofy as it seems, the "Fist of Five" has appeal even in two-person discussions. I use it at work to quickly check where we are on a topic. If I am going down a line of thinking that is completely counter to the goal of the discussion or the intent of the decision, I will no doubt see my counterpart hold up an index finger or two fingers to stop me in my tracks. Or, I can tell a colleague without a lot of negative baggage, "Sorry, that is a two for me. Can we talk about it?" We both back up and look at where we last were on track with our thinking and then move into joint brainstorming from that point to figure out how to converge on a "live with and support" solution, a solid three, four, or five. "Fast Fives" have proven to be just the jolt I needed to reenergize me on a challenging, problem-soaked day. Gradually moving to a three in a difficult situation is even better.

Make It So

A two- or three-person discussion that leads to a decision about the project or about the project team must be explicitly called out as such. To make a decision stick, declare the next steps and actions that naturally instantiate the decision. For such a small group of people, it may be enough to simply state these openly to one another and commit to one another what your actions will be as a result.

For collaborative decisions that go beyond a two-person commitment, consider explicitly capturing your personal Action Plan, wherein each of you captures your committed tasks and committed due dates. This helps you both to be clear with one another about your commitment and can also help others know the results of your discussion.

Figure out who needs to know what decisions were made based on your meeting. Sometimes your one-on-one discussions move into territory that is important and useful for others. Check in with one another about whom should be alerted to your decisions and actions. Then decide how this information will be disseminated: the project wiki, a wall chart, the online process tool, a voicemail, an email, a separate meeting, or the like.

Follow-up

As in any collaborative commitment for action, you should check in with one another with regard to your status. A mini-"Stand up" meeting serves the purpose. Whoever was involved in commitment to the decision or actions should be involved. Find out what each other has done, what is left to do, and what is getting in your way. A daily one-on-one check-in can be the simplest thing that works. Do that.

My Anecdote

In one team I worked with, we had a major deliverable due, a final analysis of user survey results regarding the system. We had to accumulate information from five different interviewers who had each interviewed up to ten people. The week that the results were due, we resolved to meet twice a day to review our progress and commitments. On the last day of the week, we had broken into pairs for completing the work. Each pair resolved to meet every hour for a quick check-in. One-on-one, we figured out what was left to do, how to do it, and what our goal would be for the next check-in. We tracked our collaboration and decisions with as little formality as possible but with an eye on both the individual commitments as well as the group commitments. For us, that meant tracking the group progress in a large Burndown Chart based on the pair reports and then posting the next check-in time. In this way, even in a small group, we made sure that we stayed focused, completed our commitments, and followed up on those commitments.

Chapter 22

Collaboration Practices for Distributed Teams

In the global marketplace of our teams and our customers, projects often have to extend collaboration into communications beyond the preferred face-to-face mode. These collaboration challenges include the following:

- Multi-site (few locales with many people at each)
- Distributed (many locales with few people at each)
- Offshore (extreme distances between roles, such as customers versus developers)

In these contexts, teams find that they can't take advantage of what Alistair Cockburn refers to as osmotic communication, the variety of sensory modalities (visual, audio, touch, sense, etc.) that provide a rich set of collaboration clues.[1] Out of visual and audio contact, teams default to a lowest common denominator of communication: paper documentation. At fault is the reliance on capturing only the explicit knowledge of the team, the data-driven details of the work. Distributed teams lose the broad flow of what Nonaka and Takeuchi describe as the tacit knowledge of the team;[2] that is, the team information that creates community and vision around the work of the team through its "sense" of what the project is about, what the team is about, and the "theory" of the solution that holds it all together.

Without face-to-face, day-to-day communication, the raging flow of tacit team information that co-located teams enjoy dwindles to a slow drip for distributed teams. Their

---

1. Cockburn, *Agile Software Development*, 81.

2. Nonaka and Takeuchi, *The Knowledge-Creating Company*, 8.

reliance on non-interactive, archival media (such as spreadsheets, documents, and models) as the team's primary communication conduit handicaps the team's ability to converge on its tacit knowledge. Distributed teams, not properly nourished with respect to their contact and tacit knowledge exchange, are deeply challenged in how they ever move through Forming and Storming into truly Performing collaborative teams.

Extending collaboration to distributed teams necessitates actions that amplify the other communication modes beyond the purely written mode. It requires a commitment to engage a rich set of tools to create, as much as possible, a virtual space for the growth of the group's tacit knowledge and trust in a team of convergent, participatory, high-performing colleagues.

Guiding Practices for Distributed Teams

Maintain a Metaphor

Extreme Programming explicitly calls out the use of a metaphor to enrich a team's sense of its work. The metaphor grabs the team imagination and applies a creative hold on the team's tacit knowledge. For that reason, metaphor is a powerful glue to apply to distributed teams: "We are a hometown newspaper" for an RSS web content manager. "We are an incubator for premature newborns" for an internal auditing system. "We are the Great Wall of China" for a security system. "We are an expedition team on K2 in the Himalayas" for project management software. These metaphors create a framework of communication, a vocabulary that can span geographies and cultures.

Applying the right metaphor in any of the non co-located team types (offshore, multi-site, distributed) creates a safety net around the communication of the detailed explicit knowledge of the project.

Apply Frequent Communications

Because distributed teams must rely on a far narrower communication pipe for collaboration than co-located teams, they must aggressively broaden their communication instances in order to exchange the same amount of information. I've watched organizations assume that increased communication means more documentation. But that is only a thin slice of the communication pipe, and a poor one at that. Increased communication can take on a number of other rich forms:

- More stand-up meetings (two a day versus one a day) when teams span more than four time zones.
- More one-on-one communications, where each team member is designated as a shadow or pair with one other member of the distributed team in order to act as a surrogate and "companion" for each other.
- More exchange of team roles, where there is a traveling customer role as well as a traveling developer and a traveling tester that is traded off among team members across the project sites.
- More retrospectives to gather feedback around what are the useful repeatable collaboration practices versus what continue to be the collaboration challenges.

One caveat about increased communication: Avoid a reliance on email, pagers, BlackBerries, and documents alone. When unsupported by other forms of communication that fill out the color, texture, and subtlety of our interactions, these tersely text-driven forms of communication create distance and distraction, both of which can actually deteriorate the collaboration of the team instead of bolstering it. Avoid an addiction to the quick sugar rush of a BlackBerry and apply liberal doses of real collaboration protein.

Intensify Facilitation

Recognize that distributed teams have a far greater challenge to move out of Forming and to navigate Storming. As a result, conflict will be the norm rather than the exception. Collaboration approaches for non-co-located teams must therefore concentrate on the Forming practices:

- Stay actively engaged as a facilitator.
- Ask frequent questions to spark discussion and consensus.
- Actively seek out opportunities to serve; don't wait for someone to ask for your service.
- Ask more questions.
- In all your audio-intense communications such as telephone calls and conference calls, repeat the responses *often*.

- Work to keep everyone engaged as much as possible in collaborating—frequent feedback and repetition of information, advance materials, surveys, detailed follow-up, and retrospectives.

Conference Call Collaboration Practices

Applying collaboration techniques to meetings conducted as conference calls isn't so much about learning a new set of tools. Rather, it is about embracing the collaboration fundamentals with greater rigor and intensity, turning it up a notch, "going to 11." Because conference calls bring out more dysfunction and breed conflict more easily than the face-to-face meetings we use for collaboration, the advice offered here emphasizes those practices that specifically address these threats.

Keep On Track—No Fuzzy Agendas

A conference call must have a specific purpose, and its agenda must specifically support that purpose. Though we talk about this in general for effective collaboration, it is all the more important for conference calls. Without visual cues for tracking how participants are staying engaged in the meeting flow, your agenda becomes your strongest guide in maintaining their participation. Publish the purpose. Publish the agenda. Start the meeting by reviewing them carefully and getting group's consensus that both are correct.

Conference calls are attention zappers. If you allow a conference call to wander off the Agenda, you run the risk of losing the trust and attention of the callers: The topic may not be of interest to the entire call, it may be controversial to some callers, or it may be completely counter to the Purpose of the call. Because you won't be able to detect any of this by looking around the room, participant dysfunctions can arise without your being aware of them. Maintain your meeting focus and the focus of the participants by keeping on track with the Agenda.

Keep a Time Limit—One Hour

Conference calls are exhausting by their nature in that they provide so little information and stimulation to keep participants engaged. Respect the burden this communication places on your participants and limit the call's duration to one hour. If the work requires more than one hour, create a break of at least 10 minutes per hour. The break creates breathing space and explicitly acknowledges the need to break away from the phone leash for sanity's sake.

Keep Track of Who Is Out There—Maintain a Seating Chart

Track who has called in by creating a seating chart such as a U-shaped conference set-up. Assign each person a seat in the chart. Tell them where they are sitting and the order around the chart so that they have a mental model about how they are virtually sitting with one another. Use the chart for managing feedback and check-ins.

To further create the sense of a room full of participants, keep pictures of each of the team's members for all virtual meetings. Send them out to each of the participants and encourage them to create their own seating chart with the pictures of each person on their place in the chart.

Finally, ask participants to provide their name each time that they respond with a comment, question, or feedback. This helps all participants keep track of who is speaking.

Keep the Decisions Flowing—No Soliloquies

Have as much information distributed in advance as possible. This includes the expert input that you might normally have presented in person for a face-to-face meeting. Reserve the time in the conference call for the work of creating decisions and actions.

Distribute the Agenda early enough to alert attendees to the purpose of the call, the flow of the call, and its time limits. Encourage early feedback about additional concerns and topics rather than discover incongruities during the call.

Send out the list of participants early. Because participants can't look around the room to see who is participating, they can do a virtual room scan by keeping an attendee list with them during the call.

Keep the Answers Coming—Engage Participants with Information Processing

Because you can't build trust among your participants with your eye contact, you must do it through your adherence to protocols, processes, and effective listening skills.

Help conference call participants stay engaged by polling them frequently for feedback. For conference calls with fewer than 20 participants, use the Round Robin approach to:

- Check who is still on the line.
- Conduct a brainstorm on a topic.
- Gather input for a listing exercise.
- Generate priorities around items.
- Conduct a consensus check.

Remember that in conducting a Round Robin, you always announce the purpose of the exercise, what responses you are looking for ("Yes," "No," or "Pass"), and explain the order in which you will call on people and who the first three people will be. Once all participants have provided their feedback, review the collected responses and ask one last time if there are any other contributions.

For larger conference calls, use an asynchronous polling option through a web conference utility that can collect feedback for you without having to ask each participant individually. Also consider having the results of the feedback available for viewing through an interactive tool. Applying visual cues to the audio will help participants stay engaged and focused.

Keep It Fair—Maintain Balanced Phone Control

Pay attention to the problems that phone technology introduces as a result of speakerphones, multiple phone lines, and phones in noisy settings. Table 22.1 lists some scenarios that can occur with conference calls and phone technology, the problems they can breed, and some facilitative solutions you can apply to avoid the problems:

Table 22.1 Conference Call Problems and Solutions

Scenario	Potential Problem	Solution
A large group of people in one location has set up a speakerphone to allow individuals in one or more other sites to "dial in" to their meeting.	The individuals who dialed in become easily forgotten by the group that is gathered together with the speakerphone; they end up being observers and missing out on much of the meeting.	Appoint a person in the large group to be the guardian of the participants who are dialed in. That person tends the phone and ensures that their questions are heard and that their input is gathered during the Round Robin exercises.
Everyone is dialing from different locations, and there is no facilitator managing the call.	One individual can end up dominating the call because the speakerphone technology makes it hard to break in on someone who has the speaker engaged.	Make sure all phones are on full duplex so that a speaker can always hear someone else trying to break in. As much as possible, act aggressively as a facilitator and use Round Robin as much as possible to manage feedback.
Participants are dialing in but not putting their phones on mute.	A lot of background noise (the "dialing in from home" participant's dog barking, a meeting in the next cubicle becoming loud) can make it hard for other participants to hear the meeting and can take over the speakerphone.	Have all participants "mute" their phones until they have a question or until they are responding in a Round Robin. Or, conduct the conference call in "listen only" mode until you are ready to seek feedback from individuals.
A participant is dialed in from a multi-line office phone.	The participant's other line rings, and when they decide to answer the other line, their "hold" music for their phone ends up dominating the call.	Create Ground Rules for the call about phone etiquette: Keep all phones on mute unless you are providing feedback; do not put the call on hold to take another call.

Continues

Table 22.1   Conference Call Problems and Solutions (*Continued*)

Scenario	Potential Problem	Solution
Participants tend to dial in up to ten minutes late.	The start of the meeting keeps being disrupted by new callers entering the line, announcing themselves, and then recapping the current list of participants and what has been covered so far. The meeting doesn't really start until 10 or 15 minutes into the call.	Encourage participants to dial into the call five to ten minutes in advance of the start time. Also let them know that there will be a cutoff time for entering into the meeting three minutes after the start of the meeting. Each minute for the three minutes prior to the start time, announce that the meeting will be starting in X number of minutes. Once you have started the meeting, put a block on any further incoming calls after three minutes.

Keep It Facilitated—Don't Take Control of the Decisions

As the chairperson or owner of a conference call, you control all the participation and flow of the call. Stay clear with yourself and with the participants about your role as their process owner and their guide for making decisions and taking actions. Avoid the temptation to take advantage of your control of the call, or just as in a face-to-face meeting, you will lose the trust of the other participants. One way to maintain objectivity and focus is to engage in a lot of reflective listening. Repeat responses from others and invite feedback on the responses.

Keep It Documented—Send Feedback as Soon as Possible

In a co-located meeting, flipcharts, projected laptop displays, and other information radiators provide feedback to participants as they make decisions and plan actions. Because conference calls lack these signals of progress and intent, you need to provide the written documentation of the call as soon as possible after the call.

Additionally, as part of how you document the call, always ask for feedback about the call before you end it. In a face-to-face meeting, you can detect issues while looking around the room; in a call, you have to request it specifically. So although this is recommended for all meetings, it is all the more important for conference call meetings. Be sure to ask: "What worked well? What could be changed for the next call? Any other issues or concerns?"

Real-Time Interactive Technologies for Collaboration

To broaden the communications pipe across distributed teams, build in as many supporting technologies as you can to adjust for the lack of face-to-face communication. Remember that the goal is to make up for non co-located meetings, not replace them. Turn to the team for its preferences and advice about which tools to use for their distributed collaboration.

As a team, select and standardize on a variety of the visually and aurally rich media as well as real-time communications tools versus asynchronous tools. In selecting technologies, consider the following:

- Frequency of collaboration (immediate problem resolution, daily team status, monthly project retrospection)
- Audience (one-on-one, group-wide)
- Purpose of the collaboration (expert input, prioritization of iteration stories, management of task status)
- Formality (casual feedback, project metrics, weekly team review)

Beyond conference calls, consider using these other forms of interactive communication and interactive documentation for team collaboration.

Web-Based Meeting Managers

As with conference calls, web-based conferencing tools need guidelines to promote their use as collaboration tools:

- Send out instructions, guidelines, and Ground Rules in advance.
- Test your setup at least 30 minutes prior to the start to make sure it is functioning properly. Have a backup plan if the service or host is not available: an email alert, conference call, or alternate service, for example.
- Encourage participants to set up their software and phone interactions five to ten minutes prior to the start of the meeting.
- Block out latecomers.
- Consider limiting the number of attendees.
- Decide how to manage comments and questions (live or chat) prior to the start of the conference, and include this guidance in the instructions you send out in advance.
- Decide in advance how to turn over control of the conference should someone need to provide expert input.
- Provide as much advance material as possible to keep the meeting flowing and interactive.
- Stay in a facilitative role; ask for frequent feedback and track information and decisions in the materials broadcast in the meeting.

Video Conferencing

Prepare, prepare, prepare. Technologies are improving, but video conferencing is still distracting. Follow the advice for conference calls and for hosted meeting etiquette. And be sure to run a test of the technologies prior to the start of the meeting to ensure that all sites are communicating properly.

Instant Messaging and Chat

Instant Messaging or "IM" promotes quick turnaround to questions or comments for one-on-one communications. As with any of the other technologies, make sure that it is broadening team collaboration, not collapsing it. Use IM when no broader means of communication (face-to-face whiteboard discussion, phone call, hosted meeting) is available.

Interactive Whiteboards

Visually rich, these applications pull distributed participants together to collaborate in the whiteboard style of brainstorming and information sharing. The interaction goes beyond a keyboard conversation or a phone conversation into the creative world of the whiteboard.

Presence-Based Applications

These applications, built on and extending the IM capabilities, manage the "currently online" status of participants to create a virtual office environment for sharing information. They can be project-based or organization-based and usually offer document and file management as well as a rudimentary project plan integration capability.

Survey Applications

Polling the team and maintaining team feedback through surveys can be a real-time or non-real-time collaboration tool. Participants can provide guiding feedback to each other about team norms, team commitments, daily project flow, release retrospectives, and project retrospectives.

Use surveys as a means to collect group feedback prior to a virtual retrospective for distributed teams. Using a hosted application will allow the teams to view their results online independent of the retrospective conference call or virtual meeting.

Non-Interactive Tools for Collaboration

Because distributed teams very often cannot rely on interactive information exchange, the non-interactive collaboration tools must be woven into the fabric of the team's communication style. As with interactive tools, have the team select the set of tools that will best suit the team members' style of collaboration with any of these applications.

Conversation Management Applications

Tools such as wikis and team intranets manage team-specific, non-interactive conversations and information. Use these tools to help teams collaborate on design discussions, process flow, schedules, team contact information, project meeting documentation, and free-form dialogues.

Process Management Applications

Typically hosted solutions, these applications are designed to specifically manage software development project team commitments and to incorporate real-time dashboard information across all project participants, beyond the technical staff alone. They in essence create virtual content-rich information radiators that maintain and broaden the collaboration information created in a planning meeting and then exchanged in a daily standup meeting.

Document Management Applications

The least collaborative of all the support applications for distributed teams, document management applications create virtual libraries for the project archive. They can manage experience reports, models, trouble logs, and other project documents, making them available for the entire project team whether co-located or distributed. Additionally, they can create relational information for the managed content.

Chapter 23

Collaboration for Organizations

Collaborative teams turn into collaborative organizations by broadening and nurturing collaboration practices beyond project boundaries. The collaborative organization builds in learning, mentoring, competence, and reflection around its collaboration expertise.

The Shu-Ha-Ri of Collaboration

Alistair Cockburn refers to the Shu-Ha-Ri model with regard to agile software development practices, communication, and learning.[1] You can think about this Aikido learning model as your guide for engendering collaboration expertise into your organization:

- **Shu**—*Following*: We understand the principles and are able to copy the practices very well.
- **Ha**—*Detaching*: We use the principles as guides and make alterations to practices that fit our circumstances.
- **Ri**—*Transcending* (a.k.a. Fluent): We just do what needs to be done for the desired effect without regard to whether we are following an exact practice or not.

Collaborative organizations foster the growth and maintenance of high-performing software teams by explicitly creating sustainable practices around participatory decision

---

1. Cockburn, *Agile Software Development*, 17.

making. You can think of expertise as the ability to move initial, highly prescriptive guidelines (Shu) for collaboration into the organization's "DNA" (Ri). Project managers, team leads, and team members no longer have to think about the explicit steps of brainstorming, prioritization, conflict resolution, or action planning; it is simply built into how they collaborate day-to-day.

I have a friend who studied fencing for several years, and he has described a similar organizational growth pattern. "Le Maître," the fencing instructor, takes on a group of students and guides them through fencing principles: physical balance, mental balance, position, timing, distance, and momentum. These principles and practices are then put into a very strict set of drills for footwork and strikes, either as a single drill or as a pair. Drill patterns are made more and more complex until the full variety of stances, strikes, and counterstrikes are simply ingrained for the student. At that point, they can fence without reference to Le Maître or to the drills. They have moved from Shu to Ha through to Ri.

Creating Organizational Shu-Ha-Ri for Collaboration

Organizations can provide "Le Maître" style mentors in collaboration by creating practices of "collaboration consultants." In one company in which I worked, we had a group referred to as "The Piranhas" whose job it was to spread the use of Extreme Programming (XP) throughout the IT organization. Although their specialty tended to be the engineering practices of XP and their ferocity about those practices (hence the name "Piranha"), they soon learned that they also had to be expert facilitators in bringing about highly collaborative, participatory decisions within the teams. The organization aggressively sought out individuals who could move from team to team as an objective facilitator to coach the teams through their initial Release Planning meetings and then through their subsequent Iteration Planning meetings. In this way, the organization created and sustained a group of individuals who were bred for high-powered, objective, facilitative guidance around the collaboration required for XP projects.

Working with the Piranhas and in other large organizations, I have seen the grace of Shu-Ha-Ri and also the guidance of Musashi, as provided by Alistair Cockburn in *Agile Software Development.*[2]

---

2. Cockburn, *Agile Software Development*, 254.

- "Do not develop an attachment to any one weapon or any one school of fighting"— Survey the canon of collaboration practices and find out what works for you.
- "Practice and observe reflectively"—Continue to build a toolkit of collaboration tools and techniques based on your own variations.
- "Win"—I call this the transcendence of decision making and decision enabling. An organization has "won" when its teams have become self-sufficient, high-performing, mighty forces fully enabled for participatory, collaborative decision making.

In applying the guidance set forth in this book, think about how to create an organizational DNA that pays attention to Musashi's advice. Use sufficiency as a guide and goal. Don't over-legislate what it takes to build collaboration in and across teams. And be extremely tolerant of variation in individual styles of collaboration for teams, for project managers, and for teams of teams.

Consider a model similar to the Piranhas. Create a practice within the Project Management Office around collaboration expertise. Or, define a career specialty in collaboration consultancy where individuals act as internal consultants to guide organization in defining and expanding their collaboration tools and techniques.

Facilitation Training and Certification

As an Agile Coach and Mentor, I consult in a variety of organizations, bringing my facilitation and collaboration style with me as a natural part of my consultancy. In many of these engagements, I end up also becoming a counselor about the specifics of collaboration and in particular the specifics outlined in this book about facilitating the meetings of collaboration. This has been particularly true in my role as an XP Coach and as a Certified Scrum Master.

Organizations ready to move into collaborative, servant leader-driven forms of decision making should seek out training in facilitation, either through public courses or through programs customized for their in-house training needs. Training can either target specific individuals (such as a group of collaboration consultants), or it can be organization-wide, wherein all members of the organization receive training about the ins and outs of acting collaboratively and facilitatively in their project teams.

Finally, you can consider building a certification around collaboration and facilitation, similar to the ScrumMaster certification. The International Association of Facilitators has a certification for professional facilitators. Or, you can craft a collaboration program specific to your organization that could include certification of general facilitation skills as well as specifics on your organization's project collaboration approach. An organizational certification should demonstrate a grasp of the collaboration fundamentals, as well as the completion of a mentoring program and set of experience reflections and retrospectives.

Measurement and Reflection (Surveys and Retrospectives)

No organizational initiative about collaboration would be complete without an explicit program for measurement of and reflection upon the success of the collaboration work. I have learned from talking with Esther Derby, Diana Larsen, Deborah Schratz, Gerhardt Ackermann, and other retrospection experts that retrospection at the organization level is the truest and most vital key to bringing collaboration into the organizational DNA.

Team successes can translate into a viral spread of collaboration as members move to new project teams. However, at the organizational level, these team learnings must be captured in survey, reflection, and retrospection that can then be tracked from team to team and from project to project. "How well do we listen? How well do we invite and respond to change? How collaborative are we in our decision making? Who is being left behind? And what can we embrace as change to bring about more high-performing teams?"

The retrospection fractal takes flight, emerging from the daily retrospection at the daily standup meeting, to the Iteration Retrospective, to the Release Retrospective, to the Project Retrospective, and finally to an organizational change management retrospective. All of these collaborative reflections host the growth of truly collaborative organizations to move them from just Forming-level sets of workgroups to High-Performing-level groups of teams.

Collaborative Facilitation Guides

Agile software development projects maintain a heartbeat of collaboration through their various meetings, from project inception to project retrospection. For this reason, the drumbeat I offer around the agile processes takes the form of agendas rather than project plans, document templates, or detailed role definitions.

This section takes you through a set of sample project meeting agendas that pull together all the guidance from Sections II and III. Along with the agendas for generic project meetings, more methodology-specific agendas are provided for Crystal Clear, Scrum, and XP and Industrial XP. These methodology-driven guides represent my particular style of defining agendas within these realms; they are not meant to be the definitive, solely sanctioned approach. As with any of the guidance around collaboration and facilitation, play with the details set forth in these agile software development contexts and discover what holds most useful and true for you and your teams. Ultimately, it comes down to what serves you best.

Agendas are presented for general project heartbeats as well as for some of the primary meetings associated with agile software development projects. Each agenda presents guidance on:

- Meeting purpose and outputs
- Meeting participants
- Agenda order and topics
- Process suggestions
- Other considerations (Comments)

These guides are purposefully detailed and so may look rigid or constricting. They are highly directive in order to define a very clear path to a very clear purpose. As such, they are the antidote to meetings with ill-defined purposes and little or no clear agenda. Additionally, the detail here is meant to obviate the need for details once captured in document templates and role descriptions. In that regard, they are minimal and open to interpretation.

For each agenda provided, you'll want to consider your own useful tweaks and variations: level of formality (minimal versus detailed documentation and preparation), timings for each agenda item, processes appropriate to your audience (a Forming team versus a High-Performing team), variations helpful to the context (small co-located groups versus large distributed groups), and your own collaboration style (processes and approaches you find the most useful and rewarding).

As a reminder, Section III holds the litany of "building blocks" for processes and tools that can be applied throughout these agenda types. Use this table as a quick reference to the chapters in Section III that hold those techniques and approaches:

Technique	Chapter
• Meeting startup	Chapter 10, "Starting the Collaborative Meeting"
• Organizing tools (Purpose, Agenda, Parking Lot, Action Plan, Decisions Board, Communication Plan, etc.)	Chapter 9, "The Organizing Tools"
• Brainstorming • Listing • Facilitator-led Callout • Post-it Notes • Round Robin • Pass the pen • Pass the card	Chapter 12, "Gathering the Information—Brainstorming and Listing"
• Grouping, Categorizing	Chapter 15, "Processing the Information"
• Prioritizing, Weighting • T-Shirt Sizing • Wideband Delphi Estimates	Chapter 15, "Processing the Information"

Technique	Chapter
• Velocity Estimates	Chapter 14, "Team Estimating Approaches"
• Individual and Dyad Work	Chapter 13, "Dialogues, Small Groups, and Expert Input Approaches"
• Small and Large Group Dialogue	Chapter 13, "Dialogues, Small Groups, and Expert Input Approaches"
• Expert Input • Timelining • Project Visioning • Giving an A	Chapter 13, "Dialogues, Small Groups, and Expert Input Approaches"
• Picture This	Chapter 16, "Visioning, Retrospection, and Other Approaches"
• Meeting closing	Chapter 20, "Closing the Collaborative Meeting"

Chapter 24

Generic Project Meetings

The guides in this chapter provide general guidance for conducting collaborative project events; they remain methodology-neutral but reflect some basic detailed steps for accomplishing each meeting's purpose collaboratively. They formulate some fundamental collaborative events within a project lifecycle:

- Status Meeting
- Strategic Action Planning
- Process Change Workshop
- Project Startup Meeting
- Project Retrospective

Typically, the Project Manager is responsible for calling the meeting, inviting the participants for the meeting, facilitating the meeting, and ensuring that all outputs of the meeting are appropriately distributed or posted.

Meeting Name:	**Status Meeting**
Meeting Purpose:	To determine the progress of the team's work and to note any actions necessary to help the team reach its goal
Meeting Outputs:	Actions for the next time period
Meeting Participants:	All members of the development team
Comments:	The Status Meeting should only collect status and create Action Items from the team. It is not a problem-solving meeting.
	If this is a daily meeting, use a timer to timebox all individual status reports as well as the length of the meeting. Always manage any problem solving by making it an Action Item for a later discussion. You may also consider maintaining a Parking Lot that can be reviewed at the end of the meeting to see if any actions should be formulated based on the parked topics.
	Standing up is a high motivator for completing status reporting quickly.

Agenda Item	
A. Opening	**Prompt Question:** n.a.
	Process: Meeting Startup
	Comments: Don't bother with Personal Objectives for such a short meeting. Just check in with everyone on the Purpose and remind them of the time limits.
	For teams that have been meeting daily, skip this formality entirely.
B. What is the status on the Action Items we gathered in the last status meeting?	**Prompt Question:** (Use the agenda question)
	Process: Facilitator-led Review
	Comments: Use the Action list from the previous meeting as the prompt for reports. Keep reports short. Make sure they don't go into problem solving or detailed solution description; that should occur in a separate or follow-on meeting as appropriate.

C. What work has been completed since the last status meeting?	**Prompt Question:** "Think back on the last status meeting we held on (date). We had a lot of work we accomplished since that time, as individuals and as a group. Now tell us, what work has been completed since the last status meeting?"
	Process: Round Robin
	Comments: Use the timer. Capture any problem solving as discussions/meetings that need to occur after the status meeting. Also capture who should be involved in the follow-on discussions/meetings.
	For a Daily Standup, skip the Prompt question and go straight to the Round Robin. Encourage participants to address one another, not you.
D. What are our next proposed actions?	**Prompt Question:** "Given what we have learned about what we have completed, we now need to think about what work still remains or has arisen as a result of the status. With this information in mind, what are our next proposed actions?"
	Process: Round Robin
	Comments: You can either perform this Round Robin independent of the previous Round Robin or have each person provide both responses at the same time.
E. What are any risks or concerns we have about our proposed actions?	**Prompt Question:** "Considering what we have completed and proposed, you may have information that could help manage our success. What are any risks or concerns we have about our proposed actions?"
	Process: Facilitator-led Brainstorming
	Comments. This is similar to the "What is getting in my way; what is distracting me?" question from the Daily Standup in Scrum. Here, the question invites broader group-wide inspection of risks or concerns.
F. What is our Action Plan?	**Prompt Question:** (No prompt question necessary)
	Process: Action Planning
	Comments: Keep this very quick and brief. But don't leave the meeting without owners of the actions that *must* take place in order for the new practices to be absorbed.

Continues

Agenda Item	
G. Close	**Prompt Question:** "Have we met our purpose today?"
	Process: n.a.
	Comments: For daily standups, a group hug is sufficient to close the meeting. : -)

Strategic Action Planning

Meeting Name:	**Strategic Action Planning**
Meeting Purpose:	To create a plan of proposed actions based on specific recommendations from a project, program, or product strategy
Meeting Outputs:	A list of actions with the owner of the action and the due date of the outcome of the action, with cost optionally listed
Meeting Participants:	All members of the team
Comments:	Conduct a strategic Action Planning session at the very start of defining a program, project, or product when you have formulated a high-level strategy or a list of recommendations to set the work in motion. This planning can either be from a previous strategy meeting or in the same meeting with the strategy formulation.
	This agenda guides you through the steps for completing the Action Plan and adds considerations not in the standard "Action Plan" organizing tool.

An Action Planning Workshop should produce one or more flipcharts with the following format:

Action Plan			
What	**When**	**Who**	**Cost**

Agenda Item	
A. Opening	**Prompt Question:** n.a.
	Process: Meeting Startup
	Comments: Once you have completed the meeting startup with Purpose, Agenda, Organizing Tools, etc., collect Personal Objectives.
	Be sure to go through the "What's In It For Me" and the Scope of Authority for the entire team.
B. What is the strategy we have set forth for this program/project/product?	**Prompt Question:** "Earlier, we completed a high-level strategy for our program/project in order to deliver the defined product. What is the strategy we have set forth?"
	Process: Expert Input
	Comments: Someone needs to represent the strategy or recommendations to the team. This may be the Executive Sponsor, the Program Manager, the Product Manager, or the Architect. They represent the high-level strategy that must be set into action.
C. What are all the actions that we need to undertake in order to support this strategy?	**Prompt Question:** "Given what we have just heard, think about all the work that we need to complete around that strategy. What are all the actions that we need to undertake in order to support this strategy?"
	Process: Brainstorming
	Comments: Do this work in dyads or in groups of three. It will generate more ideas that can be considered by the group at large when creating the actual plan.
	When the timebox is over, have each group report their results and discard any duplicates.
D. What is the high-level timeline for our strategy?	**Prompt Question:** "Based on the outline of the strategy, the dates that have been proposed, and the actions that you have just identified, what is the high-level timeline for our strategy?'"
	Process: Small Group Dialogue
	Comments: The team should be considering information revealed by the Expert Input, information already published about the strategy, and then the actions they have just accumulated.
	This should be a very high-level view of the strategy target timing: weeks, months, quarters, etc. The decision here will define the structure of the wall chart that will capture the action timeline in agenda item F.

Continues

Agenda Item	
E. What is the priority of the actions that we need to take?	**Prompt Question:** "Reviewing all these actions, think about what items must be completed, whether because of urgency, or because other actions rely on their completion. What is the priority of the actions that we need to take?"
	Process: Multi-voting
	Comments: Follow the rules of multi-voting once all the responses have been brought forward.
F. What is the order in which these priority actions should be started?	**Prompt Question:** "Some of these priorities have been set due to time dependencies or dependencies among the actions. Consider all these possible dependencies and then determine 'What is the order in which these priority actions should be started?'"
	Process: Silent Grouping
	Comments: Allow the team to rearrange the responses along the timeline in a silent grouping exercise.
	When the timebox is up, give them time to reflect on the actions and their placement in the timeline.
G. What is the due date of each of the actions that have been mapped on the timeline?	**Prompt Question:** "Each of our actions has been placed on the timeline in anticipation of the order in which each should be completed. Given this ordering and any other considerations, what is the due date of each of the actions that have been mapped on the timeline?"
	Process: Small Group Dialogue, Consensus Check
	Comments: Moving from the timeline to actual dates should only take place in this order. Get the timeline first, *then* allow and encourage the management of due dates.
	Be prepared to jump in to manage any negotiations around the final dates decided.
H. Who will be the owner for reporting on the completion of each action item on the timeline?	**Prompt Question:** "For each of our recommended actions, think about which ones for which you are willing to take responsibility to ensure it is implemented. Now, who will be the owners for reporting on the completion of each action item?"
	Process: Call-out
	Comments: Keep this short, but don't leave the meeting without owners of the actions that MUST take place in order for the strategy to be implemented.

Agenda Item	
I. What is the cost associated with each of the actions in the timeline?	**Prompt Question:** "Some of these actions may present some substantial cost. They may involve scarce resources, new hires, new hardwares, etc. What is the cost associated with each of the actions in the timeline?"
	Process: Small Group Dialogue, Consensus Check
	Comments: Keep costs at as broad a level as possible. This is a good time to keep the Parking Lot ready to hold discussions that go into detail not useful for this meeting's purpose and agenda. Budget talks should be handled in detail in a separate meeting.
J. Close	**Prompt Question:** "Have we met today's meeting purpose?"
	Process: Meeting Close
	Comments: Review the entire Action Plan and get the team's commitment to the plan. Then proceed with the rest of the closing.

Process Change Workshop

Meeting Name:	**Process Change Workshop**
Meeting Purpose:	To create a list of process improvements along with an Action Plan for implementing the plan
Meeting Outputs:	A list of practice improvements, the Action Plan to carry out the improvements
Meeting Participants:	All members of the team
Comments:	This is a good basic workshop to spark discussion around change. It can be used as the basis for defining methodology, defining team practices, reflecting on a particular strategy that has been completed, or just reviewing the communications among team members, stakeholders, vendors, etc.
	If the process steps involve more than the people currently in the room, you may need to postpone the meeting until all can be in attendance. If the steps impact external groups, consider building a detailed communication plan for introducing the new approach.

Continues

Process Change Workshop (*Continued*)

Meeting Name:	**Process Change Workshop**
	Also consider that the process may be in need of help with regard to more than steps; it may need adjustment to the defined roles, outputs, reports, etc. Help the team figure out what needs to be addressed here.

Agenda Item	
A. Opening	**Prompt Question:** n.a. **Process:** Meeting Startup **Comments:** Stick to the standard format of the Meeting Startup. Keep a flipchart available for the Communication Plan. This is a good meeting in which to collect Personal Objectives and then to recheck them at the end of the meeting.
B. What is our current set of practices and procedures in our process?	**Prompt Question:** "We have a process and set of procedures right now that we are following in our organization. To clarify our starting point, what is the current set of practices and procedures in our process?" **Process:** Expert Input, Small Group Dialogue **Comments:** The group needs to bring a common view of the current process into the meeting. After Expert Input, allow the group to talk about what they think may be different or missing from the input.
C. What is good about the process?	**Prompt Question:** "Some of what we are doing now works well for us. Think about your role in this process and how you benefit from the practices and procedures. What is good about the process?" **Process:** Facilitator-led Brainstorming **Comments:** Capture these brainstorms in a list on a flipchart.

D. What is causing us challenges about the process?

Prompt Question: "Given the definition of the process and how it is working today, think about the impact on your role and how you work. What is causing us challenges about the process?"

Process: Facilitator-led Brainstorming

Comments: Capture these responses in a list on another flipchart.

E. What are the root causes for these challenges?

Prompt Question: "For each of these challenges captured, consider what may be the underlying 'Why?' that may live below the surface of the problem. As you ask yourself why the challenge exists consider, 'What are the root causes for these challenges?'"

Process: Small Group Dialogue

Comments: Depending on the size of the group, you may want to split this work into teams of 3-5 people to engage in deeper discussion than could be possible with the entire group.

Consider having each team hold a variety of team roles: management, developers, stakeholders, testers, etc.

F. What are our recommendations for addressing these root causes?

Prompt Question: "These root causes may look very different from the actual challenge they create. Therefore, we need to think about how to address them specifically. What are our recommendations for addressing these root causes?"

Process: Small Group Dialogue, Consensus Check

Comments: You may either engage the entire team now to declare recommendations, or you may have the small teams continue their work and then report their findings and recommendations.

G. What is our Action Plan for implementing these recommendations?

Prompt Question: (No question necessary.)

Process: Action Planning

Comments: You may want to first prioritize the recommendations before moving into Action Planning, particularly if there are many recommendations and a very short window for change.

Continues

Agenda Items	
H. Close	**Prompt Question:** "Have we met this purpose today?"
	Process: Walking the walls
	Comments: Review Purpose ("Have we met this purpose today?"), process Personal Objectives, process Decisions Board, process Parking Lot, process Actions Board, create Communication Plan, and evaluate the meeting ("What worked well for you today?" "What would you change for the next meeting?").
	Celebrate!

Project Startup Meeting

Meeting Name:	Project Startup Meeting
Meeting Purpose:	To kick off a project with a vision, a charter, a set of standards and norms, identification of roles, timelines, and a commitment to all of these
Meeting Outputs:	A complete project charter with scope, norms, roles, timeline, and other useful project standards
Meeting Participants:	All members of the development team, stakeholders, product manager, Project Manager
Comments:	This is potentially the very first meeting of this group of people. Therefore, they are in a "Forming" mode of operating. This requires very strong, attentive facilitation. Pay attention to the conflicts that will arise. Keep the group focused on the work, and do frequent consensus checks.
	This meeting may take half a day or a full day, depending on the project team size. It is a very important step in helping the team gel, so be sure to take adequate time to promote the dialogue needed to gain consensus on the many project attributes: its norms, its values, its Communication Plan.

Agenda Item	
A. Opening	**Prompt Question:** n.a.
	Process: Meeting Startup
	Comments: Once you have completed the meeting startup with Purpose, Agenda, Organizing Tools, etc., collect Personal Objectives. It will be an important first instance of applying collaboration in the project context.
	Be sure to go through the "What's In It For Me" and the Scope of Authority for the entire team.
B. What is the Product Vision?	**Prompt Question:** "Given what we know about the product that this project is supporting, what is the Product Vision?"
	Process: Expert Input, Small Group Work—Product Elevator Statement
	Comments: After the Expert Input on the product has been provided, have small teams create their own Product Elevator Statement based on Geoffrey Moore's *Crossing the Chasm*:
	• For (target customer)
	• Who (statement of need)
	• The (product name) *is* a (product category)
	• That (statement of key benefit—that is, compelling reason to buy)
	• Unlike (primary competitive alternative)
	• Our product (statement of primary differentiation)[1]
C. What is the Project Scope for this project within that vision?	**Prompt Question:** "Our Project Scope should define what we intend to deliver of the Product Vision as a result of this project. Given what we understand of the Product Vision and the beginning discussions of our project, what is the Project Scope for this project within that vision?"
	Process: Small Group Dialogue
	Comments: n.a.

Continues

---

1. Moore, *Crossing the Chasm,* 159.

Agenda Item	
D. What is the project data sheet that supports that scope?	**Prompt Question:** "We can think of this Project Scope in terms of a number of attributes: who is involved, which customers are being supported, what the benefits will be. To capture these attributes, what is the project data sheet that supports the Project Scope?"
	Process: Group Dialogue
	Comments: A project data sheet is a one-page set of facts that quickly capture the essence of the project: Project Manager, Product Manager, Features, Project Objective, Key Benefits. (Consider using a template like Jim Highsmith's in *Agile Project Management* to begin to capture all this information in a very tight format.)[2]
E. What is the project schedule?	**Prompt Question:** "Review the Project Scope and the information that has been provided around the Product Vision and the scope of the project. Using a calendar as a guide, what is the project schedule?"
	Process: Facilitator-led Listing, Consensus Check
	Comments: Capture all the dates, milestones, timeboxes, and release themes from the group. Be sure to get consensus before you proceed to the next agenda item.
F. What are all the project constraints?	**Prompt Question:** n.a.
	Process: Listing, Grouping
	Comments: Teams should consider any possible constraints such as budget, geography, resources, technology, architecture, performance, costs, etc. After the listing, you can lead the team in a grouping to see the natural categories of constraints.
	This information should then feed back into the project data sheet formed earlier.

---

2. Highsmith, *Agile Project Management,* 103.

Agenda Item	
G. What are all the issues and risks that could impact this project?	**Prompt Question:** "Given these constraints and the Project Scope, think about what could derail the project. Think about what you have experienced in the past in delivering similar products. What are all the issues and risks that could impact this project?"

Process: Listing, Grouping

Comments: Just as in the constraints exercise, the group should go through listing and then grouping to discover the major areas of risk.

This information should then feed into the project data sheet. |
| **H. What are our Project Norms?** | **Prompt Question:** "As a team, you have to think about ways to work together that will make you the most successful in delivering the Project Scope. Think about practices, standards, or team techniques that you feel will help the team, especially given our constraints and risks. Given this guidance, what are our Project Norms?"

Process: Small Group Brainstorming, Group Dialogue, Consensus Check

Comments: First guide the team in brainstorming as dyads or groups of three. Resolve duplicate responses among teams.

Then lead the entire group in dialogue to weigh the pros and cons of the responses.

Gain consensus on the final list of norms before proceeding. |
| **I. What are our five Project Values?** | **Prompt Question:** "We need to declare a way that we will treat one another and that we will expect others to treat us. We call these our Project Values. Given your experiences in effective team work and given our Project Scope and norms, what are our five project values?"

Process: Facilitator-led Brainstorming, Multi-voting, Consensus Check

Comments: Lead the group in brainstorming a set of values. Have them vote using multi-voting in order to find the top five values listed. Gain consensus and post these values. |

Continues

Agenda Item	
J. What will our Project Communication Plan be?	**Prompt Question:** "In order to keep in step with one another, with our customer, and with our stakeholders, we need to commit to how we will communicate our progress, issues, distractions, and roadblocks. What will our project communication plan be?"
	Process: Listing
	Comments: Lead the team in listing all the communications that need to take place. For each communication, ask them to decide how often it needs to take place, in what format, and by whom. (You can use the guidance on the "Communication Plan" in Chapter 9, "The Organizing Tools.")
	Before closing the meeting with Action Items, consider leading the team in a "Project Name" brainstorm.
K. What is our Action Plan?	**Prompt Question:** n.a.
	Process: Action Planning
	Comments:
L. Close	**Prompt Question:** "Have we met this purpose today?"
	Process: Walking the walls
	Comments: Review Purpose ("Have we met this purpose today?"), process Personal Objectives, process Decisions Board, process Parking Lot, process Actions Board, create Communication Plan, and evaluate the meeting ("What worked well for you today?" "What would you change for the next meeting?").
	Celebrate!

Project Retrospective

Meeting Name:	**Project Retrospective**
Meeting Purpose:	To reflect on a project's timeline, members, the outcomes, the highlights, and the lowlights in order to form observations for recommendations on future projects
Meeting Outputs:	A wall chart of the project timeline, populated with events, team members, highs and lows; recommendations on what lessons were learned and what best practices were harvested
Meeting Participants:	All members of the team
Comments:	A Project Retrospective is a way of helping a project team put a project to rest, be done with it, and prepare to move on by bringing observations, recommendations, and actions out of the retrospective.

You may consider having team members fill out a survey prior to coming to the meeting if the project extended over a long time span or if team members are widely distributed.

For the mapping and timelining exercises, encourage silent activity. Each person with items for the timeline should silently place their items on the timeline.

If the project has been rough, the team could be in a "Storming" mode, not having ever achieved "Performing." Be prepared to deal with conflict and emotion. Emphasize your neutral role. Build in lots of time for silence and reflection once the timeline has been created and the team starts to populate it with their highlights and lowlights. Additionally, you may want to add an extra agenda item after the completion of the timeline with highlights and lowlights. Ask team members to draw a picture of what the project felt like to them. These can be posted on the wall along with the timeline.

Plan to conduct a two-day event if at all possible: day one for the timeline and mining of the timeline, and day two for delving into the challenges and the results of the team's responses to those challenges.

Agenda Item	
A. Opening	**Prompt Question:** n.a.
	Process: Meeting Startup
	Comments: Personal Objectives are very important in a Project Retrospective. Also, be sure to stress the WIIFM aspect of the meeting.
B. Who were the members of the project team and what were their roles?	**Prompt Question:** "I'd like you to think about this project in its many forms; in particular right now, I'd like you to think about all the people who were involved in this project. Think about the entire community of project participants from inception to completion. Who were all the members of the project team and what were their roles?"
	Process: Facilitator-led Listing
	Comments: You are looking for the full list of project participants. Pay attention to the various roles. Even if someone was only on the project a short while, they should be listed here. Their start and end times on the project will be tracked in the project timeline.
C. What was the project timeline?	**Prompt Question:** "Think back on the actual start of this project and all the events that kicked it off. Also consider what the events were that signified the end of the project. With those events in mind, what was the project timeline?"
	Process: Dialogue, Timelining
	Comments: Encourage dialogue around the actual start of the project in terms of inception of the product idea, the approval for the project funding, and then the resourcing of the project with the project kickoff. Also help the team evaluate what the actual "end" date might be: What event signified the end? For mapping, you should create a wall chart of a timeline in which each segment represents a useful measure, such as a month. Later, the team will use the segment demarcations to help them map people, events, activities, and optionally, moods.

Agenda Item	
D. When did each person join/leave the project?	**Prompt Question:** "Given the project timeline and the full list of project members, I'd like you to now form a map of when each person was involved in the project. Be thinking about events you know engaged each person. When did each person join/leave the project?" **Process:** Listing, Mapping **Comments:** You can conduct this item in two steps. First use the list of participants and record each start and end date. Then, with two sticky notes per person (one that signifies when they joined the project and one that signifies when they left the project), you can fill in the timeline wall chart. Consider using one color for when a person joins and another color for when a person leaves the project.
E. What were the key events in the project time- line (milestones, phases, and deliverables)?	**Prompt Question:** "Looking at the project timeline with its defined start and end dates, you can think about a number of very project-specific events that occurred during that time. These may have been completion of a phase, or reaching a mile- stone, or finishing a deliverable. What were these key events in the project timeline?" **Process:** Small Group Listing, Mapping **Comments.** Form several small groups and have each group brainstorm all the project timeline events. A member from each group should then map their events on the timeline wall chart. Responses are mapped on the timeline wall chart with all dupli- cates removed.
F. What were the team highlights and lowlights in the timeline?	**Prompt Question:** "In this same timeline, there are also non- deliverable oriented moments, moments when the team just felt as though it was really flowing well, or perhaps moments when the team was feeling low and struggling. Thinking about all this, what were the team highlights and lowlights in the timeline?" **Process:** Brainstorm, Mapping **Comments:** Individuals should brainstorm on their own, one response per sticky, and then silently place their contributions on the map. You may want to create a layer across the entire timeline for these team highlights and lowlights, using a differ- ent color for each.

Continues

G. What were the personal and individual highlights and lowlights in the timeline?

Prompt Question: "Now think about what was happening for you during this time in the project. What was going on with your family, your home, your career? Did you move, have a baby, get married, lose a loved one? What were your personal and individual highlights and lowlights in the timeline?"

Process: Brainstorm, Mapping, Dialogue

Comments: This agenda item and the next one may bring out emotion in a team that struggled or had to deal with the project being shut down. If there is a sense of failure about the team, the project, or the individual, this agenda item and the previous one will bring it out. Be prepared to engage in careful dialogue. Encourage sharing of reflection but discourage blame or attack.

H. What are our observations about this timeline with these key events, and the team and personal highlights and lowlights?

Prompt Question: "We now have a fairly extensive view into what our project looked like from a variety of angles. There may be surprises to you, some revelations about events and colleagues. Take some time now to review the entire timeline and reflect. What are your observations about this timeline with its highlights and lowlights?"

Process: Dialogue

Comments: Encourage people to silently walk along the timeline chart. They should take at least five minutes to look over the total set of materials. You may also want to encourage them to write down some of their observations. Once the time of observation is over, lead the group in sharing observations through group dialogue.

I. What appreciations do we have to offer one another?

Prompt Question: "Having reflected on the project and its timeline, you now have an opportunity to think about the special contributions various team members have made. Think about those very specific actions an individual took that impacted you positively during the project. What are the appreciations we have to offer one another?"

Process: Dialogue

Comments: Guide participants to respond by using the format: "I appreciate that (person's name)..." as in "I appreciate that Gail was always willing to pair on writing automated test scripts." Also consider having an awards ceremony (oldest artifact, funniest artifact, most representative artifact). You should alert people to this in advance of the retrospective.

Agenda Item	
J. What are our recommendations based on these observations?	**Prompt Question:** "Given our observations and reflection on those observations, we now have an opportunity to apply some useful interpretation to our views and create change. What are our recommendations based on all of our observations?" **Process:** Facilitator-led Listing, Dialogue **Comments:** Retrospection should create interpretation and direction. This is the pivotal agenda item in the entire retrospective. List recommendations verbatim and maintain open dialogue.
K. What is our Action Plan based on our recommendations?	**Prompt Question:** n.a. **Process:** Action Planning **Comments:** You may want to first prioritize the recommendations before moving into Action Planning, particularly if there are many, controversial, or contradictory recommendations.
L. Close	**Prompt Question:** "Have we met this purpose today?" **Process:** Walking the walls **Comments:** Review Purpose ("Have we met this purpose today?"), process Personal Objectives, process Decisions Board, process Parking Lot, process Actions Board, create Communication Plan, and evaluate the meeting ("What worked well for you today?" "What would you change for the next meeting?") Celebrate!

Chapter 25

Crystal Clear

In his book on the Crystal Clear methodology, Alistair Cockburn has captured a recommended set of "Techniques" for guiding teams in their agile and collaborative approach to software development and project management. The first three of these Crystal techniques set the project collaborative tone as team meetings or workshops: Methodology Shaping, the Blitz Planning Meeting, and the Reflection Workshop. In each of these collaborative events, teams form and grow through agendas that step them through brainstorming and communication around their project persona:

How shall we work (Methodology Shaping)

What is the size and shape of our upcoming work (Blitz Planning)

How will we continually improve as we work and deliver (Reflection Workshop)

As with any of the collaboration agendas in this section, the Crystal Clear meeting formulas documented here provide a very prescriptive approach. This level of detail supports meetings for a newly formed team with a new collaborative leader. As your teams mature and your comfort level with these meetings matures, pick your way through the materials with a practiced eye, open to guidance but seasoned enough to determine what would be most appropriate for you.

For further information about rich guidelines that accompany these Crystal Clear techniques, consult *Crystal Clear: A Human-Powered Methodology for Small Teams* by Alistair Cockburn.

Meeting Name:	**Methodology Shaping**
Meeting Purpose:	To create a list of ideas, rules, and conventions to be used by the project team at its start
Meeting Outputs:	A set of project practices that will define methodology, team standards, and norms based on what has worked well in the past and what has not worked well
Meeting Participants:	All members of the development team
Comments:	For a small team, this meeting will normally take 2-4 hours. Teams mine their collective wisdom in order to discover the most useful set of conventions they can adopt as individuals in order to work most effectively as a team. Use lots of wall charts to keep brainstorming information very visible and accessible.

Consider jumpstarting your Methodology Shaping event with project interviews, performed one-on-one in advance of the workshop with each of the project members. In the interviews, you can capture:

- A sample work product produced

- A short history of the project

- What things went wrong that you would not want to do again

- What things went right that you would want to do in your next project

- What are the critical, priority items to preserve in your next project

- Was there anything that surprised you in your last project

- Anything else useful about the project

Agenda Item	
A. Opening	**Prompt Question:** n.a.
	Process: Meeting Startup
	Comments: If this is the first time the group has gone through such an exercise, collect personal objectives. They'll need to be able to feel right from the start that they have a real voice in this process. Collecting personal objectives gets an early win for all.
B. What are the current "fixed rules" about software development for our organization?	**Prompt Question:** "Think about the projects you have participated in recently in this organization and all the built-in standards and fixed rules that guided you in those projects. Think about project startup, ongoing project procedures, and project deployment. Given your knowledge, what are the current fixed rules about software development for our organization?"
	Process: Facilitator-led Listing
	Comments: Capture items on a flipchart for reference later.
C. What are all the practices you liked and would want to keep from your last project?	**Prompt Question:** "Thinking back again on those projects, now think about the practices you felt really made the project work for you. These are things that you know you would use again. With that in mind, what are all the practices that you liked and would want to keep from your last project?"
	Process: Small Group Brainstorming
	Comments: Use flipcharts and have teams of 3-5 people keep listing very quickly with little discussion. Keep the work to a very tight timebox, 5-10 minutes.
D. What are all the practices you disliked and would want to avoid from your last project?	**Prompt Question:** "In these same projects, I want you think about situations in the projects that felt as though they just didn't work. Think back on anything that you told yourself you would never do again! What are all the practices you disliked and would want to avoid from your last project?"
	Process: Small Group Brainstorming
	Comments: Remain in the same teams as before and continue with a very quick listing of items in a tight timebox.

Continues

Agenda Item	
E. Given all this information, of the "liked/keep," which ones can we apply in our upcoming project?	**Prompt Question:** "Now let's review the suggestions you have accumulated around what to do again. Given the information we learn about each suggestion, we'll be able to prioritize which ones to take forward with us in this project."
	Process: Small Group Dialogue, Prioritizing (Multi-voting)
	Comments: In this exercise, team members need to discuss the ideas accumulated in each of the small groups, eliminating duplicates. They then prioritize what would be critically useful to adopt versus what might not be feasible to adopt.
F. What practices can we adopt that would help us avoid the "disliked/avoid" items?	**Prompt Question:** "As a group, you now have a set of recommendations for practices to maintain for this project. Review these recommendations and think about the items on your 'disliked' list. What practices or conventions might we adopt that would help us avoid the 'disliked/avoid' items?"
	Process: Large Group Dialogue, Prioritizing
	Comments: This is a first cut at bringing new approaches into the team based on the collective team wisdom.
G. Given themes that we see across our organization with regard to "likes" versus "avoids," what are our recommendations for handling these?	**Prompt Question:** "We have our team practices here now. Given what we know about the organization in which we work, and where we will want to be applying our recommended practices, think about organizational themes we should address. What are our recommendations for handling these known themes and trends?"
	Process: Large Group Dialogue, Consensus Check
	Comments: You may want to precede this agenda item with a brainstorming around organizational challenges and then categorize them to learn the major themes.
	This is a bit broader than the last agenda item. The team is looking through all the ways they succeed versus fail and then are making recommendations about practices/conventions that can take advantage of their strengths while minimizing the impact of their weaknesses.

Agenda Item	
H. What "dislike/avoid" items still remain that we can track through the course of our project?	**Prompt Question:** "Let's review the remaining items on the 'dislike/avoid' list. Given our recommendations, what should we still track through the course of the project?" **Process:** Listing **Comments:** Find out what still poses a problem but for which the group itself has no answer. Track this as an ongoing problem and check in on its impact during the "Reflection Workshops" conducted periodically through the project.
I. What is our final list of ideas, rules, and conventions?	**Prompt Question:** "Given all the information we have accumulated here, what are we prepared to declare as our methodology moving forward in terms of ideas, rules, and conventions?" **Process:** Consensus Check **Comments:** This consensus check helps the team pull together all of its work and declare the use of the methodology that has emerged. This is a good time to remind them that the "Reflection Workshops" will be used to make the useful tweaks and adjustments to help the team as they progress through the project.
J. What is our Action Plan for implementing this project timeline?	**Prompt Question:** "Consider the actionable items that have arisen as a result of our work here today. Think about which you are willing to take responsibility for seeing implemented. Now, who are the owners of each of these Action Items?" **Process:** Action Planning **Comments:**
K. Close	**Prompt Question:** "Have we met this purpose today?" **Process:** Walking the walls **Comments:** Review Purpose ("Have we met this purpose today?"), process Personal Objectives, process Decisions Board, process Parking Lot, process Actions Board, create Communication Plan, and evaluate the meeting ("What worked well for you today?" "What would you change for the next meeting?"). Celebrate!

Meeting Name:	**Blitz Planning Workshop**
Meeting Purpose:	To build an optimized project map and timeline with tasks, dependencies, and deadlines
Meeting Outputs:	All tasks with estimates, dependencies, and required task contributors; a definition of a walking skeleton by function and deadline; a set of other releases by tasks and deadlines
Meeting Participants:	Executive sponsor, expert user, business analyst, and the entire development team (lead designer, developers, testers, doc, deployment, etc.)
Comments:	The Crystal Clear Blitz Planning workshop gathers major project stakeholders and team members to collaboratively create a set of project tasks that can then be formulated into a project map and timeline through brainstorming, estimating, prioritizing, and grouping techniques. The team will know they are done when they can answer these three questions:

- In what order are we delivering what functionality?

- What are we building next?

- What are the dependencies within and between our releases?

For a small-sized team in performing mode, this meeting will normally take 2-4 hours; a newly formed team or a large team will take longer. Don't exceed six hours. Think of it as a jam session that brings the entire team together to establish their vision and their commitment to the project's success. The executive sponsor will guide prioritization decisions; the development team will guide estimation decisions. All will create the final optimized project map and timeline.

For the estimating work, stay at a high level of effort estimate (units of one week). Avoid applying staffing constraints until after dependencies have been applied. Also, consider clustering groups or tasks that can be considered focused on a particular functional component or release. You can then model dependencies from cluster to cluster.

Meeting Name:	**Blitz Planning Workshop**

Consider completing this work either at flipcharts or at a set of long tables, using sticky notes or index cards to capture and shuffle the information. Each task should be captured on its own card, with the major contributors listed on the upper left and the estimate on the lower left. Dependencies will flow from the lower-right corner of one task to the upper-right corner of the next task.

A sample task card format to use in the Blitz Planning Workshop:

Contributor Name

TASK NAME

Estimate #

Dependency (A)

Agenda Item	
A. Opening	**Prompt Question:** n.a.
	Process: Meeting Startup
	Comments: Once you have completed the meeting startup with Purpose, Agenda, Organizing Tools, etc., be sure to collect personal objectives, particularly if this is the first Blitz Planning Meeting for the participants.
	You may also want to provide five minutes to the executive sponsor to define the "What's In It For Me" for the entire team.
B. What are all the tasks associated with this project?	**Prompt Question:** "Imagine it is the end of the project and all your work is done. Think about all the specific tasks that the team completed in order to make the project a success. What are all these tasks associated with this project?"
	Process: Small Group Listing
	Comments: Blitz Planning stresses tasks. Help the team understand that this is anything that must be done, functionally or technically, for the architecture, or the documentation, or the deployment.

Continues

Agenda Item	
C. What is a natural ordering of these tasks in a map based on their chronology and dependencies?	**Prompt Question:** "Given the tasks that have been gathered, think about a natural ordering of those tasks in relation to one another. What is the ordering of these tasks based on their chronology and dependencies?"
	Process: Silent Grouping
	Comments: Allow at least 10 minutes for the silent grouping, but keep members as quiet as possible! Discussion now will bog down the flow of thought and energy.
D. What are any other tasks that we may have missed, and where do they fit in the map?	**Prompt Question:** "Review the set of accumulated and sorted tasks. Think about any other work that could support this project. What are any other tasks that we may have missed and where do they fit in?"
	Process: Dialogue
	Comments: Open dialogue is now welcome. Ask someone to scribe the new tasks as you move through the remainder of the exercise.
E. What are all the task estimates, internal and external dependents, and any required contributors?	**Prompt Question:** "Imagine once again that it is the end of the project and all your work is done. Now think about all the various aspects of each task completed: estimates, dependencies, and assigned resources. What are all these task estimates, their dependents, and their key contributors?"
	Process: Small Group Dialogue, Estimating, Consensus Check
	Comments: For estimating, the groups can use Wideband Delphi if they discover that the estimates are too broadly differing.
	Always make sure participants can come to a good consensus on all these items. A project map at this early stage of the team building leans heavily on a sense of collaboration and consensus.
F. Based on the task dependency information, what is the sorted set of parallel streams and sequential streams?	**Prompt Question:** "Review all the defined dependencies. Note what work could be started in parallel versus what work needs to be completed sequentially. What is the sorted set of parallel streams and sequential streams of the project tasks?"
	Process: Grouping
	Comments: Grouping can be functionally driven as well as dependency driven. Let the team decide what works best for their sense of flow of their project tasks.

Agenda Item	
G. What is the first and smallest set of functionality to be delivered as the walking skeleton?	**Prompt Question:** "Review the defined streams of tasks. Think about the functionality associated with the beginning tasks in the streams. Given the tasks and their dependencies, what is the first and smallest set of functionality that can be delivered as the walking skeleton?" **Process:** Large Group Dialogue, Consensus Check **Comments:** Here you are creating a "walking skeleton" piece of functionality that the team can use as a proof point, not only of the functionality, but also of the team commitment and ability to work together. A large group dialogue is the best way to do this.
H. What are all the remaining releases with their functionality and deadlines?	**Prompt Question:** "Look at all the remaining functionality defined in the project timeline. Think about natural breakpoints with regard to time or clusters of functionality. Given these considerations, what are the remaining releases with their functionality and deadlines?" **Process:** Large Group Dialogue, Consensus Check **Comments:** Keep the group working as one team once you have the walking skeleton defined. All of these remaining decisions must flow into one another as an entire team vision.
I. What is an improved, optimized version of our schedule?	**Prompt:** "Imagine that part way through the project, you were told to compress the timeline and deliver much earlier, and you in fact achieved that. Reflect on the ways in which you shifted dependencies, outsourced tasks, and reallocated work. What changes did you make to achieve this improved optimized version of the schedule?" **Process:** Large Group Dialogue, Consensus Check **Comments:** Look for individuals who have too many tasks laid on them and unload them. Look for tasks that can be split and moved forward in the schedule. Look for ways to increase parallelism and outsource work. Look for ways to deliver usable, even revenue-generating functionality earlier. This exercise is the "jamming" part of the activity. All roles present need to share and evaluate ideas.

Continues

Agenda Item	
J. Given the resulting set of release deadlines and the project priorities, what is the final recommended project timeline?	**Prompt Question:** Given the resulting set of release deadlines and the project priorities, what is the final recommended project timeline?
	Process: Large Group Dialogue
	Comments: This is just a final check on all the decisions that have accumulated to this point.
K. What is our Action Plan for implementing this project timeline?	**Prompt Question:** "Consider the actionable items that have arisen as a result of our work here today. Think about which you are willing to take responsibility for seeing implemented. Now, who are the owners of each of these Action Items?"
	Process: Action Planning
	Comments: The decisions should have created actions for the group. At the very least, you must take an action to fully document the outputs of the Blitz Planning.
L. Close	**Prompt Question:** "Have we met this purpose today?"
	Process: Walking the walls
	Comments: Review Purpose ("Have we met this purpose today?"), process Personal Objectives, process Decisions Board, process Parking Lot, process Actions Board, create Communication Plan, and evaluate the meeting ("What worked well for you today?" "What would you change for the next meeting?").
	Celebrate!

Reflection Workshop

Meeting Name:	**Reflection Workshop**
Meeting Purpose:	To create a list of proposed practices for the project's next time period
Meeting Outputs:	A list of practices to preserve, a list of new practices to try, a list of ongoing problems, and a list of "tabled" items to preserve for later discussion

Meeting Participants:	All members of the development team
Meeting Name:	**Reflection Workshop**
Comments:	The Reflection Workshop acts as a little gardening tool for the ongoing tending of the project garden. We use the Reflection Workshop to find out what to keep, what to weed out in the running of the project, and something to try right away for the next 10 days or so, keeping the goals both tactical and measurable. When running such a meeting, keep the meeting short (no more than 30 minutes) and keep the team very focused. Be sure to bring the flipchart/documentation from the last Reflection Workshop so that the team can check in on its decisions and actions.

To keep the reflection focused, hold the number of "Try These" items to six or less. Teams are looking very tactically for ideas about what to try next; they are concentrating on practices that they can absorb specifically into the team. These new ideas must be things that the team itself can act upon. Just as with "Action Items," the "Try These" items cannot be assigned to someone not present in the meeting. Instead, consider capturing an "Action Item" that compels a member of the team to approach the external organization about the issue ("Work with Group XYZ to deal with the Issue W") by a certain deadline with a response to the problem.

Ongoing problems may reflect issues that lie outside the scope of authority of the group. These must ultimately be addressed at a stakeholder/executive level and so tend to be non-actionable by the team.

A Reflection Workshop should produce one flipchart with the following format.

Keep these: Try These:

(Table These):

Ongoing Problems:

Agenda Item	
A. Opening	**Prompt Question:** n.a.
	Process: Meeting Startup
	Comments: Don't bother with personal objectives for such a short meeting. Just check in with everyone on the Purpose, Agenda, and Action Plan that will guide the meeting.
	Use one flipchart to capture all information. This emphasizes the sense of quick, immediate fixes to be fostered by the reflection.
	Keep actions limited to practices the group itself can begin to perform or act on.
B. What are all the practices/items that you would want to keep (do/use again?)	**Prompt Question:** "Think back over our last time period and all that we have accomplished. You may have learned some new things or tried some new things that you felt contributed positively to our project work. Given these reflections, what are all the practices/items that you would want to keep?"
	Process: Facilitator-led Listing
	Comments: This forms the "Keep These" list on the left side of the flipchart. This is a good place to get the group engaged in reflection. Subsequent agenda items lead them into a bit more problem solving and decision making.
C. What problems did we encounter in this last time period?	**Prompt Question:** "Some of our work may not have gone as smoothly as we would have liked. Think about areas that caused you particular difficulty. Now tell me, what problems did we encounter this last time period?"
	Process: Group Dialogue, Action Planning
	Comments: Solicit and listen to problem statements. Invite discussion around the problem to get clarity about the source of the problem. If the problem sounds like a recurring trend, ask the group if they would like you to track it as an "Ongoing Problem" on the left side of the flipchart.
	You may also begin to solicit ideas to fix it. Once the group has converged on the recommended group of solutions, ask for a recommendation (or set of recommendations) to capture either in the "Try These" section (for group-wide ongoing problems) or in the "Action Plan" if it is a one-time fix with a deadline and an owner.

Agenda Item	
D. Which of the Ongoing Problems items from the previous session can we fix, and which need escalation?	**Prompt Question:** "We had captured some ongoing problems during the last Reflection Workshop. In this session we may have seen those problems disappear, or we may have seen them intensify. Which of the ongoing problems from the previous session can we now fix, and which need escalation?"
	Process: Small Group Dialogue, Action Planning
	Comments: Review the ideas from the last session's Ongoing Problems. For each one, encourage team dialogue to brainstorm ideas about how to fix the problem. If a solution arises, capture the Action Item that will lead to the solution.
E. What are the conventions and practices you would like to try in the next time period to address these problems?	**Prompt Question:** "There may have been some of these problems in the last period that you'd like to tackle explicitly to improve our work. Think of conventions and standards you've relied upon in the past to help alleviate or avoid problems. What are some of the conventions and practices you would like to try in the next time period to fix problems we've had?"
	Process: Small Group Brainstorming, Consensus Check
	Comments: Go through each of the problem statements captured on a separate flipchart and discuss possible solutions and issues. Have the team brainstorm ideas from their bag of tricks around standards and conventions that they have used in the past (engineering practices, team communications).
	If no workable idea for fixing the problem gets suggested, ask whether the team wants to drop the problem for now or wants to capture it in the "Ongoing Problems" area.
	Continue to do this work until all problem statements have been briefly discussed. The goal is to create a "Try This," an "Action Item," or an "Ongoing Problem" entry. Remember that this technique gets applied every month or two, so the lists (after the very first session) should not be very long.

Continues

Agenda Item	
F. What are any additional practices you would like to try in the next time period?	**Prompt Question:** "Given what we have learned about what our problem areas are, and the standards and conventions you've used in the past, think about any other creative ideas you may have about this work. Thinking very creatively, what are any additional practices you would like to try in the next time period?"
	Process: Facilitator-led Brainstorming, Consensus Check
	Comments: This brainstorming continues to form the "Try These" column on the right side of the flipchart. Keep the list to six items maximum, but encourage creativity and "out-of-the-box" thinking here. Use the "Table" section to hold any overflow items that the team would still like to consider at some point in the future. Get consensus on what the team will implement in the next time period.
G. What are the practices we are going to defer?	**Prompt Question:** "With the recommendations on 'Try These' and our list of 'Ongoing Problems,' we've specifically tabled some of the suggestions. This is our opportunity to explicitly declare our intention to delay using these practices. What are the practices we are going to defer?"
	Process: Consensus Check
	Comments: The team is just validating what has emerged from all the discussions about the last time period and what practices they are willing to defer. This is simply the final check on those decisions.
H. What is our Action Plan for implementing these new practices?	**Prompt Question:** "Consider the actionable items that have arisen as a result of our recommendations here today. Think about which you are willing to take responsibility for seeing implemented. Now, who are the owners of each of these Action Items?"
	Process: Action Planning
	Comments: Keep this very quick and brief. But don't leave the meeting without assigning owners of the actions that must take place in order for the new practices to be absorbed.

Agenda Item	
I. Close	**Prompt Question:** "Have we met this purpose today?"

Process: Review the captured items in the flipchart and any Action Plan.

Comments: Perform a quick check on the Purpose of the Reflection Workshop: "Have we met this purpose today?" Confirm with the team that they are prepared to take on the actions captured. |

Chapter 26

Scrum

The Scrum methodology formulates an agile context through a series of meetings that bookend its timeboxes of software delivery:

- What product functionality can we complete in the next 30 days—Sprint Planning Meeting
- How well are we meeting our commitments—Daily Scrum
- What product functionality have we delivered—Sprint Demo and Review Meeting

While other meetings take place, these meetings form the backbone of collaboration, team building, business focus, and inspection for the Scrum team. The ScrumMaster plans the meetings, invites the attendees, facilitates the meetings, and tracks the outcomes and actions. Team members participate in each meeting. Project Stakeholders and other customers are invited as observers to the Daily Scrum; they maintain full participation in the Sprint Planning Meeting and in the Sprint Demo and Review Meeting. The thread through each of the meetings is team commitment as captured in the form of backlogs and Burndown Chart updates.

As with any of these collaboration agendas, the approach captured here is very prescriptive and provides the detail that could work for a newly formed team. As your teams mature and go through these meetings continuously over time, you'll be able to sail through the materials with the level of ballast useful to your team's profile.

For background on how these meetings reflect the work and intent of Scrum, consult these two canonical works:

- *Agile Software Development with Scrum*, Ken Schwaber and Mike Beedle
- *Agile Project Management with Scrum*, Ken Schwaber

Meeting Name:	**Sprint Planning Meeting**
Meeting Purpose:	To commit to a Sprint goal for the next 30-day Sprint with a complete Sprint Backlog of prioritized product requests, their tasks, estimates, and resource assignments
Meeting Outputs:	A Sprint Backlog with tasks, estimates, and assignments defined for the highest priority Product Backlog items and the team's commitment to the Sprint
Meeting Participants:	Executive sponsor, ScrumMaster, expert user, business analyst, and the entire development team (lead designer, developers, testers, doc, deployment, etc.)
Comments:	The Sprint Planning Meeting creates a 30-day commitment among team members and Stakeholders to deliver a certain product increment around a Sprint goal. The commitment is based on information about the prioritized Product Backlog, the team's current members and their capabilities, the current business conditions, the architectural and technology framework, and the definition and demonstration of an executable product increment.

Because Scrum emphasizes self-organizing, cross-functional teams, the group uses the Sprint Planning Meeting to formulate their team structure: who will perform what tasks and roles, what their working mode will look like, and how they will self-manage.

The first agenda items of the meeting gather factual data about how the Sprint will move forward. Because these are not brainstorming, detailed listing, or dialogue events, they do not require a "Prompt" question and should be kept as brief as possible.

Process suggestions:

- For Sprints with small teams, you can have all the brainstorming as a facilitator-led, group-wide activity.

- If the Product Backlog has not yet been prioritized, you may want to insert an agenda item of Silent Grouping that creates time for the Product Owner to move items in priority with silent collaboration of interested parties.

Agenda Item	
A. Opening	**Prompt Question:** n.a.
	Process: Meeting Startup
	Comments: Once you have completed the meeting startup with Purpose, Agenda, Organizing Tools, etc., collect personal objectives if this is the first Sprint Planning Meeting for the participants.
	You may also want to provide five minutes to the executive sponsor to define the "What's In It For Me" for the entire team.
B. What is the product vision for the Sprint?	**Prompt Question:** n.a.
	Process: Expert Input with Question and Answers
	Comments: Always kick off the Sprint Planning Meeting with a product vision statement from the Product Owner. This sets the tone and motivation for the entire meeting. It also sets the "What's In It For Me" context for each member of the team. As the ScrumMaster, be sure to capture any Action Items or Parking Lot items that may come out of this Q&A.
C. What is the team composition for this Sprint?	**Prompt Question:** "Considering all our roles and the product vision we have just outlined, what is the team composition expected to be for this Sprint?"
	Process: Facilitator-led Listing
	Comments: Because team makeup can shift from Sprint to Sprint, explicitly collect the names of each of the team members who will be involved in this next 30-day Sprint.
D. What is the total team capacity for the Sprint?	**Prompt Question:** "As a team, consider what your capacity was for the last team Sprint (using the Burndown Chart as a guide). Now also consider what your individual capacity is expected to be in this Sprint. With this information, what is the total team capacity for the Sprint?"
	Process: Facilitator-led Listing

Continues

	Comments: For each of the team members listed, determine what their availability and capacity will be for the Sprint. Use the previous Sprint Burndown Chart as a guide for estimating capacity. Accumulate the number of ideal effort hours per person per day for the total number of working days in the 30-day Sprint. Or, you may choose to work with ideal days or points as a starting point for this estimate.
	Combined, this number defines the total capacity of the team to take on work tasks for the Sprint. Post this on a wall chart.
E. What are all the prioritized items in the Product Backlog and what information supports their priority?	**Prompt Question:** "We've been accumulating entries in our Product Backlog in a prioritized fashion. These entries represent any of the functional and non-functional items that could define the product increment. They are prioritized based on the Product Owner's vision for the Sprint. Given this list of entries, what are all the prioritized items in the Product Backlog and what information supports their priority?"
	Process: Expert Input, Dialogue
	Comments: The Product Owner reviews the top items in the Product Backlog, providing descriptive information with regard to the intent of each of the items. Each item is also explained in the context of the product vision of the Sprint. This debrief helps the team to prepare for their tasking and estimating exercise.
	Keep this overview brief and focused. Team members will be able to go into detail into each item in subsequent agenda items. Any dialogue here should be quickly captured by the ScrumMaster on flipcharts in order to proceed to the small group work.
F. What are the technical concerns around the priority items in the Product Backlog?	**Prompt Question:** "Based on the information we have just heard about the priority items in the Product Backlog, think about what the technical aspects of the product are that must be in place to support these priorities. Think about the architecture, the language, the testing, etc. Given this understanding, what are the technical concerns around the priority items in the Product Backlog?"
	Process: Small Group Brainstorming, Dialogue, Facilitator-led Listing

Comments: Groups of three should brainstorm with one another about all their concerns about the technical aspects of the product. Once the brainstorming is complete (take no more than five minutes for this part of the agenda item), engage the entire group in debriefing their responses and discussing the impacts of these concerns. Capture concerns on a flipchart.

G. What are the other concerns or risks associated with the project team and the goal of the Sprint?

Prompt Question: "We've looked at the technical concerns around the priority items in the Product Backlog. But you may have other issues and concerns about the goal for the Sprint: business, team, organizational, logistics, etc. What are these other concerns or risks associated with the project team and the goal of the Sprint? "

Process: Round Robin, Dialogue

Comments: Use a round-robin brainstorming survey of all participants to collect a broad view into any other concerns or risks. The round robin will keep things moving, given that the team has already done some small group brainstorming. Collect items first, then invite discussion once all items have been documented on a flipchart. Collect any recommendations or actions so that, when the group is asked to commit to the Sprint later in the agenda, they will have a clear view of the commitment they are making around managing the issues.

H. Given all of this information, what are the tasks, estimates, and assignments for these items that will form the Sprint Backlog?

Prompt Question: "Imagine it is the end of the Sprint and all your work is done. Think about all the specific tasks that the team completed in order to make the Sprint a success with the highest priority items from the Product Backlog. What were all the tasks, estimates, and assignments that formed the Sprint Backlog?"

Process: Small Group Listing, Wideband Delphi Estimating

Comments: This part of the planning works best when groups can work in small teams, collecting major backlog items for which they are most qualified to provide task, estimate, and assignment values. Encourage visiting from group to group so that all contributing experts can provide guidance around the collected information. Once each small group has completed its work, hold a group-wide readout of the results so that all information is shared at a high level with all participants.

Continues

Agenda Item	
I. Given these estimates, what priorities have shifted that would impact the Sprint Backlog?	**Prompt Question:** "Now that we have created a set of tasks, estimates, and assignments, we may have discovered complexity or effort that is larger than was initially expected. Given these estimates, what priorities have shifted that would impact the Sprint Backlog?" **Process:** Group Dialogue **Comments:** This dialogue seeks feedback from the Product Owner to consider changing priorities if some tasks are taking too much of the team effort. The team members are invited to give any additional information to help the Product Owner make a final decision about the priorities. This may involve determining new tasks, estimates, and assignments to accommodate the shift in priorities.
J. What is our final commitment for this Sprint?	**Prompt Question:** "Based on this inspection and dialogue around our work, are we prepared to declare this set of tasks and estimates as our Sprint Backlog?" **Process:** Consensus Check **Comments:** This is the final statement by the entire group that they are prepared to commit to the product vision for the Sprint, the team makeup, the plans for managing issues and concerns, and the detailed Sprint Backlog. Before asking for this consensus check, you may want to survey the team one last time for any recommendations about the running of the Sprint that were not expressed as backlog, vision, issues, or concerns. Once the full consensus is reached, celebrate! Take a picture of the team showing their "Fist of Five" and hang it on the wall. It is a great way to kick off the high visibility of the team's Sprint commitment.
K. What actions do we need to take from this meeting as a result of our commitment, and who are the owners of those actions?	**Prompt Question:** "Consider the actionable items that have arisen as a result of our planning here today. Think about which you are willing to take responsibility for seeing them implemented. Now, what actions do we need to take from this meeting as a result of our commitment, and who are the owners of those actions?" **Process:** Action Planning **Comments:** n.a.

L. Close	**Prompt Question:** "Have we met our meeting purpose today?"
	Process: Walk the walls
	Comments: Review Purpose ("Have we met this purpose today?"), process Personal Objectives, process Decisions Board, process Parking Lot, process Actions Board, create Communication Plan, and evaluate the meeting ("What worked well for you today?" "What would you change for the next meeting?").
	Celebrate!

Daily Scrum (Standup)

Meeting Name:	**Daily Scrum**
Meeting Purpose:	To determine the progress of the team's commitments from the previous Scrum and to note any actions necessary to help the team reach its 30-day Sprint goal
Meeting Outputs:	An updated Sprint Backlog and/or Burndown Chart with remaining effort hours per task; the team's commitment for the day's work; and, a list of post-meeting actions
Meeting Participants:	Team members provide their status; the ScrumMaster documents updates and actions. Project Stakeholders observe.
Comments·	The Daily Scrum is the standup status meeting that keeps the team focused on its Sprint commitments, as individuals and as a team. The purpose of the meeting is to determine what impediments need to be removed and to eliminate distractions that may be harming the team's progress. Though the meeting guidance here might appear to suggest that the ScrumMaster asks all the questions, these are just a guide for the flow of the meeting. Team members provide this information to one another and to the stakeholder observers at the meeting.
	(Stakeholders are invited to observe but are not allowed to participate/speak; they consult with the ScrumMaster about their observations after the meeting.)

Continues

Daily Scrum (Standup) (*Continued*)

Meeting Name:	Daily Scrum
	During the meeting, the ScrumMaster listens for action items and documents these, both for team actions and for personal follow-up with Stakeholders. Additionally, the ScrumMaster updates the Sprint documentation (Burndown Chart, Sprint Backlog, Task Board, etc.). Participants should stick to status only, no problem solving. The meeting is always conducted standing up.

Agenda Item	
A. Opening	**Prompt Question:** "Are we ready to start the Daily Scrum?"
	Process: n.a.
	Comments: Because it occurs daily, don't bother with a formal opening. Instead, use the opening as the time to enforce the "Starting on time" rules the team has agreed to use (penalty, fine, singing, charity).
	Once the meeting is ready to start, use round robin to query each team member for his or her status. Each team member provides status to the three agenda questions B, C, and D before the Round Robin continues to the next participant.
B. What did you do since the last Daily Scrum?	**Prompt Question:** "What did you do since the last Daily Scrum?"
	Process: Round Robin
	Comments: Keep participants specific to their commitments that they made in the last Standup meeting. Did they meet their commitments or not?
C. What are you committing to completing before the next Scrum?	**Prompt Question:** "What are you committing to completing before the next Scrum?"
	Process: Continuation of the Round Robin
	Comments: Here again, keep team members focused on the commitments they are willing to make to other team members with regard to the team's Sprint Backlog.

Agenda Item	
D. What is getting in your way?	**Prompt Question:** "What is getting in your way?"
	Process: Continuation of the Round Robin
	Comments: This is the ScrumMaster's chance to find out how to serve the team. Find impediments and remove them. Any blockage or impediment reported here should become an Action Item, either for the ScrumMaster to handle outside of the team, or for a subset of the team to resolve as prompted and arranged by the ScrumMaster. The ScrumMaster always tracks these Action Items.
E. What is the update to the team Burndown Chart?	**Prompt Question:** "Based on all the status provided here, what is the update to the team Burndown Chart or Task Board?"
	Process: Listing
	Comments: The ScrumMaster ensures that each team member has provided "To Do" estimates and records the responses in the Sprint's Burndown Chart. Any changes to story, task, or test status are also noted in the Task Board.
F. Close	**Prompt Question:** "What are all our actions as a result of this status information?"
	Process: Action Planning
	Comments: Close the Daily Scrum by reviewing any collected action items with their due dates and the owner of the actions. These should be part of the round-robin review for each subsequent Daily Scrum.
	Limit the meeting to 15 minutes.

Meeting Name:	**Sprint Demo and Review**
Meeting Purpose:	To demonstrate the potentially shippable functionality completed by the team during the Sprint, to update the Product Backlog based on information from the demo, and to learn about team practices to keep, change, or add
Meeting Outputs:	Updated Product Backlog with new items and priorities, any new team practices, recommendations for the next Sprint
Meeting Participants:	Product Owner, ScrumMaster, Development Team, Stakeholders
Comments:	The Sprint Demo and Review meeting brings the team's Sprint commitment to life. Planned by the ScrumMaster, team members demonstrate the functionality that they have completed for the Sprint increment and then collect feedback from the Product Owner and Stakeholders. Based on the demo and discussion, the meeting participants then review the impact of the Sprint on any subsequent Sprints: What priorities have changed, what team structure has altered, what team practices should shift, what issues and concerns must be addressed?

Don't allow the team to take more than four hours to prepare the demo for the meeting; keep the meeting under two hours.

Some process suggestions:

- Demo should be prepared in advance.
- Members should take turns running the meeting.
- The person who accepted the item should demo its acceptance.
- Keep the meeting to two hours.
- What did this Sprint look like? ("Picture This" Exercise).
- What are our appreciations from the Sprint? ("I appreciate that…").

Agenda Item	
A. Opening	**Prompt Question:** n.a.
	Process: Meeting Startup
	Comments: Once you have completed the meeting startup with Purpose, Agenda, Organizing Tools, etc., be sure to go through the "What's In It For Me" and the Scope of Authority for the entire team.
B. What was our commitment for this Sprint?	**Prompt Question:** n.a.
	Process: Expert Input
	Comments: The ScrumMaster or a team member reviews all the items that had been put in the Sprint Backlog during the last Sprint Planning meeting.
C. What was our final set of completed items for the Sprint?	**Prompt Question:** "Given what we have accomplished in our work with the Sprint Backlog, what were all our completed, accepted items?"
	Process: Expert Input
	Comments: The ScrumMaster or a team member reads out the total set of Sprint Backlog items that were completed during the 30-day Sprint. This will set up the set of demos of functionality.
D. What is our demonstration of these items from the Sprint?	**Prompt Question:** "Given the work that has been completed and accepted, who has work to demonstrate for this Sprint?"
	Process: Expert Input, Dialogue
	Comments: Have each team member demonstrate the functionality that has been delivered as part of the product increment from the Sprint. Open dialogue is now welcome. Ask someone to scribe any recommendations or Action Items that come out of the dialogue.
	Keep a close eye on the agenda item and encourage use of the Parking Lot in order to keep the demonstration flowing without digging into problem solving that should occur in subsequent meetings.

Continues

Agenda Item	
E. What was our final Burndown Chart?	**Prompt Question:** n.a.
	Process: Expert Input, Dialogue
	Comments: The ScrumMaster reviews the details of the Burndown Chart with regard to daily trends, overall trends, exception situations, and major turning points.
	Capture any insights from the team and Stakeholders on a flipchart.
F. What did we learn about our estimates?	**Prompt Question:** "Looking at the backlog items we were able to complete, the demos we were able to conduct, and our Burndown patterns, think about what we have observed. What did we learn about our estimates?"
	Process: Facilitator-led Brainstorm
	Comments: The team reviews the results of the demo and the trend of the Burndown Chart in order to make recommendations about how they will estimate their next Sprint Backlog. This may also impact the high-level estimates for items currently in the Product Backlog. The facilitator captures results on a flipchart.
G. What changes are there in the Product Backlog items, priorities, or estimates?	**Prompt Question:** "Given what we have learned about the product, we may want to recommend some changes in the Product Backlog. This may be due to technology, functionality, usability, etc. Thinking about these things, what changes are there in the Product Backlog items, priorities, or estimates?"
	Process: Large Group Dialogue
	Comments: Here you are explicitly drawing out guidance from the team and the Stakeholders to the Product Owner in order to make recommendations or decisions about the state of the Product Backlog. This may include adding items, removing items, reprioritizing items, or reestimating items.
	Be sure each recommendation is recorded explicitly and that the group has consensus about each change. If not, put the item in the Parking Lot for later consideration, or create an Action Item to hold a separate meeting to determine backlog changes.

Agenda Item	
H. What documented issues/concerns were we able to address?	**Prompt Question:** "Looking back on the issues and concerns we had documented at the start of the Sprint, think about how we either managed those issues or watched them end up being non-issues. What documented issues/concerns were we able to address?"
	Process: Large Group Dialogue
	Comments: Keep the group working as one team to talk through how they faced their documented issues and concerns. This will feed recommendations about team practices for the next Sprint or Action Items following this meeting.
I. What are our current issues/concerns?	**Prompt Question:** "Think about how we were able to meet our commitment and what may still be a challenge in terms of meeting future Sprint commitments. You may recognize either a persistent problem or a newly emerging one. What are our current issues/concerns?"
	Process: Small Group Listing Dialogue
	Comments: Have each group work through their own set of issues and concerns. This promotes open dialogue that then helps the entire group understand what the total set of issues and concerns are. For a small enough team, use Facilitator-led Listing.
J. What worked well that we'd do again?	**Prompt Question:** "During the 30 days of the Sprint, we engaged in any number of team practices to help us get to this demo and review. Considering how our Sprint worked, what worked well that we'd do again?"
	Process: Facilitator-led Brainstorming
	Comments: Capture all recommendations on a flipchart that can be posted for use in the next Sprint Planning meeting.
K. What practices would we alter or drop?	**Prompt Question:** "Thinking back over the Sprint, we may have had some difficulties in how we were working, communicating, delivering, committing, etc. Considering the ways that we chose to work, what practices would we alter or drop?"
	Process: Facilitator-led Brainstorming, Dialogue

Continues

	Comments: Encourage open dialogue around brainstorm responses so that the team can fully agree on what practices really should be altered or dropped. In particular, pay attention to any suggestion that would alter a fundamental practice of Scrum. Only a high-performing team should alter or change these basic practices.
L. What new practices would we want to introduce into our next Sprint?	**Prompt Question:** "Given our list of what to keep and what to change or drop, you may also be able to think about new practices, either something you have tried in a different team, or something you have learned since the last Sprint Planning meeting. What new practices would we want to introduce into our next Sprint?"
	Process: Faciliitator-led Brainstorming, Dialogue
	Comments: Lead the team in brainstorming any new ideas without remarking on their applicability, positive or negative. Then go through the items one-by-one to gain consensus around which practices to absorb for the next iteration. Use this information captured on a flipchart in the next Sprint Planning meeting.
M. Based on our work over the last 30 days, what appreciations do we have for individuals?	**Prompt Question:** "Before we close the meeting, we have an opportunity to openly extend gratitude to others for something they did that had a particularly valuable impact on the success of the Sprint. This may be a team member, a stakeholder, or someone outside the team who had supported the team. Based on our work over the last 30 days, what appreciations do we have for individuals?"
	Process: Brainstorming
	Comments: Ask participants to form their sentences in a way that directly applies to a particular individual and an action that person took: "I appreciate that Michele created the calendar of team events and commitments and didn't complain about doing it for everyone else."

Agenda Item	
N. What is our Action Plan for next steps?	**Prompt Question:** "Based on all the information and recommendations we have accumulated here, what is our set of actions for next steps?"
	Process: Action Planning
	Comments: Work with the team to ensure that they have the appropriate set of actions that can move their decisions forward from the demonstration and review.
O. Close	**Prompt Question:** "Have we met this purpose today?"
	Process: Walking the walls
	Comments: Review Purpose ("Have we met this purpose today?"), process Personal Objectives, process Decisions Board, process Parking Lot, process Actions Board, create Communication Plan, and evaluate the meeting ("What worked well for you today?" "What would you change for the next meeting?").
	Celebrate!

Chapter 27

XP and Industrial XP

Extreme Programming (XP) and Industrial XP teams rely on the Planning Game to create the Release Plans and Iteration Plans that time box the team's work and commitments. In these contexts, planning is intended to be a concise, disciplined, highly focused collaboration with the various members of the project community. Customers prioritize stories of customer value. Developers estimate the work it will take to complete the stories. Testers provide guidance to both about how to ensure delivery of the expected functionality. Together, these project team members form a commitment about how to deliver the work and how to communicate progress around that commitment.

You can think of this highly focused planning activity almost as a continuous process, an ongoing game. Teams move from the highest-level plan (Project Charter) into the next level of plan (Release Plan) that then sets a series of plans together (Iteration Plan) each of which ultimately tracks to daily planning (Daily Standup). Improving the quality of the ongoing planning comes from adaptation at all levels, the highest being Release Retrospective.

Therefore, the main meetings that form the backbone of planning and adoption for XP and Industrial XP teams are:

- Project Chartering (Industrial XP) meeting
- Release Planning meeting
- Iteration Planning meeting
- Daily Standup
- Iteration Demo and Review
- Release Retrospective

The XP Coach is responsible for planning the meeting, inviting all participants to the meeting, facilitating the meeting, and assuring that the meeting results are appropriately distributed and posted.

As in all the agile approaches, many other collaborations occur day-to-day in XP and Industrial XP. These particular collaboration events and their focused agendas serve to establish the necessary heartbeat of timeboxes through which those daily collaborations mature in nature and content. It is through these meetings that XP and Industrial XP create the specific moments in time where we aggressively plan, inspect, and retrospect.

For more information on the values, principles, and practices of XP that guide the fabric of these meetings, consult these three guides on implementing XP:

- *Extreme Programming Explained: Embracing Change*, Kent Beck
- *Planning Extreme Programming*, Martin Fowler and Kent Beck
- *Extreme Programming Explored*, William Wake

Project Chartering

Meeting Name:	**Project Chartering Meeting**
Meeting Purpose:	To declare a project community around a common purpose and set of values
Meeting Outputs:	A list of all members of the project community, a prioritized list of project values, and a statement of the project purpose and goals
Meeting Participants:	Customer, development team, testers, project sponsor, and any other key personnel needed to successfully complete the project
Comments:	The Project Chartering Meeting sets a project in motion by declaring the key attributes of the project, ensuring that the entire project team understands the purpose of the project, how they will be able to judge their own success, and how they will coordinate as a team. Because it precedes the first Release Planning meeting of the project, it plays a pivotal role in creating trust and commitment among the project team members. Additionally, it establishes communication norms or working agreements that are applied in the other Planning Game meetings.

Agenda Item	
A. Opening	**Prompt Question:** n.a.
	Process: Meeting Startup
	Comments: Once you have completed the meeting startup with Purpose, Agenda, Organizing Tools, etc., collect personal objectives if this is the first Project Chartering Meeting for the participants. You may also want to provide five minutes to the executive sponsor to define the "What's In It For Me" for the entire team.
B. What is the vision for this project?	**Prompt Question:** n.a.
	Process: Expert Input with Question and Answers
	Comments: This is the time for the primary or executive sponsor of the project to step forward with their vision for the project. This should be a concise "elevator statement" declaration that should invite clarification from the team members.
C. What are our measures of success?	**Prompt Question:** "For the defined vision and the scope of this project, think about the various ways that we would be able to tell that we have succeeded. This might be in terms of functionality, budget, delivery date, or other project attributes. With this in mind, what are our measures of success?"
	Process: Small Group Listing, Grouping, Prioritizing
	Comments: Have each group debrief the rest of the team. Perform a grouping exercise to discover the categories of these measurements. The team may want to then prioritize which category is the most critical or important.
D. What are the values that guide this project team?	**Prompt Question:** "We need to declare what we hold most valuable and worthy about our project, how we define ourselves to others. We call these our Project Values. Given your experiences in effective team work and given our project scope and resources, what are our project values?"
	Process: Facilitator-led Brainstorming, Multi-voting, Consensus Check
	Comments: Lead the group in brainstorming a set of values. Have them vote using multi-voting in order to find the top five values listed. Gain consensus and post these values.

Continues

Agenda Item	
E. Who are all the members of the project community?	**Prompt Question:** "Each project's success relies on a group of people larger than the immediate project team. We are supported by a broad net of people around us in a variety of roles, from stakeholders to end-users to support staff. Thinking about the many people who will be supporting our success, who are all the members of the project community?"
	Process: Small Group Listing
	Comments: Have each group of three people list all the possible members of the project community. When each team debriefs, remove all duplicates and gain consensus on the accumulated list.
F. What are all the project constraints?	**Prompt Question:** "We have set a vision and a set of measures of success within that vision. This may bring to mind roadblocks or limitations that we know about even before we start the project. What are all these project constraints?"
	Process: Listing, Grouping
	Comments: Teams should consider any possible constraints such as budget, geography, resources, technology, architecture, performance, costs, etc. After the listing, you can lead the team in a grouping to see the natural categories of constraints.
	This information should then feed into the project data sheet.
G. What are our working agreements?	**Prompt Question:** "As a team, you have to think about ways to work together that will make you the most successful in delivering the project scope despite the constraints and the various levels of committed resources. Think about practices, standards, or team techniques that you feel will help the team, especially given our constraints and risks. Given this guidance, what are our working agreements for this project?"
	Process: Small Group Brainstorming, Group Dialogue, Consensus Check
	Comments: First guide the team in brainstorming as dyads or groups of three. Resolve duplicate responses among teams.
	Then lead the entire group in dialogue to weigh the pros and cons of the responses. You may want to guide them to include a sort of "Communication Plan" as part of their working agreements. Gain consensus on the final list of working agreements before proceeding.

Agenda Item	
H. What is our Action Plan?	**Prompt Question:** "Based on all the work that we have done in defining our Project Charter, are there actions we should plan now that can contribute to our success?"
	Process: Action Planning
	Comments: n.a.
I. Close	**Prompt Question:** "Have we met this purpose today?"
	Process: Walking the walls
	Comments: Review Purpose ("Have we met this purpose today?"), process Personal Objectives, process Decisions Board, process Parking Lot, process Actions Board, create Communication Plan, and evaluate the meeting ("What worked well for you today?" "What would you change for the next meeting?").
	Celebrate!

Release Planning

Meeting Name:	**Release Planning Meeting**
Meeting Purpose:	To commit to a release goal in a set of iterations, their stories, and team velocity
Meeting Outputs:	A release theme and metaphor, a release date, a roadmap of time-boxed iterations, a set of User Stories per iteration, and a rough estimate for each story
Meeting Participants:	Customer, development team, testers, and any other key personnel needed to appropriately assess the high-level priorities and estimates for the release goal
Comments:	The Release Planning Meeting creates a timeboxed commitment among team members and stakeholders to deliver a certain series of product increments (iterations) around a release goal. The commitment is based on the formation of prioritized User Stories, the team's current members and their velocity, the current business conditions, the architectural and technology framework, and the definition of a shippable product increment.

Continues

Meeting Name:	Release Planning Meeting

Release Planning sets the collaborative tone in motion for the remainder of the release. For this reason, it invites tremendous interaction, communication, feedback, and consensus building. For teams that have an extensive history of product delivery, the processes described here should be far less formal, far more relaxed. Newer, forming teams need a clear, facilitative guide as a life raft for moving among the new currents of agile software development: accepting incompleteness, taking responsibility, letting go of old power domains, and learning to come to sustainable, collaborative agreements prior to moving forward with the project.

Process suggestions for large teams:

- For very large teams, you will have to manage breakout sessions across the various team domains, such as component by component.

- Use the same information-gathering processes and timings for all teams.

- Always have the entire group check in after each agenda item.

- Provide lots of extra time in the agenda in order to allow for these logistics and regroupings.

- Plan to have mini-checkins throughout the meeting ("What is working well; what needs improvement; what would you like to try new?") in order to keep the meeting productive, collaborative, and on target for its purpose.

- Use multiple coaches, one for each team breakout session if possible, to make sure each team can get guidance and sufficient check-in.

- The final release commitment will need ample time to create consensus across teams and to compare issues and concerns that have been gathered from each team. Similarly, dependencies across teams must be resolved before the final commitment can be taken.

Agenda Item	
A. Opening	**Prompt Question:** n.a.
	Process: Meeting Startup
	Comments: Once you have completed the meeting startup with Purpose, Agenda, Organizing Tools, etc., collect personal objectives if this is the first Release Planning meeting for the participants.
	You may also want to provide five minutes to the executive sponsor to define the "What's In It For Me" for the entire team.
B. What is the Release theme and product metaphor for this Release?	**Prompt Question:** n.a.
	Process: Expert Input with Question and Answers
	Comments: Always kick off the Release Planning meeting with a look into the Release theme. This should be based on a product metaphor. If a metaphor has not been defined in a previous Release Planning meeting, consider adding an agenda item here to conduct a small-group brainstorm exercise around the metaphor.
	The product metaphor creates a language for simple explanation of the product concept. The Release vision becomes the guiding light and true measure of success for the release within that metaphor. The customer should present this theme and invite questions from the team.
	For teams that have already completed a Release, the subsequent Release Planning meetings should include a debrief on the status of the just-completed Release and the Release Retrospective that occurred at its end:
	• What was our theme from the last release?
	• What was our commitment?
	• What were our total accepted stories?
	• What other metrics did we accumulate (points, actuals, number of automated tests, number of defects)?
	• What did we learn from the Release Retrospective?
	• How can this information guide us in this Release Planning meeting?

Continues

Agenda Item	
C. What is the timebox for this Release and its Iterations?	**Prompt Question:** "Given the defined theme for the Release and any other driving factors, what is the timebox for the Release?" **Process:** Facilitator-led Dialogue **Comments:** The Customer should present a view of the Release timebox based on the theme and any other driving factors (customer requests, marketing events, major technical changes). The Customer and the team then determine the number of iterations and the length of each iteration. Keep a calendar on hand to help track the start and stop date of the Release as well as for each Iteration within the Release. Post the table of dates on the wall.
D. What is the expected team composition for this Release?	**Prompt Question:** "There will be a number of people assumed to be involved in the successful delivery of this release vision. That means they are committed to the rest of the team and their work. With that in mind, what is the expected team composition for this Release?" **Process:** Facilitator-led Listing **Comments:** Because team makeup can shift from release to release, create a list of all team members and their roles. Find out if there is other team member information that would be useful for the list (location, full or part time). Use this as a reference when the team has completed the Release Planning and is ready to commit to the Release. All of these people must be able to personally commit (i.e., no one can accept their commitment for them).
E. What is the expected team velocity for the Release?	**Prompt Question:** "Given the team makeup defined on the team list, think about your expected team velocity. This is your capacity to create commitments around the Release based on what we know today. What is the expected team velocity for the Release?" **Process:** Dialogue, Consensus Check

Comments: For new teams, list each of the team members and determine what their availability and capacity will be for the Release. This may be in terms of points, ideal weeks, or ideal days. Keep teams estimating at a high level. Do not let them go into detailed resource allocations or total dedicated hours. These numbers are first best guesses at expected release velocity per individual, or by team, not a final detailed commitment. Moreover, because the list of stories for the Release is assumed to be incomplete, a detailed resource allocation is a wasted investment. Combine all individual gross estimates. This number defines the total velocity (or capacity) of the team to take on stories for the Release. Post this on a wall chart.

For teams that have already completed a release, this agenda item should instead be a dialogue around "Yesterday's Weather"—What was our average team velocity in the last Release (how many points were we able to accept over the course of the Release)? How can that velocity help us determine our team velocity for this Release?

F. What are all the current prioritized stories for this Release?

Prompt Question: "We've been accumulating stories for this project as a means to understand the vision for the product and hence the theme for this Release. These stories may also already have been prioritized with a bit of background on their priority and intent. What are all the current prioritized stories for this Release?"

Process: Expert Input, Dialogue

Comments: The Customer provides high-level information about all the currently identified, prioritized stories that may be planned into the Release.

Help the group stay focused on the current stories and specific information around these stories by gathering discussion topics on a flipchart; later agenda items will bring out other stories and lists of issues and concerns.

Continues

Agenda Item	
G. What additional stories can contribute to the theme of this Release?	**Prompt Question:** "Based on the information we have just heard about the stories, think about what additional information we may have learned about the business climate, market shifts, requested functionality, etc. Given what we know about these factors and influences, what additional stories can contribute to the theme of this Release?"
	Process: Small Group Brainstorming, Dialogue, Grouping
	Comments: Groups of three should brainstorm with one another any new stories they may have. After all teams have completed their stories (use a timer to timebox this), have each team debrief with open dialogue about the stories and their content. Resolve duplicates. Then have the Customer arrange the stories in a priority order either through silent grouping or with engagement of other team members as appropriate.
H. What are the technical concerns around these stories?	**Prompt Question:** "Based on the information we have just heard about the stories, think about what the technical aspects of the product are that must be in place to support these priorities. Think about the architecture, the language, the testing, etc. Given this understanding, what are the technical concerns around the stories we have accumulated?"
	Process: Facilitator-led Brainstorming, Grouping
	Comments: Capture brainstorm items on a flipchart. If the list becomes very long, you also may want to lead the team in grouping the responses in order to better understand the general sense of technical risk.
I. What are the other concerns or risks associated with the project team and the theme of the Release?	**Prompt Question:** "We've looked at the technical concerns around the priority stories and added new stories. But you may have other issues and concerns about the goal for the Release: business, team, organizational, logistics, etc. What are these other concerns or risks associated with the project team and the goal of the Release?"
	Process: Round Robin, Dialogue
	Comments: Use a round robin brainstorming survey of all participants to collect a broad view into any other concerns or risks. The round robin will keep things moving, given that the team has already done some small group brainstorming.

Agenda Item	
	Collect items first, then invite discussion once all items have been documented on a flipchart.
	Listen for and capture any recommendations or actions around the concerns so that, when the group is asked to commit to the Release later in the agenda, they will have a clear view of the commitment they are making with regard to managing the identified issues.
J. Given all of this information, what are the estimates for these stories?	**Prompt Question:** "Think about how the team has worked in the past and what its observed velocity has been for particular story types. You may have noticed which stories are bigger or more complex than other stories. We've now just reviewed the stories and our issues and concerns around them. Given all this information, what are the estimates for these stories?"
	Process: Small Group Listing, Wideband Delphi Estimating
	Comments: This part of the planning works best when groups can work in small teams, collecting stories for which they are most qualified to provide task, estimate, and assignment values. The customer, developers, and testers work together to share information so that the developers can then create estimates for each story under consideration.
	Encourage visiting from group-to-group so that all contributing experts can provide guidance around the collected information. Once each small group has completed its work, hold a group-wide readout of the results so that all information is shared at a high level with all participants.
K. Given these estimates, what priorities have shifted that would impact the set of Release stories?	**Prompt Question:** "Now that we have created a set of estimates for the stories, we may have discovered complexity or effort that is larger than was initially anticipated. Given these estimates, what priorities have shifted that would impact the stories committed to the Release?"
	Process: Group Dialogue
	Comments: This dialogue seeks feedback from the Customer to consider changing priorities if some stories appear to monopolize the team's commitment. The development team is invited to give any additional information to help the Customer make a final decision about the priorities.

Continues

Agenda Item	
L. What is the mapping of these stories to each of the Release's iterations?	**Prompt Question:** "We have declared a set of iterations for this Release, and we have declared a set of prioritized, estimated stories for the Release. What is the mapping of these stories to each of the Release's iterations?"
	Process: Small Group Listing and Grouping, Dialogue
	Comments: This work, coupled with the estimating work is some of the real heart of Release Planning. In large teams, the small-group approach encourages parallel work that can be evaluated once all teams come back together. For a small team, have all members work at flipcharts together to discuss and arrange stories from iteration to iteration.
	When the mapping of stories across iterations is complete, make sure all participants of the meeting review the work. Then lead the group in a dialogue around the mappings.
M. What is the final set stories and velocity for this Release?	**Prompt Question:** "Based on this inspection and dialogue around our mapping of stories across the Release iterations, are we prepared to declare this as our Release Plan?"
	Process: Consensus Check
	Comments: This is a final check-in on all the work that has been accomplished in the meeting. By now, the stories, their priorities, their estimates, and their mapping into iterations should be ready for a consensus commitment by the team. This may include revising the original Release theme to accommodate what has been learned.
	Make sure that you have full consensus on this agenda item before you move to close the meeting. Once the full consensus is reached, celebrate! Taking a picture of the team showing their "Fist of Five" and hanging it on the wall is a great way to kick-off the high visibility of the team's Release commitment.
N. Based on this commitment, what are our actions from this Release Planning meeting?	**Prompt Question:** "Based on all the information and recommendations we have accumulated here, what is our set of actions for next steps?"
	Process: Action Planning
	Comments: Work with the team to outline each action and its owner. These actions from the Release Planning meeting set the plan in motion.

Agenda Item	
0. Close	**Prompt Question:** "Have we met our meeting purpose today?"
	Process: Walk the walls
	Comments: Review Purpose ("Have we met this purpose today?"), process Personal Objectives, process Decisions Board, process Parking Lot, process Actions Board, create Communication Plan, and evaluate the meeting ("What worked well for you today?" "What would you change for the next meeting?").
	Celebrate!

Iteration Planning

Meeting Name:	**Iteration Planning Meeting**
Meeting Purpose:	To commit to a set of stories, their tasks, their estimates, and a team velocity to support these
Meeting Outputs:	Stories with tasks, estimates, and assignments defined for the highest priority Release stories
Meeting Participants:	Customer, other stakeholders who may hold information about the requested stories, and the entire development team (lead designer, developers, testers, doc, deployment, etc.)
Comments:	

Agenda Item	
A. Opening	**Prompt Question:** n.a.
	Process: Meeting Startup
	Comments: For a new team, detail the WIIFM aspect of the Iteration Planning meeting.

Continues

Agenda Item	
B. What are all the stories planned for this Iteration?	**Prompt Question:** n.a.
	Process: Expert Input with Question and Answers
	Comments: Always kick off the Iteration Planning Meeting with a recount by the Customer about what was originally planned for the iteration (during Release Planning), and what has changed as a result of preceding iterations and their results.
C. What is the team composition for this Sprint?	**Prompt Question:** n.a.
	Process: Facilitator-led Listing
	Comments: Because team makeup can shift from iteration to iteration (vacations, roles needed), explicitly collect the names of each of the team members who will be involved in this next iteration.
D. What is the total team velocity for the Sprint?	**Prompt Question:** n.a.
	Process: Facilitator-led Listing
	Comments: If you have used points for estimating stories in the past, use "Yesterday's Weather" to declare your velocity (how many points have we tended to deliver in past iterations?"). Otherwise, for each of the team members listed, determine what their availability and capacity will be for the iteration (number of days they will be available and number of ideal hours per day). The sum of these velocity estimates from each person represents the team velocity for the iteration.
	Post this information on the wall for use in the remainder of the planning.
E. What information do we need in order to estimate these stories?	**Prompt Question:** "The stories we have are just the start of a conversation. Further elaboration may be needed in order to declare tasks and estimates for the work of each story. What information do we need in order to estimate these stories?"
	Process: Dialogue
	Comments: As the XP Coach, you should go through each story and ask the group what questions they may have around the story, and what elaboration they may need from the customer for that story. Have someone record information as useful for later work and testing.

Agenda Item	
F. What are all the tasks and their estimates for each story?	**Prompt Question:** "Based on the information we have just heard, we can now move to the next level of detail about the story estimates. Think about how you have completed similar work in the past, the tasks that you used and the estimates for those tasks. What are all the tasks and their estimates for each story.
	Process: Small Group Dialogue, Listing, Wideband Delphi Estimating
	Comments: Small groups should be formed based on components or expertises. Each group should discuss story content and components, as well dependencies and any other factors around story acceptance. For each story, list all the tasks necessary to complete the story through to acceptance. Then use Wide-Delphi Estimating to converge on useful estimates for each task.
	Complete a listing of all stories and tasks and estimates for debrief to the entire team. You can do this in a marketplace setting, where each team shares its set of stories, tasks, and estimates around the room and collects feedback from all the other team members visiting their "stall."
G. What are the concerns or risks associated with these task estimates?	**Prompt Question:** "Given the information you have shared in creating each story's tasks and estimates, you may have learned about some concerns or risks that weren't known during the Release Planning that originally mapped out this iteration. What are the concerns or risks associated with these task estimates?"
	Process: Round Robin Brainstorm
	Comments: Use a round robin brainstorming survey of all participants to collect a broad view into any other concerns or risks. The round robin will keep things moving, given that the team has already done some small group brainstorming and dialogue work. Collect items first, then invite discussion once all items have been documented on a flipchart.
	Collect any recommendations or actions so that, when the group is asked to commit to the iteration in the next agenda item, they will have a clear view of the commitment they are making to managing the issues.

Continues

Agenda Item	
H. Given all of this information, what is our commitment to this iteration's timebox, velocity, and stories?	**Prompt Question:** "Imagine it is the end of the iteration and all your work is done. Think about all the specific tasks that the team completed in order to make the iteration a success with its accepted stories. Also think about the concerns and risks we maneuvered during the iteration in order to accomplish this. Given all this information, what is our commitment to this iteration's timebox, velocity, and stories?"
	Process: Consensus Check
	Comments: This is a final check-in on all the work that has been accomplished in the meeting. By now, the stories, their tasks, and their estimates should be ready for a consensus commitment by the team.
	Use a "Fist of Five" consensus, take a picture of the team, and hang it on the wall as a way to kick-off the iteration.
I. Close	**Prompt Question:** "Have we met our meeting purpose today?"
	Process: Walk the walls
	Comments: Review Purpose ("Have we met this purpose today?"), process Personal Objectives, process Decisions Board, process Parking Lot, process Actions Board, create Communication Plan, and evaluate the meeting ("What worked well for you today?" "What would you change for the next meeting?").
	Celebrate!

Daily Standup

Meeting Name:	**Daily Standup**
Meeting Purpose:	To determine the progress of the team's commitments from the previous status meeting and to note any actions necessary to remove impediments and to help the team reach its iteration goal
Meeting Outputs:	An updated "To Do" list and/or Burndown Chart with remaining effort hours per task; a list of post-meeting actions based on any impediments raised as obstacles

Meeting Name:	**Daily Standup**
Meeting Participants:	Team members provide their status; the XP Coach/Tracker documents updates and actions. Project Stakeholders observe.
Comments:	The Daily Standup is the stand-up status meeting that keeps the team focused on its iteration commitments, as individuals and as a team. The purpose of the meeting is to determine what impediments need to be removed and to eliminate distractions that may be harming the team's progress. Team members provide this information to one another and to the stakeholder observers at the meeting; the XP coach simply facilitates these communications. (Stakeholders are invited to observe but are not allowed to participate/speak; they consult with the XP Coach about their observations after the meeting.)
	During the meeting, the XP Coach listens for action items and documents these, both for team actions and for personal follow-up with Stakeholders. Additionally, the Coach updates any Iteration documentation (Burndown Chart, Task Board, etc.). Participants should stick to status only, no problem-solving. The meeting is always conducted standing up.

Agenda Item	
A. Opening	**Prompt Question:** "Are we ready to start the Daily Standup?"
	Process. n.a.
	Comments: Because it occurs daily, don't bother with a formal opening. Instead, use the opening as the time to enforce the "Starting on time" rules the team has agreed to use (penalty, fine, singing, charity).
	Once the meeting is ready to start, use round robin to query each team member for his or her status. Each team member provides status to the three agenda questions B, C, and D before the Round Robin continues to the next participant.
B. What did you do since the last meeting?	**Prompt Question:** "What did you do yesterday?"
	Process: Round Robin
	Comments: Keep participants specific to their commitments that they made in the last status meeting. Did they meet their commitments or not?

Continues

Agenda Item	
C. What are you committing to completing before the next meeting?	**Prompt Question:** "What are you committing to completing today?"
	Process: Continuation of the Round Robin
	Comments: Here again, keep team members focused on the commitments they are willing to make to other team members with regard to the team's Iteration Backlog.
D. What is getting in your way?	**Prompt Question:** "What is getting in your way?"
	Process: Continuation of the Round Robin
	Comments: This is the XP Coach's chance to find out how to serve the team. Find impediments and remove them. Any blockage or impediment reported here should become an Action Item, either for the XP Coach to handle outside of the team, or for a subset of the team to resolve as prompted and arranged by the Coach. The XP Coach or Tracker always tracks these Action Items.
E. What is the update to the team Burndown Chart?	**Prompt Question:** "Based on all the status provided here, what is the update to the team Burndown Chart?"
	Process: Listing
	Comments: The XP Coach ensures that each team member has provided "To Do" estimates from each member and records the responses in the Iteration's Burndown Chart.
F. Close	**Prompt Question:** "What are all our actions as a result of this status information?"
	Process: Action Planning
	Comments: Close the Daily Standup by reviewing any collected action items with their due date and the owner of the action. These should be part of the round robin review for each subsequent Daily Standup.
	Limit the meeting to 15 minutes.

Meeting Name:	Iteration Demo and Review
Meeting Purpose:	To learn feature functionality from the accepted stories in the iteration, and to determine the impact on the Release plan, priorities, and subsequent iterations
Meeting Outputs:	New list of prioritized stories, further elaboration of intended functionality, a list of issues and concerns, and a list of recommendations about team practices
Meeting Participants:	Customer, Stakeholders, developers, testers, XP Coach, and any other interested parties
Comments:	The Iteration Demo and Review meeting demonstrates the team's iteration commitment to the Customer and any other Stakeholders. Planned by the XP Coach, team members demonstrate the functionality that they have completed during the iteration and collect feedback from the Customer and stakeholders. Based on the demo and discussion, the meeting participants then review the impact of the iteration on the Release and any subsequent iterations: what priorities have changed; what team structure has altered; what team practices should shift; what issues and concerns must be addressed? Finally the meeting ends with an Iteration Retrospective that draws out the team's recommendations about its practicess that can be applied in the next Iteration.

Don't allow the team to take more than four hours to prepare the demo for the meeting. Keep the meeting under two hours.

Some process suggestions:

- Demo should be prepared in advance.

- Members should take turns running the meeting.

- The person who accepted the story could be the person who demos its acceptance; this is a powerful statement about acceptance.

- Consider adding an agenda item: "What did this iteration look like? " ("Picture This" Exercise) for teams just starting XP or for teams when the iteration has been particularly hard.

Agenda Item	
A. Opening	**Prompt Question:** n.a.
	Process: Meeting Startup
	Comments: Once you have completed the meeting startup with Purpose, Agenda, Organizing Tools, etc., collect personal objectives. It will be an important point for bringing out retrospection and reflection.
	Be sure to go through the "What's In It For Me" and the Scope of Authority for the entire team.
B. What was our commitment of stories for this Iteration?	**Prompt Question:** "We kicked off this iteration with a planning meeting that defined a set of stories with their tasks and estimates. What was our commitment of stories for this iteration?"
	Process: Expert Input
	Comments: The XP Coach or a team member reviews all the stories to which the team had committed in the Iteration Planning meeting.
C. What was our final set of accepted stories for this iteration?	**Prompt Question:** n.a.
	Process: Expert Input
	Comments: The XP Coach or team member reviews which stories had been completed through to acceptance. This helps set up which demos will be presented.
D. What is our demonstration of these stories?	**Prompt Question:** "Given the stories that have been accepted, what is our demonstration of these stories?"
	Process: Expert Input, Dialogue
	Comments: Here, the Customer or team members demonstrate what has been accepted during the iteration. Observers and team members provide feedback and recommendations based on the demonstrated functionality.
	Make sure this does not turn into problem solving. Use the Parking Lot to table lengthy discussions, or create an Action Item for a follow-up meeting around the issue.

Agenda Item	
E. What was our estimated velocity versus our actual velocity?	**Prompt Question:** "At the beginning of the Iteration, we estimated a velocity based on detailing of tasks for each of the stories in the Iteration. Our actual velocity is based on the stories that were accepted. What was our estimated velocity versus our actual velocity?"
	Process: Expert Input, Dialogue
	Comments: The XP Coach reviews the details of the team's original velocity estimate and then covers the details of the actual velocity: daily trends, overall trends, exception situations, major turning points, unexpected complexities, or impediments.
F. What did we learn about our estimates?	**Prompt Question:** "Given what we had proposed as our velocity versus what we have been able to observe as our velocity, what did we learn about our estimates?"
	Process: Large Group Dialogue
	Comments: The team reviews the results of the demo and the comparison of the estimated velocity versus the actual velocity in order to make recommendations about how they will estimate their next iteration. This may also impact the high-level estimates for items currently planned for the Release.
G. What changes are there in the set of prioritized stories?	**Prompt Question:** "The demo helps us not only to see functionality in action, but also to ponder the current vision for the Release and the stories that support it. Given what we have seen in the demo and what we have learned from our estimates, what changes are there in the set of prioritized stories?"
	Process: Large Group Dialogue
	Comments: In this agenda item, the Customer provides feedback on what she has learned based on all the meeting work to this point. This includes dialogue to draw out guidance from the team and the Stakeholders in order to make useful changes. This may include adding stories, removing stories, reprioritizing stories, or reestimating stories.
	Keep this activity extremely focused and away from in-depth problem solving. The team should provide guidance that is specific to the high-level view of stories. When discussion becomes in-depth, use the Parking Lot, or create an Action Item for a later conversation.

Continues

Agenda Item	
H. What documented issues/concerns were we able to address?	**Prompt Question:** "Looking back on the concerns and risks we had documented at the start of the iteration, think about how we either managed those concerns or watched them end up becoming non-issues. What documented concerns and risks were we able to address?"
	Process: Large Group Dialogue
	Comments: Keep the group working as one team to talk through how they faced their documented issues and concerns. This will feed recommendations about team practices for the next Iteration or action items following this meeting.
I. What are our current issues/concerns?	**Prompt Question:** "Think about how we were able to meet our commitment and what may still be a challenge in terms of meeting future iteration commitments. You may recognize either a persistent problem or a newly emerging one. What are our current issues and concerns?"
	Process: Small Group Listing
	Comments: Have each group work through their own set of issues and concerns. This promotes open dialogue that then helps the entire group understand what the total set of issues and concerns are. For a small enough team, use Facilitator-led Listing for the entire group.
J. What worked well that we'd do again?	**Prompt Question:** "During the iteration, we engaged in any number of team practices to help us get to this demo and review. Considering how our iteration worked, what worked well that we'd do again?"
	Process: Brainstorming
	Comments: This is the group's chance to validate their practices and standardize as appropriate. You are now inviting the team to move beyond the mechanics of the Iteration and to retrospect about its own norms, team practices, standards, etc.
K. What practices would we alter/drop?	**Prompt Question:** "Think back over the iteration. We may have had some difficulties in how we were working, communicating, delivering, committing, etc. Considering the ways that we chose to work, what practices would we alter or drop?"
	Process: Facilitator-led Brainstorming, Dialogue

	Comments: Encourage open dialogue around brainstorm responses so that the team can fully agree on what practices really should be altered or dropped. In particular, pay attention to any suggestion that would alter a fundamental practice of XP. Only a high-performing team should alter or change these basic practices.
L. What new practices would we want to introduce into our next Iteration?	**Prompt Question:** "Given our list of what to keep and what to change or drop, you may also be able to think about new practices, either something you have tried in a different team, or something you have learned since the last Iteration Planning meeting. What new practices would we want to introduce into our next iteration?" **Process:** Facilitator-led Brainstorming, Dialogue **Comments:** Lead the team in brainstorming any new ideas without remarking on their applicability, positive or negative. Then go through the items one-by-one to gain consensus around which practices to absorb for the next iteration. Document the recommendations on a flipchart for use in the next Iteration Planning meeting.
M. Based on our work over the last iteration, what appreciations do we have for individuals?	**Prompt Question:** "Before we close the meeting, we have an opportunity to openly extend gratitude to others for something they did that had a particularly valuable impact on the success of the Iteration. This may be a team member, a stakeholder, or someone outside the team who had supported the team. Based on our work over the last iteration, what appreciations do we have for individuals?" **Process:** Brainstorming **Comments:** Ask participants to form their sentences in a way that directly applies to a particular individual and an action that person took: "I appreciate that Biada pulled together all the test data and made sure that the test platform was set up in time for us to get our final acceptance completed before the end of the iteration."

Continues

Agenda Item	
N. What is our Action Plan for next steps?	**Prompt Question:** "Based on all the information and recommendations we have accumulated here, what is our set of actions for next steps?"
	Process: Action Planning
	Comments: Work with the team to ensure that they have the appropriate set of actions that can move their decisions forward from the demonstration and review.
O. Close	**Prompt Question:** "Have we met this purpose today?"
	Process: Walking the walls
	Comments: Review Purpose ("Have we met this purpose today?"), process Personal Objectives, process Decisions Board, process Parking Lot, process Actions Board, create Communication Plan, and evaluate the meeting ("What worked well for you today?" "What would you change for the next meeting?").
	Celebrate!

Release Retrospective Meeting

Meeting Name:	**Release Retrospective**
Meeting Purpose:	To reflect on a release's timeline, members, the outcomes, the highlights, and the lowlights in order to form observations for recommendations on subsequent releases for the team
Meeting Outputs:	A wall chart of the project timeline, populated with events, team members, highs, and lows; recommendations on what lessons were learned and what best practices were harvested
Meeting Participants:	All members of the team
Comments:	Because XP and Industrial XP are so fundamentally linked to creating and absorbing change, the Release Retrospective creates a critical health check for the team. Through the reflection gained in this meeting, the team can take a larger view of their set of ongoing practices and how this impacts their long-term viability as an XP team.

Meeting Name:	Release Retrospective

The Release Retrospective differs slightly from the Iteration Retrospective that takes place with the Iteration Demo and Review in that it is more focused on the passage of time and the events that occurred during that time. Iteration Retrospectives tend to focus on specific metrics and practices around the Iteration; a Release Retrospective may draw that out based on information in the timeline, but it doesn't necessarily focus on metrics that have already been accumulated in each Iteration Retrospective meeting.

If the release involved a number of organizations, or if the work involved distributed sub-teams, you may consider having team members fill out a survey prior to coming to the meeting.

As in a silent grouping exercise, for the mapping and timelining exercises of the retrospective, encourage silent activity. Each person with items for the timeline should silently place their items on the timeline.

If the release has proven to be a rough one, the team could be in a "Storming" mode, not having ever achieved "Performing." Be prepared to deal with conflict and emotion. Emphasize your neutral role. Build in lots of time for silence and reflection once the timeline has been created and the team starts to populate it with their highlights and lowlights. Additionally, you may want to add an extra agenda item after the completion of the timeline with highlights and lowlights. Ask team members to draw a picture of what the release felt like to them. These pictures can be posted on the wall along with the timeline.

Plan to conduct a one-day event if at all possible. This allows ample time to create the timeline and to mine the information it holds. Additionally, the team will need time to delve into the specific release challenges and the results of the team's responses to those challenges. Finally, a release retrospective must produce actions that can directly and positively impact the team's success in the next Release.

Agenda Item	
A. Opening	**Prompt Question:** n.a.
	Process: Meeting Startup
	Comments: Personal objectives are very important in a Release Retrospective. Also be sure to stress the WIIFM aspect of the meeting.
B. Who were the members of the project team, and what were their roles?	**Prompt Question:** "I'd like you to think about this release in its many forms; in particular right now, I'd like you to think about all the people who were involved in the release. Think about the entire community of team members, customers, and others who contributed to the release at some point in the release timeline. Who were all the members of the project team, and what were their roles?"
	Process: Facilitator-led Listing
	Comments: You are looking for the full list of people who contributed to the Release. Pay attention to the various roles. Even if someone was only involved in the Release for one iteration, they should be listed here. Their start and end times in the Release will be tracked in the release timeline.
C. What was the timeline of this Release?	**Prompt Question:** "Think back on the actual start of this Release and how it was subdivided into multiple iterations that ended on the Release end-date. There may have been other significant dates during that time as well. What was the timeline of the Release?"
	Process: Facilitator Timelining
	Comments: Create a wall chart with the Release start and end dates on it. This is divided into large segments, one for each iteration of the Release. Now solicit important dates from the team and list those as well.
D. When did each person join/leave the Release?	**Prompt Question:** "Given the release timeline and the full list of team members, I'd like you to now form a map of when each person was involved in the Release. Be thinking about events you know that engaged each person. When did each person join or leave the Release?"
	Process: Listing, Mapping

	Comments: If this was a short release, or if the team was whole for the duration of the Release, you can skip this agenda item.
	Conduct this item in two steps. First use the list of participants and record each start and end date. Then, with two sticky notes per person (one that signifies when they joined the project and one that signifies when they left the project), you can fill in the timeline wall chart. Consider using one color for when a person joined and another color for when a person left the Release.
E. What were the team highlights and lowlights in the timeline?	**Prompt Question:** "In this timeline of iteration timeboxes, there are also non-timebox–oriented events worth noting, moments or events when the team just felt as though it was really flowing well. Or perhaps there were specific events or times when the team was feeling low and struggling. Thinking about all this, what were the team highlights and lowlights in the timeline?"
	Process: Brainstorm, Mapping
	Comments: Individuals should brainstorm on their own, one response per sticky, and then silently place their contributions on the map. You may want to create a layer across the entire timeline for these team highlights and lowlights, using a different color for each
	Make sure to give this activity a good amount of time for the brainstorming. A team not used to reflecting on its highlights and lowlights will need time to have these emerge.
F. What were the personal and individual highlights and lowlights in the timeline?	**Prompt Question:** "Now think about what was happening for you during this Release. What was going on with your family, your home, your career? Did you move, have a baby, get married, lose a loved one? What were your personal and individual highlights and lowlights in the timeline?"
	Process: Brainstorm, Mapping, Dialogue
	Comments: This agenda item and the next one may bring out emotion in a team that struggled or had to deal with a very stressful Release. If there is a sense of failure about the team, the Release, or the individual, this agenda item and the previous one will bring it out. Be prepared to engage in careful dialogue. Encourage sharing of reflection but discourage blame or attack.

Continues

Agenda Item	
G. What are our observations about this timeline with these key events, and the team and personal highlights and lowlights?	**Prompt Question:** "We now have a fairly extensive view into what our Release looked like from a variety of angles. There may be some things that surprise you, perhaps some revelations about events and colleagues. Take some time now to review the entire timeline and reflect. What are your observations about this timeline with its highlights and lowlights?"
	Process: Dialogue
	Comments: Encourage people to silently walk along the timeline chart. They should take at least five minutes to look over the total set of materials. You may also want to encourage them to write down some of their observations. Once the time of observation is over, lead the group in sharing observations through group dialogue.
	This is another agenda item that needs lots of time. Give this an hour in a full-day retrospective. Reflection on the timeline should bring out a lot of dialogue and observation as well as moving into interpretation of why events, high or low, occurred in the Release as they did.
H. How did we address our issues and risks that were identified at the start of the Release?	**Prompt Question:** "During Release Planning, we captured issues and risks that could potentially have a negative impact on the team's commitment to the Release theme. Reviewing these items, how did we address our issues and risks that were identified at the start of the Release?"
	Process: Dialogue
	Comments: Bring the Release Planning meeting issues and risks to this meeting as a flipchart so that the team can be reminded of what they had documented. Engage the team in reflecting on the flow of the timeline events and where they were able to address particular issues or risks. Find out what were ongoing issues or risks that didn't go away and capture these on a flipchart.

Agenda Item	
I. Based on these observations, what practices would we keep for the next Release?	**Prompt Question:** "Having reflected on the project and its timeline as well as the issues and risks of the Release, you now have an opportunity to think about modes of working, reporting, or creating decisions that worked well for you. Based on these observations, what practices would you keep for the next Release?" **Process:** Facilitator-led Brainstorm, Dialogue **Comments:** This is a pivotal agenda item for the Retrospective: learning what the team would bring forward to subsequent releases. After the brainstorming, invite dialogue so that the group can create some consensus on their recommendations.
J. What practices would you alter or drop?	**Prompt Question:** "Think back over the release. We may have had some difficulties in how we were working, communicating, delivering, committing, etc. Considering the ways that we chose to work, what practices would we alter or drop?" **Process:** Facilitator-led Brainstorming, Dialogue **Comments:** Encourage open dialogue around brainstorm responses so that the team can fully agree on what practices really should be altered or dropped. In particular, pay attention to any suggestion that would alter a fundamental practice of XP. Only a high-performing team should alter or change these basic practices.
K. What new practices would you like to try in the next Release?	**Prompt Question:** "Given our list of what to keep and what to change or drop, you may also be able to think about new practices, either something you have tried in a different team, or something you have learned since the last Release Planning meeting. What new practices would we want to introduce into our next release?" **Process:** Facilitator-led Brainstorming, Dialogue **Comments:** Lead the team in brainstorming any new ideas without remarking on their applicability, positive or negative. Then go through the items one-by-one to gain consensus around which practices to absorb for the next release.

Continues

Agenda Item	
L. What appreciations do we have to offer one another?	**Prompt Question:** "Having reflected on the Release and its timeline, you now have an opportunity to think about the special contributions various team members have made. Think about those very specific actions an individual took that impacted you positively during the Release. What are the appreciations we have to offer one another?" **Process:** Brainstorming **Comments:** Guide participants to respond by using the format: "I appreciate that (person's name)…" as in "I appreciate that Gail was always willing to pair on writing automated test scripts." Also consider having an awards ceremony (oldest artifact, funniest artifact, most representative artifact). You should alert people to this in advance of the retrospective.
M. What is our Action Plan from our retrospection?	**Prompt Question:** "Based on all the information and recommendations we have accumulated here, what is our set of actions for next steps?" **Process:** Action Planning **Comments:** You may want to first prioritize the recommendations about altered practices, dropped practices, and new practices before moving into action planning, particularly if there are many controversial, or contradictory recommendations.
N. Close	**Prompt Question:** "Have we met this purpose today?" **Process:** Walking the walls **Comments:** Review Purpose ("Have we met this purpose today?"), process Personal Objectives, process Decisions Board, process Parking Lot, process Actions Board, create Communication Plan, and evaluate the meeting ("What worked well for you today?" "What would you change for the next meeting?"). Celebrate!

Bibliography

Abrashoff, Captain D. Michael. *It's Your Ship: Management Techniques from the Best Damn Ship in the Navy*. New York: Warner Books, 2002.

Ambler, Scott. *Agile Modeling: Effective Practices for Extreme Programming and the Unified Process*. New York: John Wiley & Sons, 2002.

Beck, Kent. *Extreme Programming Explained. Embrace Change.* Upper Saddle River, NJ: Pearson Education, 2005.

Beck, Kent and Martin Fowler *Planning Extreme Programming*. Upper Saddle River, NJ: Pearson Education, 2001.

Bens, Ingrid. *Facilitating with Ease! A Step-By-Step Guidebook with Customizable Worksheets on CD-ROM*. San Francisco: Jossey-Bass, 2000.

Booch, Grady and Alan W. Brown. *Collaborative Development Environments*. Rational Software Corporation, October 28, 2002.

Cloke, Kenneth and Joan Goldsmith. *Resolving Conflicts at Work: A Complete Guide for Everyone on the Job*. San Francisco: Jossey-Bass, 2000.

Cockburn, Alistair. *Agile Software Development*. Boston: Addison-Wesley, 2002.

———. *Surviving Object-Oriented Projects*. Boston: Addison-Wesley, 1998.

———. *Crystal Clear: A Human-Powered Methodology for Small Teams*. Boston: Addison-Wesley, 2005.

Cohn, Mike. *Agile Estimating and Planning*. Boston: Pearson Education, 2005.

———. *User Stories Applied: For Agile Software Development*. Boston: Pearson Education, 2004.

Collins, Jim. *Good to Great: Why Some Companies Make the Leap...and Others Don't*. New York: HarperCollins, 2001.

Danforth, Janet and Robert Moir. "Facilitation4Results." Facilitator4Hire Inc. course material, 2000.

DeGrace, Peter, and Leslie Hulet Stahl. *Wicked Problems, Righteous Solutions: A Catalogue of Modern Engineering Paradigms*. Upper Saddle River, NJ: Prentice Hall, 1998.

DeMarco, Tom and Tim Lister. *Peopleware: Productive Projects and Teams*. New York: Dorset House, 1999.

Fowler, Martin, and Jim Highsmith. "Agile Methodologists Agree on Something." *Software Development* 9, no. 8 (August 2001): 28-32.

Goldratt, Eliyahu M. and Jeff Cox. *The Goal: Excellence in Manufacturing*. Croton-on-Hudson, NY: North River Press, 1984.

Gottesdiener, Ellen. *Requirements by Collaboration: Workshops for Defining Needs*. Boston: Pearson Education, 2002.

Greenleaf, Robert. *Servant Leadership: A Journey into the Nature of Legitimate Power & Greatness*. New York: Paulist Press, 1977.

Highsmith, James A. III. *Adaptive Software Development: A Collaborative Approach to Managing Complex Systems*. New York: Dorset House, 2000.

Highsmith, Jim. *Agile Project Management: Creating Innovative Products*. Boston: Addison-Wesley, 2004.

———. *Agile Software Development Ecosystems*. Boston: Addison-Wesley, 2002.

Hoefling, Trina. *Working Virtually: Managing People for Successful Virtual Teams and Organizations*. Sterling, VA: Stylus Publishing, 2003.

Jackson, Phil. *Sacred Hoops: Spiritual Lessons of a Hardwood Warrior*. New York: Hyperion, 1996.

Jeffries, Ron, Ann Anderson, and Chet Hendrickson. *Extreme Programming Installed.* Boston: Addison-Wesley, 2001.

Justice, Thomas, and David W. Jamieson. *The Facilitator's Fieldbook.* New York: HRD Press Inc., 1999.

Kaner, Sam with Lenny Lind, Catherine Toldi, Sarah Fisk, and Duane Berger. *Facilitator's Guide to Participatory Decision-Making.* Philadelphia: New Society Publishers, 1996.

Karsten, Naomi. *Communication Gaps and How to Close Them.* New York: Dorset House, 2002.

Katzenbach, Jon R., and Douglas K. Smith. *The Wisdom of Teams: Creating the High-Performance Organization.* Boston: Harvard Business School Press, 1993.

Kerth, Norman L. *Project Retrospectives: A Handbook for Team Members.* New York: Dorset House, 2001.

Manns, Mary Lynn and Linda Rising. *Fearless Change: Patterns for Introducing New Ideas.* Boston: Addison-Wesley, 2004.

McBreen, Pete. *Software Craftsmanship: The New Imperative.* Boston: Addison-Wesley, 2001.

McConnell, Steve. *Rapid Development: Taming Wild Software Schedules* Redmond, WA: Microsoft Press, 1996.

Moore, Geoffrey A. *Crossing the Chasm: Marketing and Selling High Tech Products to Mainstream Customers.* New York: HarperBusiness, 1991.

Nonaka, Ikujiro and Hirotaka Takeuchi. *The Knowledge-Creating Company: How Japanese Companies Create the Dynamics of Innovation.* Oxford University Press, 1995

Owen, Harrison. *Open Space Technology: A User's Guide.* San Francisco: Berrett-Koehler, 1997.

Poppendieck, Mary and Tom Poppendieck. *Lean Software Development.* Boston: Addison-Wesley, 2003.

Reina, Dennis S. and Michelle L. Reina. *Trust & Betrayal in the Workplace: Building Effective Relationships in Your Organization.* San Francisco: Berrett-Koehler, 1999.

Ruiz, Don Miguel. *The Four Agreements: A Practical Guide to Personal Freedom.* Amber-Allen Publishing, 1997.

Schneider, William. *The Reengineering Alternative: A Plan for Making Your Current Culture Work.* Burr Ridge, IL: Irwin Professional Publishing, 1994.

Schwaber. Ken. *Agile Project Management with Scrum.* Redmond, WA: Microsoft Press, 2004.

Schwaber, Ken and Mike Beedle. *Agile Software Development with Scrum.* Upper Saddle River, NJ: Prentice Hall, 2002.

Senge, Peter. *The Fifth Discipline: The Art & Practice of The Learning Organization.* New York: Currency Doubleday, 1990.

Strübing, Jörg. "Designing the Working Process—What Programmers Do Besides Programming." NATO Advanced Research Workshop on User-Centered Requirements for Software Engineering Environments, Toulouse, 5-10 September 1991.

————. "Negotiation—A Central Aspect of Collaborative Work in Software Design." 5ème Workshop sur la Psychologie de la Programmation, Institut National de Recherche en Informatique et en Automatique (Ed.). 10-12 Décembre 1992, Paris, S. 31-39.

Takeuchi, Hirotaka and Ikujiro Nonaka. *Hitotsubashi on Knowledge Management.* Singapore: John Wiley & Sons (Asia) Pte Ltd, 2004.

Thomas, Kenneth W. and Ralph H. Kilmann, The Thomas-Kilmann Conflict Mode Instrument (TKI), http://www.cpp.com/detail/detailitem.asp?ic=4813. CPP, Inc., and Davies-Black® Publishing, 1055 Joaquin Rd., Suite 200, Mountain View, CA 94043.

Wake, William. *Extreme Programming Explored.* Boston: Addison-Wesley, 2002.

Watkins, Jane Magruder and Bernard J. Mohr. *Appreciative Inquiry: Change at the Speed of Imagination.* San Francisco: Jossey-Bass, 2001.

Weeks, Dudley. *The Eight Essential Steps to Conflict Resolution: Preserving Relationships at Work, at Home and in the Community.* New York: Penguin Putnam, 1992.

Whitney, Diana, Amanda Trosten-Bloom, and David Cooperrider. *The Power of Appreciative Inquiry: A Practical Guide to Positive Change.* San Francisco: Berrett-Koehler, 2003.

Zander, Rosamund Stone and Benjamin Zander. *The Art of Possibility: Transforming Professional and Personal Life.* New York: Penguin Books, 2000.

Index

Bens, Ingrid, 123, 181, 199, 209, 214
Best Thinking, 35
big design up front (BDUF), 98
blame, eliminating, 82-83
Blitz Planning Workshop, 330-334
bolters, managing, 250
Booch, Grady, 47
brainstorming, 156-157
 dyad mode, 179-180
 group brainstorming of labels, 198-199
 individual mode, 179-180
 small-group work, 171
  delegating, 172
  dialogues, 174-178
  Personal Objectives Exercise,
   173-174
 techniques, 158-166
breakout room lists (as organizing
 tools), 134
breaks (meetings), providing food and
 drinks for, 139
bridging meetings, 275
business scope meetings, 61-62
butcher paper, 111

C

carbohydrates, 140
categories
 of information, 193-194
  creating timelines, 197
  defining Impact/Effort Grids,
   199-201
  facilitator-led, 194-195
  facilitator-led labeling, 198
  group brainstorming of labels,
   198-199

 MoSCoW PRL, 203-205
 multi-voting/dot voting PRL,
  205-207
 Pass the Cards PRL, 207-208
 prioritizing and weighting, 201-202
 priority/weighting grids, 209-211
 silent grouping, 196
 of meetings, 47
  Agile modeling design, 65
  Agile Practices Planning, 61
  business scope, 61-62
  design, 62
  Iteration Planning, 60
  one-on-one, 66-67
  planning, 54-58
  Release Planning, 58
  retrospection, 67-69
  status, 48-54
  unnecessary, 70
celebrating the work, 271
Center for Applied Ethics, 18
certification, facilitation of, 299
change
 collaborative teams responses to, 29
 Process Change Workshops, 311-314
characteristics
 of bad status meetings, 48
 of collaboration cultures, 12
 of collaborative teams, 36
  commitment, 39
  consensus-driven, 41-42
  constructive and useful
   disagreements, 43
  empowerment, 38
  participatory in decision making,
   40-41
  self-organizing, 37

Q–R

questions
  asking, 76-77
  Prompt, 150-151
  sequential questioning, 181-183
  stating agenda items as, 101-104

rambles, managing someone who, 245-246

reactions to conflict, 232-233

real-time interactive technologies, distributed teams, 293-295

rectangular tables, 138

reevaluation of decision making, 235

refactoring, frequent, 101

reflection
  applying, 30
  meetings, 274
  organizational reflection, 300

Reflection Workshop, 69, 334-339

Release Planning Meetings, 58, 361-372

Release Retrospective Meeting, 380-386

removing team members, 29

requirements modeling sessions, 63

resolution modes (conflicts), 258

resolving conflict, 257-261

retrospectives, 67-69, 300
  applying, 30
  Project Retrospective Meetings, 319-323
  Release Retrospective Meeting, 380-386

reviewing
  agendas, 270
  Iteration Demo and Review Meeting, 375-380
  meetings, 68

  organizing tools, 143
  personal objectives, 271
  purpose of meetings, 270
  Sprint Demo and Review Meeting (Scrum), 350-355

Rising, Linda, 139

Rodman, Dennis, 14

roles of meeting participants, 93

rooms (meeting venues), setting up, 137-138

Rostal, Pam, 216

Round Robin
  brainstorming, 161
  listing, 166

round tables, 138

Ruiz, Don Miguel, 21

rules
  Action Plan, 127-129
  Ground Rules, 120-123
  self-governance through, 233-234

S

Sacred Hoops: Spiritual Lessons of a Hardwood Warrior, 14

sanctity of teams, preserving, 31

Schneider, William, 7

Schratz, Deborah, 216, 300

Schwaber, Ken, 19

scope of authority, 142

Scrum, 18-19, 202
  meetings, 50, 341
    Daily Scrum Meeting, 347-349
    Sprint Demo and Review Meeting, 350-355
    Sprint Planning Meeting, 57-58, 342-345
  teams, defining, 24

Reach for a Classic in Agile Project Management

Agile Project Management: Creating Innovative Products

Jim Highsmith

One of the field's leading experts brings together all the knowledge and resources you need to use Agile Project Management (APM) in your next project. Jim Highsmith shows why APM should be in every manager's toolkit, thoroughly addressing the questions project managers raise about agile approaches. He systematically introduces the five-phase APM framework, then presents specific, proven tools for every project participant. Coverage includes

- Six principles of Agile Project Management
- How to capitalize on emerging new product development technologies
- Putting customers at the center of your project, where they belong
- Creating adaptive teams that respond quickly to changes in your project's "ecosystem"
- Which projects will benefit from APM—and which won't
- APM's five phases: Envision, Speculate, Explore, Adapt, Close
- APM practices, including the Product Vision Box and Project Data Sheet
- Leveraging your PMI skills in Agile environments
- Scaling APM to larger projects and teams
- For every project manager, team leader, and team member

Praise for *Agile Project Management*

"Jim Highsmith is one of a few modern writers who are helping us understand the new nature of work in the knowledge economy."
— ROB AUSTIN, Assistant Professor, Harvard Business School

"This is the project management book we've all been waiting for—the book that effectively combines Agile methods and rigorous project management. Not only does this book help us make sense of project management in this current world of iterative, incremental Agile methods, but it's an all-around good read!"
— LYNNE ELLEN, Sr. VP & CIO, DTE Energy

"Finally a book that reconciles the passion of the Agile Software movement with the needed disciplines of project management. Jim's book has provided a service to all of us."
— NEVILLE R(OY) SINGHAM, CEO, ThoughtWorks, Inc.

"The world of product development is becoming more dynamic and uncertain. Many managers cope by reinforcing processes, adding documentation, or further honing costs. This isn't working. Highsmith brilliantly guides us into an alternative that fits the times."
— PRESTON G. SMITH, principal, New Product Dynamics/coauthor, *Developing Products in Half the Time*

0-321-21977-5 • © 2004 • 312 pages

The Agile Software Development Series

Patterns for Effective Use Cases
0201721848

Agile Software Development
0201699699

Crystal Clear
0201699478

Surviving Object-Oriented Projects
0201498340

Writing Effective Use Cases
0201702258

Configuration Management Principles and Practice
0321117662

Agile Software Development Ecosystems
0201760436

Agile Project Management
0321219775

Agile & Iterative Development
0131111558

Improving Software Organizations
0201758202

Lean Software Development
0321150783

Collaboration Explained
0321268776

Sustainable Software Development
0321286081